I Never Knew That
About

ROYAL BRITAIN

Christopher Winn

I Never Knew That
About

ROYAL BRITAIN

ILLUSTRATIONS
BY
Mai Osawa

EBURY
PRESS

1 3 5 7 9 10 8 6 4 2

Published in 2018 by Ebury Press an imprint of Ebury Publishing,
20 Vauxhall Bridge Road,
London SW1V 2SA

Ebury Press is part of the Penguin Random House group of companies
whose addresses can be found at global.penguinrandomhouse.com

Copyright © Christopher Winn 2018

Christopher Winn has asserted his right to be identified as the author of this
Work in accordance with the Copyright, Designs and Patents Act 1988

First published by Ebury Press in 2012
This edition published by Ebury Press in 2018

www.penguin.co.uk

A CIP catalogue record for this book is available from the British Library

ISBN 9781785039829

Printed and bound in Great Britain by Clays Ltd, St Ives PLC

Penguin Random House is committed to a sustainable
future for our business, our readers and our planet. This
book is made from Forest Stewardship Council® certified
paper.

For Dids – 80 amazing years
and Jo Jo –
so many Happy Christmases

Contents

PREFACE ix

MONARCHS xi

1: QUEEN ELIZABETH II 1

2: ROYAL CELEBRATIONS & PAGEANTRY 11

3: ROYAL WESTMINSTER 24

4: ROYAL ST JAMES'S & WHITEHALL 34

5: ROYAL LONDON 46

6: ROYAL THAMES 59

7: ROYAL WINDSOR 72

8: ROYAL ENGLAND HOMES & PALACES 84

9: ROYAL ENGLAND BIRTHS, BURIALS & BETWEEN 96

10: ROYAL SCOTLAND – PRESENT 110

11: ROYAL SCOTLAND – PAST 119

12: ROYAL WALES 131

13: ROYAL VILLAINS 145

14: ROYAL ROGUES 159

15: ROYAL STICKY ENDS 167

GAZETTEER 187

INDEX OF PEOPLE 196

INDEX OF PLACES 204

ACKNOWLEDGEMENTS 210

Preface

To paraphrase King Farouk of Egypt, 'Soon there will only be five queens left in the world: the Queen of Spades, the Queen of Clubs, the Queen of Hearts, the Queen of Diamonds – and the Queen of England.'

He was almost correct. There are still a number of queens in the world, in addition to those in a pack of cards, but to most of the world 'the Queen' is Queen Elizabeth II, Queen of Great Britain and the Commonwealth, Queen of one of the world's most ancient monarchies and, most fittingly, the longest living monarch in British history.

For much of the world, Royal Britain is the Britain they know and recognise – the historic Britain of battlefields and castles, of romance and intrigue, of larger-than-life heroes and villains, the glamorous Britain of glittering palaces and tragic love stories, of pageantry and pomp, the modern Britain of royal weddings and royal celebrations that captivate record television audiences all over the world.

The origins of Royal Britain are lost in the mists of time. For the romantic, Royal Britain began 4,000 years ago when the legendary Trojan Prince Brutus stood on the Brutus stone in Totnes, Devon, and declared himself king of the land he had named for himself, Brut, or Brit. For the pragmatic, Royal Britain begins with the first recorded Royal Briton, Cassivellaunus, King of the Catevellauni, who was overcome by the Roman legions of Julius Caesar in 54 BC.

Whichever view you take, Britain's history is inextricably wrapped up in its royal past. Britain's kings and queens, good and bad, are the reference points by which we navigate Britain's history, and have played an essential role in creating the Britain of today. They have moulded and shaped Britain's laws and customs, its architecture and tastes, its dynamics and destiny. The royal dynasties define the great eras of Britain's history, Elizabethan, Georgian, Victorian.

Royal Britain has survived by adapting and modernising with the times, by remaining relevant, yet without losing the magic and the mystery of the past, or unravelling the threads that bind us to our royal ancestry. Royal Britain is both ancient and modern. And therein lies its glory.

Monarchs

Queen Elizabeth II can trace her ancestry back to the Saxon House of Wessex, which became the dominant Saxon dynasty during the reign of Egbert in the early 9th century, and from which the first Kings of England emerged.

ENGLISH MONARCHS

House of Wessex

	Reign
Egbert	802–839
Aethelwulf	839–858
Aethelbald	858–860
Aethelbert	860–865
Aethelred	865–871
Alfred the Great	871–899
Edward the Elder	899–924
Athelstan	924–939
Edmund the Magnificent	939–946
Eadred	946–955
Eadwig	955–959
Edgar the Peaceful	959–975
Edward the Martyr	975–978
Ethelred the Unready	978–1013
	1014–1016
Edmund Ironside	1016

House of Denmark

Canute	1016–1035
Harold Harefoot	1035–1040
Harthacnut	1040–1042

House of Wessex (restored)

Edward the Confessor	1042–1066
Harold II	1066

House of Normandy

William the Conqueror	1066–1087
William II (Rufus)	1087–1100
Henry I	1100–1135
Stephen	1135–1154

House of Plantagenet

Henry II	1154–1189
Richard I (Lionheart)	1189–1199
John (Lackland)	1199–1216
Henry III	1216–1272
Edward I (Longshanks)	1272–1307
Edward II	1307–1327
Edward III	1327–1377
Richard II	1377–1399

House of Lancaster

Henry IV	1399–1413
Henry V	1413–1422
Henry VI	1422–1461

House of York

Edward IV	1461–1470

House of Lancaster (restored)

Henry VI	1470–1471

House of York (restored)

Edward IV	1471–1483
Edward V	1483
Richard III	1483–1485

House of Tudor

Henry VII	1485–1509
Henry VIII	1509–1547
Edward VI	1547–1553
Mary I	1553–1558
Elizabeth I	1558–1603

SCOTTISH MONARCHS

House of Alpin	Reign
Kenneth MacAlpin	843–858
Donald I	858–862

Constantine I	862–877
Aed	877–878
Giric and Eochald	878–889
Donald II	889–900
Constantine II	900–943
Malcolm I	943–954
Indulf	954–962
Dubh	962–966
Culen	966–971
Kenneth II	971–995
Constantine III	995–997
Kenneth III	997–1005
Malcolm II	1005–1034

House of Dunkeld

Duncan I	1034–1040
Macbeth	1040–1057
Lulach	1057–1058
Malcolm III	1058–1093
Donald III	1093–1094
Duncan II	1094
Donald III (restored)	1094–1097
Edgar	1097–1107
Alexander I	1107–1124
David I	1124–1153
Malcolm IV	1153–1165
William I (the Lion)	1165–1214
Alexander II	1214–1249
Alexander III	1249–1286
Margaret (Maid of Norway)	1286–1290

Interregnum	1290–1292
John de Balliol	1292–1296
Interregnum	1296–1306

House of Bruce

| Robert I (the Bruce) | 1306–1329 |
| David II | 1329–1371 |

House of Stewart

Robert II	1371–1390
Robert III	1390–1406
James I	1406–1437
James II	1437–1460
James III	1460–1488
James IV	1488–1513
James V	1513–1542
Mary, Queen of Scots	1542–1567
James VI	1567–1603

UNION OF CROWNS

House of Stuart	**Reign**
James I (VI of Scotland)	1603–1625
Charles I	1625–1649

Commonwealth

| Oliver Cromwell | 1653–1658 |
| Richard Cromwell | 1658–1659 |

House of Stuart (restored)

Charles II	1660–1685
James II (VII of Scotland)	1685–1689
Mary II (with William III)	1689–1694
William III	1694–1702
Anne	1702–1707

BRITISH MONARCHS

| Anne | 1707–1714 |

House of Hanover

George I	1714–1727
George II	1727–1760
George III	1760–1820
George IV	1820–1830
William IV	1830–1837
Victoria	1837–1901

House of Saxe-Coburg and Gotha

| Edward VII | 1901–1910 |

House of Windsor

George V	1910–1936
Edward VIII	1936
George VI	1936–1952
Elizabeth II	1952–present

CHAPTER ONE

Queen Elizabeth II

In December 2007 Elizabeth II became
THE OLDEST REIGNING BRITISH MONARCH,
passing Queen Victoria, who died at 81.

'I declare before you all that my whole
life, whether it be long or short, shall
be devoted to your service and the
service of our great imperial family to
which we all belong.'
QUEEN ELIZABETH II

Elizabeth II

r. 1952 – present

ELIZABETH II was born on 21 April 1926
at 17 Bruton Street, Mayfair, the
London home of her maternal grandparents the Earl and Countess of
Strathmore. Her birth was attended by
the Home Secretary, Sir William
Joyson-Hicks, to ensure that it was a
genuine birth. Her grandfather, George
V, gave her the nickname 'Lilibet'.

Elizabeth was the daughter of the
Duke of York, who was a younger son
of George V and therefore not expected
to become King. When she was ten years
old, her uncle Edward VIII abdicated,
her father became King George VI, and
Elizabeth became heir to the throne.

Elizabeth grew up in the White Lodge in Richmond Park and later in the Royal Lodge in Windsor Great Park.

In 1939 Princess Elizabeth made THE FIRST ROYAL TRANSATLANTIC TELE-PHONE CALL, to her parents, who were touring Canada.

During the Second World War Princess Elizabeth became THE FIRST FEMALE MEMBER OF THE BRITISH ROYAL FAMILY TO ACTUALLY SERVE IN THE ARMED FORCES when she joined the ATS, learning mechanics and becoming THE ONLY BRITISH QUEEN ABLE TO CHANGE A SPARK PLUG. As a 14-year-old she delivered a radio broadcast to the children of the British Empire.

On 20 November 1947 Princess Elizabeth married LIEUTENANT PHILIP MOUNTBATTEN at Westminster Abbey, in the first royal celebration since the end of the war. The couple had met at the wedding of Philip's cousin Princess Marina of Greece, when Elizabeth was just 13 years old. Philip proposed in 1946 during a walk around the grounds of Balmoral. They honeymooned at BROADLANDS, in Hampshire, the home of Philip's uncle Lord Mountbatten, and at BIRKHALL, on the Balmoral estate in Aberdeenshire.

One year later Princess Elizabeth gave birth to a son, CHARLES, at Buckingham Palace, and then in 1950 she gave birth to her only daughter, ANNE, at Clarence House. (ANDREW and EDWARD were both born at Buckingham Palace in 1960 and 1964 respectively.)

In 1952 Princess Elizabeth was staying at a safari lodge in Kenya called TREETOPS when she was given the news that her father had died during the night of 6 February, and that she was Queen.

Queen Elizabeth II's coronation in Westminster Abbey on 2 June 1953 was THE FIRST CORONATION SERVICE EVER TO BE TELEVISED.

Later in 1953 Queen Elizabeth became THE FIRST REIGNING MONARCH TO VISIT AUSTRALIA AND NEW ZEALAND and gave THE FIRST EVER CHRISTMAS BROADCAST FROM OUTSIDE BRITAIN. During the tour she became THE FIRST BRITISH MONARCH TO CIRCUMNAVIGATE THE WORLD.

Commonwealth

In 1957 the Gold Coast became THE FIRST BRITISH COLONY IN AFRICA TO GAIN ITS INDEPENDENCE, taking the name Ghana. Elizabeth II remains Queen of 16 former British colonies,

Broadlands

including Australia, New Zealand and Canada, and is said to regard the greatest achievement of her reign as being the peaceful establishment of the Commonwealth, of which she is the Head. Today it consists of 53 independent states, only two of which were not part of the British Empire, and contains 1.8 billion people, 30 per cent of the world's population.

She has been served by 12 Prime Ministers during her reign so far, second only to George III, who lived through 14.

Royal Horse Racing

Queen Elizabeth is known for her love of horses, which began in 1930 when her grandfather George V gave her a Shetland pony called Peggy. Since she inherited the royal racing stables in 1952 the Queen's racehorses have won every 'Classic' race except the Derby. Her racing colours are a purple shirt with gold braid and scarlet sleeves and a black cap with gold fringe.

Suspicious Royal Births

The requirement for a government minister to be in attendance at a royal birth dated from 1566, when Mary, Queen of Scots, gave birth to her son Charles James (later James VI of Scotland and I of England) at Edinburgh Castle. It was rumoured that the baby was stillborn and that Mary had the tiny corpse dropped down the palace well, while a surrogate was hauled up the cliffs in a basket and then presented as the young prince (*see* Royal Scotland).

In 1688 there was consternation amongst English Protestants when Mary of Modena, wife of the Catholic James II, gave birth to a boy at St James's Palace, with the result that there was now a Catholic heir to the throne. The story was put about that Mary hadn't been pregnant at all, but had been feigning pregnancy, using a 'false belly', and that a changeling had been smuggled into the room in a warming pan, despite there being at least 50 observers watching the Queen's every move.

The last royal birth at which a government minister was present was that of PRINCESS MARGARET, at Glamis Castle in 1930.

Newmarket

The Queen perhaps inherited her passion for the turf from her ancestor JAMES I, WHO INTRODUCED HORSE-RACING INTO ENGLAND and was responsible, in 1604, for founding NEWMARKET in Suffolk as THE WORLD CENTRE FOR THOROUGHBRED HORSE-RACING. James was out hunting near what was then a tiny village, when he made the judgement that the flat heathland around the village would be excellent for racing, as well as for hunting and hawking. So he bought a couple of old local inns, the Griffin and the Swan, demolished them and built himself a palace, in front of which he laid out a flat racecourse. THE FIRST RACE AT NEWMARKET took place on 18 March 1622.

Formal race meetings were established by Charles I, and the royal palace was enlarged by Charles II, who was a regular visitor, often riding in races himself. To avoid being dazzled by the low sun in the spring and autumn months Charles had a new course laid out, known as the ROWLEY MILE after Charles's own nickname 'Old Rowley', which was taken from the name of his favourite horse.

In October 1666 Charles II inaugurated THE FIRST EVER HORSE RACE RUN UNDER WRITTEN RULES, the NEWMARKET TOWN PLATE, which he himself won in 1671. The Town Plate is still run every year and is THE OLDEST SURVIVING HORSE RACE IN THE WORLD.

The first RACETRACK IN AMERICA was named Newmarket after the Suffolk racecourse. It was founded by RICHARD NICOLLS, appointed by Charles II as the FIRST GOVERNOR OF NEW YORK in 1664.

Royal Ascot

While not having much of a reputation as a sports lover, QUEEN ANNE adored horse-racing and kept a string of racehorses at Newmarket. While out riding near Windsor Castle in 1711 she came across a patch of open heathland at a place called East Cote, which she thought might be a good place for 'horses to gallop at full stretch'. She bought the land and ordered a course to be laid out on it for racing, and on 11 August 1711 THE FIRST RACE, HER MAJESTY'S PLATE, was run over the royal racecourse.

The ASCOT GOLD CUP was run for the first time in 1807, and in 1825 George IV initiated THE FIRST ROYAL CARRIAGE PROCESSION along the course, a tradition that has been followed ever since.

The first race on opening day of Royal Ascot is called the QUEEN ANNE STAKES in memory of the monarch who founded this integral part of the English Summer Season.

Royal Corgis

In 1933, King George VI (then Duke of York) bought his seven-year-old daughter a Pembrokeshire corgi named DOOKIE and Elizabeth has been associated with the breed ever since.

A later dog, SUSAN, an 18th birthday

Royal Pets

The royal fascination with animals and pets goes back to HENRY I, who in 1129 put up 7 miles (11 km) of wall around his hunting lodge at WOODSTOCK, near Oxford, creating THE FIRST ENCLOSED PARK IN ENGLAND. The walls were built to keep in his menagerie, which included lions, camels, leopards and THE FIRST PORCUPINE SEEN IN ENGLAND.

present from her father, travelled with Elizabeth and Philip in their open carriage as they drove through London on the way to their honeymoon in Hampshire. Susan eventually produced 30 royal puppies, all of whom inherited her naughty temperament.

The royal corgis have a reputation for unruly behaviour. Amongst other misdemeanours, they have knocked out a royal butler, Paul Burrell, by toppling him on the stairs, torn the seat out of a Guards officer's trousers, savaged the leg of a royal clock winder and even bitten the Queen herself, during a dogfight in 1991, after which she required three stitches in her hand.

The Queen is usually accompanied by a pack of four or five corgis and has even developed her own special breed of 'dorgi', a cross between a corgi and a dachshund.

The gourmet daily menu enjoyed by the corgis, or dorgis, consists of Pedigree Chum embellished with fresh steak, rabbit or chicken, which is customarily fed to them by the Queen using a silver spoon and fork. For breakfast there is toast and marmalade with Her Majesty, and at tea-time, crumbled fresh baked scones and butter.

In 1255 King Louis IX of France presented HENRY III with an elephant, THE FIRST ELEPHANT SEEN IN ENGLAND since the Roman Emperor Claudius's invasion in AD 42, when Claudius is believed to have used elephants to frighten the Celtic defenders during the siege of Colchester. Henry's elephant was brought up the Thames by boat and then walked to the Tower of London, where the King already kept quite a menagerie, with leopards and a polar bear given by Haakon IV of Norway in 1252.

After MARY, QUEEN OF SCOTS, was executed at Fotheringhay Castle in Northamptonshire in February 1587, her limp, headless body began to move causing much alarm – hidden under Mary's gown was her little terrier GEDDON, Mary's constant friend during those last years of imprisonment, who had stayed with her to the end.

Like his grandmother, CHARLES I went to his death accompanied by his dog. On the morning of 30 January 1649, after Charles had taken Communion in the Chapel Royal at St James's Palace, his faithful hound ROGUE bounded happily along behind the King as Charles was escorted across St James's Park to his doom at the Banqueting House in Whitehall.

CHARLES II gave his name to a breed of spaniel from the Far East of which he was particularly fond, the KING CHARLES SPANIEL.

Royal Thespians

As a young girl in the Second World War, Princess Elizabeth acted in a number of pantomimes, which were usually performed in the Waterloo Chamber in Windsor Castle.

She was following in a noble royal tradition. In 1516 HENRY VIII took a leading part in THE FIRST MASQUERADE SEEN IN ENGLAND, performed in the park surrounding Greenwich Palace.

JAMES I and his wife ANNE OF DENMARK were particularly fond of masques, theatrical performances in which everyone could dress up and there was plenty of song and dance. They were mainly held at the Queen's residence SOMERSET PALACE, by the River Thames in London. Playwright BEN JONSON gained great favour by writing a number of masques especially for the Royal Family, which included

Somerset House, as it now appears

roles for the Queen and for James's eldest son PRINCE HENRY. Jonson was given a paid position at court and a lifetime pension, and is regarded as perhaps THE FIRST EXAMPLE OF A POET LAUREATE, although the position would not be officially established until Charles II made JOHN DRYDEN Poet Laureate in 1668.

The architect INIGO JONES made his name by designing the sets and costumes for Ben Jonson's court masques.

Royal Performances

In November 2004, Elizabeth II invited the West End cast of LES MISERABLES to perform in front of JACQUES CHIRAC, the French President, at Windsor Castle, THE FIRST TIME THE CAST OF A WEST END MUSICAL HAD PERFORMED IN A ROYAL RESIDENCE.

ELIZABETH I was a great patron of the theatre and ordered her Lord Chamberlain to grant a licence to a troupe of actors, led by WILLIAM SHAKESPEARE, who became known as the LORD CHAMBERLAIN'S MEN. While staying at Windsor Castle Elizabeth asked Shakespeare to write a play for her, 'in a fortnight', and the result was THE MERRY WIVES OF WINDSOR, which in 1602 had its FIRST PERFORMANCE IN FRONT OF ELIZABETH I IN WINDSOR CASTLE.

JAMES I promoted the troupe from the Lord Chamberlain's to THE KING'S MEN, and many of Shakespeare's plays were premiered in front of James's royal court at Whitehall Palace and in the Great Hall at Hampton Court.

Childhood Homes

White Lodge

The WHITE LODGE in Richmond Park, originally known as the New Lodge, was built as a hunting lodge for GEORGE II and his wife QUEEN CAROLINE in 1729. In 1751 their daughter PRINCESS AMELIA moved in there when she became Ranger of Richmond Park and caused much consternation by closing the park to the public, a decision that was reversed in 1758. In the meantime she added two flanking wings to the lodge.

On Princess Amelia's death, the Prime Minister, the 3RD EARL OF BUTE, became Ranger and lived in the lodge until he died in 1792. During this time it became known as the White Lodge, and George III and Queen Charlotte were frequent visitors for Sunday lunch.

Another Prime Minister, HENRY ADDINGTON, took over the lodge and created a private garden there in 1805. In the same year he was visited at the lodge by Lord Nelson just before Nelson sailed to fight the French at the Battle of Trafalgar.

Queen Victoria gave the White Lodge to her aunt, PRINCESS MARY, last surviving daughter of George III, and then Prince Albert decided to send the 17-year-old EDWARD, PRINCE OF WALES there to study, away from the distractions of London. Not surprisingly, Edward found life at the White Lodge deadly dull.

In 1861 Queen Victoria stayed at the lodge with Prince Albert while grieving over the death of her mother, and only a few months later Albert was dead too.

In 1869 PRINCESS MARY ADELAIDE, DUCHESS OF TECK, a granddaughter of George III and cousin of Queen Victoria, was given the lodge. In 1893 Victoria's grandson George, Duke of York married the Duchess of Teck's daughter Mary, and in 1894 Mary gave birth at the White Lodge to her first child, the future Edward VIII. Queen Victoria came to the lodge to see the new baby.

In 1923 Edward's younger brother Prince Albert, Duke of York, the future George VI, and his new bride Elizabeth spent part of their honeymoon at the White Lodge and loved it so much they eventually took up residence there, enlarging the house to make it into a family home and landscaping the gardens. Their daughter Princess Elizabeth spent her early years there, and on her birth certificate the White Lodge is given as her parents' address.

The White Lodge is now the home of the ROYAL BALLET SCHOOL.

Royal Lodge Windsor

There has been a house on the site of the ROYAL LODGE in Windsor Great Park, 3 miles (5 km) south of Windsor Castle, since the mid 17th century, but the first royal to occupy the site was the PRINCE REGENT, who moved there in 1815 after alterations were undertaken by John Nash to turn the property into an elaborate rustic cottage, or summer house, known as a cottage orne. Sir Jeffrey Wyattville made additions and the house became known as the Royal Lodge.

Much of the house was demolished on the orders of William IV in 1830, but since then the lodge has been developed piecemeal around the surviving conservatory. In 1931 the Royal Lodge was granted to the future George VI and his wife Elizabeth, who enlarged it with flanking wings and entrance lodges. The house now has some 30 rooms, including seven bedrooms and the original conservatory.

After the death of George VI, his widow, now known as the QUEEN MOTHER, continued to use the Royal Lodge as her Windsor home. She died there in her sleep in March 2002 at the age of 101, THE LONGEST LIVING QUEEN IN BRITISH ROYAL HISTORY and, at the time, THE LONGEST LIVING MEMBER OF THE BRITISH ROYAL FAMILY IN HISTORY – the latter title later went to her sister-in-law PRINCESS ALICE, DUCHESS OF GLOUCESTER, who died in 2004 at the age of 102.

Before being taken to London, where the Queen Mother would lie in state in Westminster Hall, her coffin rested in the tiny ROYAL CHAPEL OF ALL SAINTS in the grounds of the Royal Lodge. The chapel had been originally converted out of a porter's lodge by George IV and then rebuilt in the reign of Queen Victoria, with an east window dedicated to the memory of Victoria's mother the Duchess of Kent. Members of the Royal Family still attend services in the chapel when they wish to be private.

In 2004 the Royal Lodge became the official residence of PRINCE ANDREW, DUKE OF YORK, the second son of Queen Elizabeth II.

Y Bwthyn Bach

In 1932 a small straw-thatched cottage called Y BWTHYN BACH (the Little

House) was erected in the gardens of the Royal Lodge as a gift from the people of Wales to Princess Elizabeth and Princess Margaret, the daughters of the Duke of York, the future George VI, and his wife Elizabeth. The cottage, fully furnished and with its own scaled-down garden, is still standing today. The house is so tiny that when the Princesses' grandmother Queen Mary paid a visit she got stuck in the sitting room.

Well, I never *knew this*
about
QUEEN ELIZABETH II

The Queen's birthplace, 17 BRUTON STREET, built in 1742, was demolished in 1937 and replaced with an office block, Berkeley Square House. A small plaque commemorates the birth.

While Elizabeth II was sitting in a tree house in Kenya when she heard that she had become Queen, her namesake Elizabeth I was sitting under an oak tree in the grounds of Hatfield Palace when she heard that she had become Queen.

ELIZABETH II was 25 years old when she became Queen in 1952, the same age as her namesake ELIZABETH I when the latter succeeded her sister Mary in 1558.

Sir Edmund Hillary and Sherpa Tensing became THE FIRST MEN TO REACH THE TOP OF MOUNT EVEREST just four days before Queen Elizabeth II's coronation in 1953.

Elizabeth II is the FORTIETH MONARCH since William the Conqueror.

Elizabeth II is 5 ft 4 in (1.63 m) tall, the same height as Elizabeth I and Charles I, who is BRITAIN'S SHORTEST KING. The TALLEST BRITISH MONARCH to date is Edward IV, who was 6 ft 4 in (1.93 m) tall.

TONY BLAIR, born in May 1953, is THE FIRST PRIME MINISTER TO HAVE BEEN BORN DURING ELIZABETH II'S REIGN. DAVID CAMERON, born in 1966, is THE ONLY PRIME MINISTER TO HAVE BEEN BORN SINCE HER CORONATION.

Elizabeth II is a keen pigeon racer and Patron of the ROYAL PIGEON RACING ASSOCIATION. In 1990 one of the Queen's birds won a section of the INTERNATIONAL PAU RACE, held in southern France, one of the four 'classic' pigeon races, and was afterwards named SANDRINGHAM LIGHTNING.

In 1986 Elizabeth II became THE FIRST BRITISH MONARCH TO VISIT CHINA.

Elizabeth II is a fluent French speaker.

In 2007 Elizabeth II became THE FIRST BRITISH MONARCH TO CELEBRATE A DIAMOND WEDDING ANNIVERSARY.

The Queen once demoted a footman for feeding the royal corgis whisky.

An earlier Queen Elizabeth, ELIZABETH OF YORK, was THE ONLY ENGLISH QUEEN to have been not only the wife of an English monarch (Henry VII), but also the daughter (Edward IV), sister (Edward V), and niece (Richard III) of an English monarch. A portrait of her by an unknown artist that hangs in the National Portrait Gallery in London is thought to be THE MODEL FOR THE QUEEN IN A PACK OF CARDS.

CHAPTER TWO

ROYAL CELEBRATIONS & PAGEANTRY

JUBILEES ✦ ENTHRONEMENTS AND CORONATIONS

Jubilees

2012 marks the DIAMOND JUBILEE of Queen Elizabeth II, celebrating 60 years of her reign.

No British king has achieved a Diamond Jubilee and Elizabeth II is only the second British monarch to achieve one, the other being Queen Victoria. Only Victoria, who reigned for 63 years and 216 days, has reigned for longer then Elizabeth II.

Diamond Jubilees

Queen Victoria

Queen Victoria's Diamond Jubilee in 1897 was a celebration of the British Empire, with particular regard to Victoria's role as Empress of India. The highlight was the Queen's Procession from Buckingham Palace to St Paul's Cathedral escorted by soldiers from all parts of the Empire. At St Paul's, the thanksgiving service was held outside because the Queen was too frail to leave her carriage and mount the steps into the church. Eleven colonial prime ministers were present. Victoria also reviewed the Royal Navy at Spithead from Osborne House on the Isle of Wight, through a telescope.

Queen Elizabeth II

After much debate it was decided that Queen Elizabeth's Diamond Jubilee should be celebrated with a Jubilee Woods project, namely the planting of 60 woods of 60 acres (24 ha), the issuing of a Queen's Diamond Jubilee Medal, the lighting of thousands of Jubilee Beacons around the world on 4 June, and THE MOST SPECTACULAR RIVER PAGEANT EVER WITNESSED ON THE THAMES, consisting of over 1,000 boats and stretching for over 7 miles.

Golden Jubilees

Four British kings reached their Golden Jubilee. The first was HENRY III, who reigned for 56 years and 29 days from 1216 to 1272, and the next was EDWARD

III, who reigned for 50 years and 147 days from 1327 to 1377. It is not known if either of these kings celebrated the occasion.

JAMES VI OF SCOTLAND (James I of England) reigned as King of Scotland for 57 years and 246 days from 1567 to 1625, THE LONGEST REIGN OF ANY KING OF SCOTLAND. When James left Scotland to become James I of England in 1603, he promised to return to his homeland every three years. In fact, he only went back once, in 1617, to celebrate his 50 years as King of Scotland.

GEORGE III reigned for 59 years and 96 days from 1760 to 1820. His Golden Jubilee was THE FIRST ROYAL JUBILEE TO BE CELEBRATED as such, with a fete and firework display at Frogmore.

Queen Victoria's Golden Jubilee was celebrated with a large family dinner at Buckingham Palace for 50 foreign kings and princes, all of whom were related to Victoria. The following day Victoria processed to Westminster Abbey escorted by the Indian cavalry along a route lined with soldiers from across the Empire. She then made an appearance on the balcony of Buckingham Palace before watching fireworks in the palace gardens.

Elizabeth II

Elizabeth II's Golden Jubilee in 2002 was celebrated with a weekend of events and festivities throughout Britain and the Commonwealth.

The Queen held a thanksgiving service at St George's in Windsor while other members of the Royal Family attended services elsewhere throughout Britain, the Prince of Wales and Princes William and Harry in Swansea.

In London the BUCKINGHAM PALACE GARDENS were OPENED TO THE PUBLIC FOR THE FIRST TIME, for two public concerts, starting with a classical PROM AT THE PALACE, attended by 12,500 people and THE LARGEST EVENT EVER HELD ON ROYAL PROPERTY. This was followed the next evening by the PARTY AT THE PALACE, highlighting 50 years of British pop music, during which Elizabeth II was serenaded by Paul McCartney, and guitarist Brian May of Queen performed 'God Save the Queen' from the palace roof.

At the end of the concert, echoing Queen Victoria's Golden Jubilee, Elizabeth II lit the National Beacon at the Victoria Memorial in front of the Palace, the last in a chain of over 2,000 beacons lit around the world.

The next day the Queen processed in the Golden State Coach to St Paul's Cathedral for the National Thanksgiving Service, and this was followed in the afternoon by a parade of floats illustrating British life over 50 years accompanied by schoolchildren from every Commonwealth country in National dress. Over a million people filled the Mall as the Queen and Royal Family gathered on the balcony at Buckingham Palace to watch the flypast, which included every kind of aircraft in service with the Royal Air Force, as well as Concorde and the Red Arrows.

Enthronements and Coronations

Early monarchs were invested with sovereign power at enthronements. Coronations, where the monarch was crowned, began later with the Saxon kings – the word 'king' comes from the Saxon word 'cyning' meaning an elected sacred and military leader.

The first enthronements known about in Britain were held at the Iron Age hill fort of DUNADD in Argyllshire in the 6th century. Dunadd was the capital of the Scotii, settlers from the ancient Irish Gaelic kingdom of Dalriada in the north of Ireland. The name Scot comes from the Roman word for the Irish, Scotii, and the first Kings of Scotland emerged from the kings who were crowned at Dunadd.

Dunadd is a 175 ft (53 m) high crag that rises out of the eerily flat, brown and barren area of bog known as Crinan Moss, a few miles north of Lochgilphead. A rocky path winds uncertainly to the summit through a series of fortified terraces and gateways, and at the top there are carvings, Ogham writings, a basin scooped out of the rock, and what appears to be a seat or throne – all indications that this was somewhere special.

The Kings of Dalriada were enthroned right here, seated on the Stone of Destiny, brought with them from Ireland. Following the Irish tradition a king was inaugurated by placing his foot into an imprint carved in the rock and there is just such an imprint here, in which you can still place your own foot.

AIDAN, THE FIRST CHRISTIAN KING OF SCOTLAND, was enthroned here in 574 by ST COLUMBA, the Irish monk who founded the monastery on Iona. This was THE VERY FIRST CHRISTIAN ENTHRONEMENT IN BRITAIN.

Dunadd is a wonderfully evocative place to be at dusk. Apart from a small farm at the foot of the rock, the stupendous view from Dunadd is probably much the same now as it was for King Aidan and his court. The landscape is still, empty and mystical. To the north and east are the hills of Argyll. To the west, across the gold, glittering sea, lie the fiery Paps of Jura, and all around the ghosts of ancient kings moan from beneath the mossy ground.

In 843 the Stone of Destiny was taken from Dunadd to Scone in modern Perthshire by THE FIRST KING OF SCOTLAND, KENNETH MACALPIN.

Scone

Kenneth moved his capital from Dunadd to SCONE, in Perthshire, which thus became THE FIRST CAPITAL OF SCOTLAND. He also set up the Stone of Destiny there, and for the next 450 years all the Kings of Scotland were enthroned on the Moot Hill at Scone.

Macbeth's stepson LULACH was THE FIRST SCOTTISH KING TO HAVE A CORONATION AT SCONE, being crowned there rather than just enthroned in 1057. A century later, an abbey was founded there by ALEXANDER I.

JOHN BALLIOL was THE LAST SCOTTISH KING TO BE CROWNED ON THE STONE OF DESTINY, AT SCONE, in 1292.

Although the Stone of Destiny was removed by Edward I in 1296 Scone remained the coronation site of the Scottish kings for another 350 years. Robert the Bruce was crowned at Scone in 1306, as was the first Stewart king, Robert II, in 1371 – two years later a parliament met in the abbey at Scone to declare Robert and his line as legitimate heirs, thus confirming the Stewart line.

The LAST CORONATION AT SCONE was that of CHARLES II, on New Year's Day in 1651, just before he was temporarily deposed by Oliver Cromwell at the Battle of Worcester.

Kingston-upon-Thames

Before 1066 coronations in England were held in a number of different places including Bath, Winchester, Kingston-upon-Thames, Canterbury and Gloucester.

[14]

Stone of Destiny

The Stone of Destiny, or Stone of Scone, as it became known, is a block of sandstone from the Holy Land, upon which successive Dalriadan, Scottish, English and British kings and queens have been enthroned. The stone is reputed to have been used as a pillow by the biblical figure Jacob and then brought to Dunadd through Egypt, Sicily, Spain and Ireland. After Kenneth MacAlpin took the stone to Scone in 843, it remained there until 1296, when Edward I removed it to Westminster Abbey. There it was placed in a compartment below the wooden chair Edward had commissioned as a coronation chair, called King Edward's Chair after Edward the Confessor. Every monarch since Edward II has been seated in this chair, above the Stone of Destiny, for the coronation ceremony.

There is a rumour that the Scots didn't hand over the real Stone of Destiny to Edward in 1296 at all, but rather the capstone to the palace privy. They then hid the genuine Stone under Dunsinane Hill where it awaits the next true, independent King of Scotland to retrieve it.

In 1950 the Stone of Destiny was stolen from Westminster Abbey by nationalist students and recovered from beneath the altar at Arbroath Abbey, where it had been placed as a symbolic gesture.

In 1996 the Stone was finally returned to Scotland for good, and it now sits amongst the crown jewels of Scotland in Edinburgh Castle. It will be taken down to Westminster Abbey for the next coronation and then sent back to Edinburgh until it is needed again.

One of the earliest established coronation sites in England was at Kingston-upon-Thames in Surrey, where during the 10th century seven Saxon kings were crowned while standing upon the ancient KING'S STONE, a large boulder that now sits behind railings outside Kingston's Guildhall. This stone may not be much to look at, but it is THE EARLIEST THRONE OF ENGLISH KINGS.

The dimensions of the Saxon chapel of St Mary where the coronations took place are marked out beside the present Norman church of All Saints next to the market-place. The chapel fell down in 1730, undermined by grave-digging.

Kingston has since grown into a bustling market town and hides its venerable heritage well, but in 1977 during her Silver Jubilee year, the present Queen of England, Elizabeth II, came to the town where the first Kings of England were crowned and unveiled a stone to her ancestor Edward the Elder.

Edgar, King of England

In 973, EDGAR was crowned as the FIRST KING OF ENGLAND in the Benedictine abbey of the imperial Roman city of BATH.

The abbey stood right beside the Roman baths, and the imperial symbolism was deliberate: although the unification of England had been begun

Bath Abbey today

The seven kings crowned at Kingston were

EADWEARD THE ELDER in 902

ATHELSTAN in 925

EDMUND I (THE MAGNIFICENT) in 940

EADRED, Edmund's brother, in 946

EDGAR THE PEACEFUL in 959. In 973 Edgar was crowned as THE FIRST OFFICIALLY RECOGNISED KING OF ENGLAND (as opposed to King of Wessex) in Bath Abbey.

EADWEARD THE MARTYR in 975. In 978 he was murdered at Corfe Castle by his stepmother ELFRIDA to clear the way for her son,

ETHELRED THE UNREADY, who was crowned in 979.

by his great-grandfather Alfred the Great, and was largely achieved by Edgar's predecessors, Edgar's coronation was the culmination of their work and he was being crowned as THE FIRST RULER OF A UNITED ENGLAND since the end of the Roman occupation.

Coronation Service

The coronation service was devised by DUNSTAN, the Archbishop of Canterbury, as a religious ceremony, in which Edgar was anointed as if by God, in the same way that King David of Israel had been, and the service has remained substantially unchanged ever since. The same rituals were performed, the same oaths were sworn and many of the same words were spoken (including the words of 'Zadok the Priest') at the coronation of Elizabeth II in Westminster Abbey in 1953 as at the coronation of Edgar in Bath Abbey almost 1,000 years earlier.

Westminster Abbey

Although it is believed that King Harold was crowned in Westminster Abbey in January 1066, the day after Edward the Confessor died, THE FIRST RECORDED CORONATION AT WESTMINSTER ABBEY was that of WILLIAM I (the Conqueror) on Christmas Day 1066. William chose to be crowned in Edward the Confessor's church to reinforce his position as the Confessor's legitimate successor.

William's coronation established Westminster Abbey as the coronation church, and every subsequent English

and British monarch has been crowned there except for two – Edward V, who was murdered in the Tower before his coronation in 1483, and Edward VIII, who abdicated before his in 1936.

When Henry III rebuilt Edward the Confessor's church in 1245, he copied the design of the French coronation church, Reims Cathedral, in recognition of Westminster Abbey's role as England's coronation church, leaving a large central space in front of the High Altar suitable for the theatrical element of the ceremony.

Coronation Chair

The FIRST KING TO BE CROWNED IN HENRY III'S NEW GOTHIC ABBEY was EDWARD I in 1274. In 1298 Edward had the CORONATION CHAIR built to house the Stone of Destiny that he had brought down from Scotland, and this chair has been used for the actual moment of crowning at every coronation since. It has only been removed from the abbey once, for the installation of Oliver Cromwell as Lord Protector in Westminster Hall in 1653. In the 18th century, Westminster choirboys are said to have carved their names on the chair and in the early 20th century a suffragette hung a handbag containing a bomb on the chair, which blew off one of the pinnacles.

King Edgar's coronation service in Bath Abbey was spoken in Latin. THE FIRST CORONATION SERVICE IN WHICH ENGLISH WAS SPOKEN was that of ELIZABETH I in 1558, which was a mixture of Latin and English. Because of this the Archbishop of Canterbury refused to crown Elizabeth and the Bishop of Carlisle did so instead.

At the coronation of James I (James VI of Scotland) the Liturgy was read entirely in English. In 1689 the service was adapted to take account of the fact that William and Mary were joint monarchs and a second coronation chair was constructed so that both monarchs could be crowned simultaneously.

Crown Jewels

Crown Jewels, or Regalia, have been used at coronations in England, Scotland and Wales since Saxon times. The British monarchy is THE ONLY EUROPEAN MONARCHY TO STILL USE ITS CROWN JEWELS FOR CORONATIONS.

The Crown Jewels held in the Tower of London are THE LARGEST AND MOST VALUABLE COLLECTION OF REGALIA IN USE IN THE WORLD, containing 23,578 gems, including two of the world's most famous diamonds, the CULLINAN I and the KOH-I-NOOR.

In 1649, after the execution of Charles I, the Crown Jewels were destroyed on the instructions of Oliver Cromwell, although it was rumoured that Henrietta Maria, widow of Charles I, had in fact

The CULLINAN I, or GREAT STAR OF AFRICA, was given to Edward VII by the government of the Transvaal in 1907. It is mounted in the Royal Sceptre and was, until 1985, THE LARGEST CUT DIAMOND IN THE WORLD. The Cullinan I was the largest of the polished gems to be cut from THE LARGEST ROUGH GEM-QUALITY DIAMOND EVER FOUND, THE CULLINAN DIAMOND, which was discovered in the Premier Mine near Pretoria in South Africa in 1905. Currently, the largest cut diamond in the world is called the Golden Jubilee, which was cut from a stone found in the same South African mine and now resides with the Crown Jewels of Thailand. In 2007 a new diamond, said to be twice the size of the Cullinan I, was discovered in South Africa's North-West Province.

The KOH-I-NOOR diamond, which came to Britain from the Punjab in 1850, is mounted in the crown of the Queen Consort (originally for Edward VII's consort, Queen Alexandra in 1902). It was first recorded in the 14th century, although is said to date from before the time of Christ and at some point belonged to the great Mughal emperors. It is said that whoever owns the Koh-i-Noor can rule the world but that only 'God, or a woman, can wear it without misfortune', hence its use in the Queen's crown.

smuggled the Regalia out of the country and sold it in France. Since then it has been illegal to take any of the Crown Jewels out of the country.

Only four items of the original Regalia survived – the three coronation swords, of Temporal Justice, of Spiritual Justice and of Mercy, and a gold 12th-century Anointing Spoon used to anoint the sovereign with holy oil, which is the oldest piece of the Regalia remaining.

At the Restoration Charles II ordered that new Crown Jewels should be made, modelled on the lost Regalia, and these were ready in time for his coronation on St George's Day, 23 April 1661. Principal amongst these are the Royal Orb and Sceptre, and the St Edward's Crown.

Crowns

The Crown Jewels include several crowns. The official coronation crown, which is actually placed on the sovereign's head at the coronation, is the ST EDWARD'S CROWN, set with 444 precious stones. The original St Edward's Crown was used by Edward the Confessor, from whom it takes its name, and incorporated gold from the crown of Alfred the Great. It was used at the coronations of all the Norman kings, William the Conqueror, William II, Henry I and Stephen and also for the early Plantagenet Kings, Henry II, Richard the Lionheart and John. John is thought to have lost St Edward's Crown in the Wash (see page 151) although some believe the crown survived until the Civil War when it

was destroyed by Oliver Cromwell. The current St Edward's Crown is extremely heavy and uncomfortable and a number of monarchs since 1661 have chosen to be crowned with their own specially made crowns, including Queen Victoria and Edward VII who were both crowned with a more manageable custom-made diamond crown. Monarchs who have been crowned with the 1661 St Edward's Crown are Charles II, James II, William of Orange, George V, George VI and Elizabeth II.

The IMPERIAL STATE CROWN, similar to the small diamond crown made for the coronations of Queen Victoria and Edward VII, was created for the coronation of George VI in 1937 and includes 2,868 diamonds, 273 pearls, 17 sapphires, 11 emeralds and 5 rubies. Amongst the jewels are a sapphire taken from Edward the Confessor's ring, the Black Prince's ruby, given to the Black Prince in 1367 and allegedly worn by Henry V at the Battle of Agincourt in 1415, the CULLINAN II, or Lesser Star of Africa, cut from the same stone as the Cullinan I, and two pearls worn by Elizabeth I. The Imperial State Crown is worn at the conclusion of the coronation service and at the State Opening of Parliament.

The IMPERIAL CROWN OF INDIA, set with over 6,000 diamonds, was created for George V to wear for his coronation as Emperor of India at the Delhi Durbar of 1911. It has never been worn since.

The Honours of Scotland

Scotland's royal Regalia, THE HONOURS OF SCOTLAND, are THE OLDEST ROYAL

REGALIA IN EUROPE. They consist of a sceptre and a sword of state with an elaborate belt given to James IV of Scotland by the Pope in the early 16th century and a crown of Scottish gold refashioned in its present form for James V in 1540. They were first used all together for the coronation of the infant Mary, Queen of Scots, at Stirling Castle in 1543. They are now on permanent display in the Crown Room at Edinburgh Castle.

The Honours of the Principality of Wales
The crowns and coronets used by the rulers of Wales's most powerful kingdom, Gwynedd, have all been lost. LLYWELYN'S CORONET, the crown used by Llywelyn ap Gruffudd, the last independent Prince of Wales, was seized by Edward I in 1284 and put with the rest of the English Crown Jewels, which were subsequently destroyed by Oliver Cromwell.

Charles II ordered Regalia, consisting of a coronet, a ring, a rod and a mantle, to be made for the investiture of future Princes of Wales, and in 1911 a new set of honours was made for the investiture of Prince Edward (later Edward VIII). These honours were used for the investiture of Prince Charles in 1969 and are at present on loan to the National Museum of Wales in Cardiff.

Well, I never knew this about
ROYAL CELEBRATIONS & PAGEANTRY

The stretch of the River Thames between Westminster Bridge and London Bridge was named KING's REACH in celebration of the Silver Jubilee of George V in 1935.

At 76 years of age in 2002, Elizabeth II was THE OLDEST MONARCH TO CELEBRATE A GOLDEN JUBILEE. The youngest was James VI of Scotland (James I of England) at the age of 51.

THE FIRST RECORDED CONSECRATION, as opposed to coronation, in English royal history, was the consecration of King Offa's son ECGFRITH in the Saxon church at Lichfield in 787. In order to ensure the succession, Offa had his son consecrated while he, Offa, was still alive. The ceremony was a mixture of Anglo-Saxon tradition, Ecgfrith being 'crowned' with a royal warrior's helmet, and Christian ritual as used for the inauguration of the Old Testament kings.

At WILLIAM THE CONQUEROR'S coronation in 1066 there was chaos when the Norman soldiers on guard outside heard shouting, as the mixed congregation of Norman and English nobles cried out their salutations at the moment of crowning. The guards thought the King was being attacked and panicked, setting fire to the houses outside, causing riots and sending smoke billowing into the abbey. Despite the pandemonium William forced the terrified Archbishop of York, Eadred, to complete the ceremony.

HENRY III was crowned in Gloucester in 1216 because London and Winchester were still in the hands of the French Dauphin, who had been invited in by the barons opposed to Henry's father King John. A simple gold bracelet belonging to Henry's mother was used in place of the grand St Edward's Crown

that John had lost in the Wash. Later, in 1220, Henry was crowned again in a proper ceremony at Westminster Abbey.

In 1377 RICHARD II held THE FIRST EVER CORONATION PROCESSION, from the Tower of London to Westminster Abbey. Hanging from one of the pillars in the nave of the abbey is a wooden panel painting representing his coronation. The painting shows Richard wearing coronation robes, seated in the coronation chair and holding the orb and sceptre. It dates from the 1390s and is THE OLDEST KNOWN CONTEMPORARY PORTRAIT OF A MONARCH.

HENRY IV, THE FIRST KING OF ENGLAND TO HAVE ENGLISH AS HIS MOTHER TONGUE SINCE THE NORMAN CONQUEST, gave the FIRST CORONATION ADDRESS IN ENGLISH.

The anthem 'I Was Glad' was first sung at the coronation service of CHARLES I in 1626.

Bad omens attended the coronation of JAMES II in 1685 – the crown almost fell from his head and the royal standard on the Tower of London was ripped by the wind. James reigned for just four years before being deposed by William and Mary.

The coronation of WILLIAM AND MARY was the first double coronation at Westminster Abbey. During the investiture their coronation rings were muddled up and Mary's ruby ring was placed on William's finger by mistake.

QUEEN ANNE, at her coronation in 1702, was so racked with gout that she had to be carried to the abbey in a sedan chair, with the back cut out for the 20 ft (6 m) train of her dress.

GEORGE II's coronation at Westminster Abbey in October 1727 was a glamorous affair. A blue carpet strewn with flowers and herbs was laid along the route from Westminster Hall to the Abbey, and Handel composed four new anthems for the service, including 'ZADOK THE PRIEST', a musical setting of the words of the biblical account of the anointing of Solomon, which had been spoken at every coronation since that of King Edgar at Bath Abbey in 973. Handel's

'Zadok the Priest' has been sung at every subsequent coronation, during the anointing of the new monarch.

GEORGE IV's coronation in 1821 was the most extravagant and sumptuous coronation ever held. The ageing and corpulent King required 19 handkerchiefs to mop his brow as he sweated in his heavy robes, long wig and specially created crown, which contained over 12,000 diamonds. George barred his unloved queen, CAROLINE OF BRUNSWICK, from the service, but she pounded on the door of the abbey, demanding to be let in, before being hustled away by embarrassed courtiers. Caroline took ill that same day, and died three weeks later in Brandenburgh House by the Thames at Hammersmith. George later had the house razed to the ground.

Such was the public disapproval at the lavishness of George IV's coronation that in 1831 WILLIAM IV had to be persuaded to have a coronation at all, and it was kept a very low-key affair, with no banquet afterwards.

QUEEN VICTORIA's coronation service in 1838 was chaotic. Her ring was placed on the wrong finger; an elderly peer, Lord Rollie, fell down the steps while paying homage to the Queen; and Victoria left her seat after being told the ceremony was over by a confused bishop, and then had to return to it. She still called it 'the proudest day of my life'.

EDWARD VII's coronation had to be postponed when he got appendicitis.

He was operated on in Buckingham Palace, in one of the rooms overlooking the garden, by Sir Frederick Treves, famous for his work with Joseph Merrick, the Elephant Man.

Richard the lionheart was the first King of England to use the 'Three Lions' in his royal coat of arms. He combined the Angevin lion of his father Henry II with his mother's lion of Aquitaine and added his own as King of England. The lion depicted on the Royal Standard of Scotland was taken from the heraldic symbol of William I of Scotland, a red lion rampant on a yellow background. William himself became known as William the Lion.

CHAPTER THREE

ROYAL WESTMINSTER

WESTMINSTER ABBEY ✦ THE PALACE OF WESTMINSTER

Westminster Abbey

For nearly 1,000 years, since Edward the Confessor decided to build an abbey and a palace there, WESTMINSTER has been the scene of coronations, royal weddings and funerals, processions, state occasions and sumptuous royal pageantry, ceremony and drama.

On 29 April 2011 WESTMINSTER ABBEY hosted a spectacular Royal Wedding as Queen Elizabeth's grandson PRINCE WILLIAM married CATHERINE (KATE) MIDDLETON in front of 2,000 invited guests and an estimated worldwide television audience of some 200 million. The best man was Prince William's brother PRINCE HARRY, while the Maid of Honour was Catherine's sister PIPPA. The abbey was decorated with an avenue of real maple and hornbeam trees, which were arranged on either side of the main aisle of the nave.

There was a poignancy about the venue, as 14 years earlier Westminster Abbey had held the funeral for Prince William's mother, DIANA, PRINCESS OF WALES.

After the service Prince William and

his bride processed in an open carriage to Buckingham Palace for a reception hosted by the Queen. The bride and groom later emerged on to the balcony of Buckingham Palace and recreated the famous kiss with which Prince William's parents Charles and Diana had delighted the watching crowds on their own wedding day in 1981.

Royal Marriages at Westminster Abbey

Westminster Abbey is a relatively recent venue for royal weddings. Traditionally they were held in the Chapel Royal at St James's Palace or in St George's Chapel at Windsor. Royal weddings in the abbey have included:

PRINCESS ELIZABETH (later Elizabeth II) and PRINCE PHILIP in 1947

PRINCESS MARGARET and ANTHONY ARMSTRONG-JONES in 1960

PRINCESS ANNE and CAPTAIN MARK PHILLIPS in 1973

PRINCE ANDREW and SARAH FERGUSON in 1986

Saxon Westminster Abbey

The first Westminster Abbey was built in 1050 by Edward the Confessor. Early on in his reign Edward had sworn to make a pilgrimage to the tomb of St Peter in Rome, but affairs of state had left him no time, so the Pope released Edward from his vow on condition that he raised an abbey to St Peter instead. Edward determined to build the greatest abbey ever seen. It would be built in the grand Romanesque style that Edward had so admired during his exile in Normandy and would be unlike any church ever seen before in England.

He decided he would build his 'west minster' on what was then an island in the Thames to the west of London, called Thorney Island, where there was already a small Saxon monastery, founded in 620 by Sebert, King of the East Saxons. This was sacred ground because legend had it that St Peter had miraculously appeared to consecrate that church himself. On the floor of the present Chapter House there are depictions of the salmon with which St Peter rewarded the ferryman who had rowed him over to the island.

Work began on Edward's new abbey in 1050. The Saxon monastery buildings were torn down and in their place arose THE FIRST ROMANESQUE BUILDING IN ENGLAND, a vast edifice, some 320 ft (98 m) long, as big as the present-day abbey. It was completed in 1065 and consecrated on 28 December – Edward died just one week later, on 5 January 1066, and was buried by the high altar of his masterpiece.

Within 24 hours Edward's brother-in-law HAROLD GODWINSON was crowned in the abbey. He was followed, on Christmas Day that same year, by WILLIAM THE CONQUEROR – and Westminster Abbey's role as the CORONATION CHURCH was established.

Edward the Confessor was the FIRST SOVEREIGN TO CARRY OUT THE CUSTOM OF TOUCHING HIS PEOPLE TO HEAL THEM – a custom that continued until the time of Queen Anne – and he was canonised in 1161.

Although the shrine of Edward the Confessor remains at the heart of the abbey, only the undercroft and the CHAPEL OF THE PYX, used to house the royal treasury, survive from Edward's Saxon church. In 2005 archaeologists uncovered the Confessor's actual tomb and vaulted burial chamber beneath the abbey's 13th-century mosaic pavement.

Chapel of the Pyx

A New Abbey

In 1245 Henry III, who venerated St Edward the Confessor and even named his eldest son after him, decided to honour England's then patron saint by replacing Edward's abbey at Westminster with an even more glorious church in the Gothic style popular on the Continent, and within which he would build Edward a magnificent shrine. The result was a wonder of early English

Edward the Confessor's Shrine

Gothic, with THE LOFTIEST NAVE IN ENGLAND, 104 ft (32 m) high, and forms the core of the abbey as we see it today. Edward the Confessor's shrine, decorated with golden images of saints and kings, was placed at the heart of the new abbey.

Chapter House

Henry was also responsible for building Westminster Abbey's famous CHAPTER HOUSE. In 1257, not long after it was completed, Henry's GREAT COUNCIL met in the Chapter House and Parliament continued to meet there until 1547, when it moved out to St Stephen's Chapel in Westminster Palace. Unusually, because of its importance as 'the cradle of representative and constitutional government throughout the world', the Chapter House, which boasts THE FINEST MEDIEVAL TILED FLOOR IN ENGLAND, is under the control of Parliament, not Westminster Abbey.

Royal Burials

Henry, THE FIRST PLANTAGENET KING TO BE BURIED IN ENGLAND, chose to be buried in the abbey near to Edward, and so established Westminster Abbey as principal royal burial place, which it remained for the next 500 years.

Henry III's magnificent abbey was completed by his great-great-great-grandson RICHARD II. When his beloved wife ANNE OF BOHEMIA died in 1394 at just 28, Richard was heartbroken and had a resplendent tomb built for her and placed near his grandfather Edward III in the Chapel of St Edward the Confessor. Richard himself, who was probably murdered on the orders of his successor Henry IV, was originally buried out of sight in a friary at King's Langley near his uncle's home, but his body was removed to Westminster Abbey by Henry V and laid to rest beside Anne. The tomb is crowned with twin effigies of Richard and Anne, with their hands once linked – but, alas, the hands have long since been chipped away by vandals.

Also in the Chapel of St Edward the Confessor lie EDWARD I and his wife ELEANOR OF CASTILE, EDWARD III and his wife PHILIPPA OF HAINAULT, and HENRY V and his wife CATHERINE DE VALOIS.

Henry VII's Chapel

In 1503 HENRY VII created a lovely new chapel at the east end of Westminster Abbey, which he intended to dedicate

to HENRY VI. It became, instead, his own burial place. The chapel boasts some of the finest fan vaulting in Britain, described by Washington Irving as having the 'wonderful minuteness and airy security of a cobweb'. Henry lies there with his wife Elizabeth of York, in a tomb sculpted by PIETRO TORRIGIANI, THE FIRST EXAMPLE OF RENAISSANCE ART IN BRITAIN.

Edward VI lies in Henry VII's chapel, as do his sisters Queen Mary and Elizabeth I, so bitterly divided by religion while they were alive, but resting in eternity together in the same tomb in the north aisle. Above them is a large white marble monument put there in memory of Elizabeth by her successor James I – Elizabeth I was THE LAST MONARCH TO HAVE A MONUMENT ERECTED ABOVE HER IN WESTMINSTER ABBEY.

Nearby is the pathetic 'INNOCENTS CORNER', supposed resting place of the two little Princes murdered in the Tower, EDWARD V and his brother RICHARD, and two of James I's daughters, three-day-old SOPHIA, lying in a cradle, and MARY, two years old, portrayed reclining on her elbow.

Stuart Burials

James I's mother, MARY, QUEEN OF SCOTS, lies in the south aisle, under a grand marble tomb James had erected for her. Mary was originally buried in Peterborough Cathedral, after her execution at Fotheringhay Castle, but James brought her to Westminster Abbey and had her laid to rest opposite her cousin Elizabeth.

James I himself lies in the vault below Henry VII, beneath a simple modern inscription, while his wife Anne of Denmark is buried in the southeastern corner of the chapel.

Charles II lies in the Stuart vault in the south aisle, as do William and Mary and Queen Anne.

Final Burial

George II was THE LAST MONARCH TO BE BURIED IN THE ABBEY. He ordered that the sides of his coffin, and that of his wife Caroline of Ansbach, should be left open within their tomb so that their dust could mingle forever.

The Palace of Westminster

THE PALACE OF WESTMINSTER today serves as the Houses of Parliament, but it is nevertheless LONDON'S OLDEST ROYAL PALACE and still goes by the name Palace of Westminster. The first palace was built by Edward the Confessor in 1050 so that he could be on hand to watch over the construction of Westminster Abbey.

Edward's decision to move his court here from London had far-reaching consequences. As an early example of the Separation of Powers, it set apart the political power of the King and the royal court from commercial power of London.

In 1512 much of the palace was burned down and Henry VIII moved his court along the road to Whitehall Palace, leaving Westminster to be rebuilt as a home for the developing English Parliament. In 1834 another great fire virtually destroyed the rebuilt palace and this was replaced by the present building, designed by Sir Charles Barry, which opened in 1860.

The only parts of the medieval royal palace to survive are WESTMINSTER HALL, the CHAPEL OF ST MARY UNDERCROFT and the JEWEL TOWER of Edward III.

Westminster Hall

'The Most Capacious Room in Christendom'

In 1097 WILLIAM II (Rufus) determined to build himself a resplendent new palace at Westminster to rival Edward

the Confessor's abbey. He began with a vast hall, 240 ft (73 m) long and 68 ft (21 m) wide, with stone walls 6 ft (1.8 m) thick, THE LARGEST HALL IN EUROPE at that time and described as 'the most capacious room in Christendom'. According to William, though, it was 'only a bedchamber in comparison with the building I intend to make'.

In the end Westminster Hall was the only part of his dream that William got to complete and it stands today as his greatest memorial. It is THE OLDEST SURVIVING PART OF THE PALACE OF WESTMINSTER, and THE OLDEST CEREMONIAL HALL IN BRITAIN.

Richard II

In 1394, Richard II began remodelling WESTMINSTER HALL. The walls were elevated and new windows were put in to accommodate the hall's most striking feature, a magnificent oak hammer beam roof, which rises to a height of 92 ft (28 m), is 240 ft (73 m) long and has a span of 68 ft (21 m). When completed it was THE LARGEST ROOF IN EUROPE, and even now it is THE LARGEST MEDIEVAL TIMBER ROOF IN

King's Champion

Originally designed as a banqueting hall, Westminster Hall hosted coronation banquets from the time of Henry II right up until George IV in 1821 – William IV refused to hold a coronation banquet in 1830 on the grounds of expense, and there has not been one since. During the coronation banquet the KING'S CHAMPION would ride through the hall in full armour, throw down his gauntlet and challenge anyone to come forward and dispute the King's right to succeed to the throne. If no challenge was issued the champion would have to reverse his horse out of the hall – no mean feat. At George IV's banquet in 1821, the champion hired a trained circus horse for the purpose, and when the crowd applauded, the horse went into its routine of circus tricks.

The position of King's Champion was created by William the Conqueror and has been held by the same family ever since, the Dymocks, who came over with William in 1066 and settled in Dymock in Gloucestershire, from where they took their name. Since they were no longer required to perform the ceremony after the last banquet in 1821, the Dymocks were appointed to the role of Standard Bearer of England, and the champion now carries the banner at the coronation.

NORTHERN EUROPE, with the WIDEST UNSUPPORTED WOODEN SPAN IN BRITAIN.

Richard's personal emblem, the white hart, is carved on the stone course running beneath the eaves, and there are stone statues of all the kings from Edward the Confessor to Richard himself standing in niches and on window sills around the building. The statues were ordered by Richard in 1385. Ironically, THE FIRST EVENT TO TAKE PLACE UNDER RICHARD'S NEW HAMMER-BEAM ROOF was his own trial in 1399, when the Lords of the Council met there to depose him and declare Henry IV King.

Significant Royal Events in Westminster Hall

In 1265 THE FIRST ELECTED PARLIAMENT, under SIMON DE MONTFORT, met in Westminster Hall.

In 1327 an assembly of earls, knights and bishops met there to announce the abdication of EDWARD II and proclaim his son KING EDWARD III.

In 1461 Edward IV proclaimed himself King there.

In 1649 the trial of CHARLES I took place in Westminster Hall. A brass plaque on the steps at the south end marks where the King stood as he was condemned. When the silver top of his cane fell off no one stooped to pick it up for him, and at that point he must have finally realised that he was doomed. A tablet on the east wall of the hall indicates the position of the door through which Charles I passed when he came to arrest the Five Members of Parliament in 1642 – the act that finally sealed his fate and brought him to trial.

In 1653 OLIVER CROMWELL was installed as Lord Protector in Westminster Hall, dressed in purple and holding a Bible and a gold sceptre, while seated in King Edward's Coronation Chair – brought across from Westminster Abbey. At the Restoration Cromwell's severed head was stuck up on a pole outside the hall, where it remained for 25 years before being blown down in a storm.

Royals who have lain in state in Westminster Hall are EDWARD VII in 1910, GEORGE V in 1936, GEORGE VI in 1952, QUEEN MARY in 1953 and QUEEN ELIZABETH THE QUEEN MOTHER in 2002. The only non-royals to have lain in state there are Prime Ministers WILLIAM GLADSTONE in 1898 and WINSTON CHURCHILL in 1965.

*Well, I never knew this
about*
ROYAL WESTMINSTER

In 1413 HENRY IV suffered a fit while praying at the shrine of Edward the Confessor in Westminster Abbey. He was carried into the JERUSALEM CHAMBER of the Abbot's House, and as he lay by the fire he asked where he was. On hearing the answer 'Jerusalem', Henry knew he was going to die, as it had been prophesied that he would die in Jerusalem.

Although Henry died in Westminster Abbey he is THE ONLY MONARCH TO BE BURIED IN CANTERBURY CATHEDRAL. His second wife, JOAN OF NAVARRE, joined him there in 1437.

Henry IV's tomb in Canterbury Cathedral

ANNE OF CLEVES is the only one of Henry VIII's six queens to be buried in Westminster Abbey.

The western towers of Westminster Abbey, which give the abbey its familiar profile, were not added until 1745, five

Burial Places of the Wives of Henry VIII

Catherine of Aragon – Peterborough Cathedral

Anne Boleyn (beheaded) – Chapel of St Peter ad Vincula in the Tower of London

Jane Seymour – St George's Chapel, Windsor, next to Henry VIII

Anne of Cleves – Westminster Abbey

Catherine Howard (beheaded) – Chapel of St Peter ad Vincula in the Tower of London

Catherine Parr – Chapel at Sudeley Castle in Gloucestershire

hundred years after Henry III's new church was begun. They were designed by NICHOLAS HAWKSMOOR.

Tucked away in the shadow of Westminster Abbey, and often overlooked, the JEWEL TOWER, along with Westminster Hall, is one of only two buildings to survive from the medieval Palace of Westminster. It was built in 1365 by Edward III to accommodate his treasury and today it houses a permanent exhibition about the history of Parliament.

During maintenance work in the 1920s, some medieval tennis balls were found in the rafters of Richard II's roof at Westminster Hall, suggesting that the hall was once used for real tennis.

Richard II's personal emblem of a WHITE HART, seen carved beneath the eaves of Westminster Hall, and painted on pub signs throughout England, can more clearly be seen on a clasp, modelled in the shape of white hart, which Richard is shown wearing in the WILTON DIPTYCH, a hinged altar-piece from Wilton House, painted by an unknown artist in the late 14th century for Richard himself. The Diptych is now on display in the National Gallery and is THE OLDEST KNOWN CONTEMPORARY PORTRAIT OF AN ENGLISH KING.

Richard II built THE FIRST ROYAL BATHHOUSE, at Westminster, and was THE FIRST ENGLISH KING TO USE A SPOON AT MEAL-TIMES. He is also recorded in contemporary documents as using square pieces of cloth to wipe his nose, and is hence credited with INVENTING THE HANDKERCHIEF.

THE GORING HOTEL, where Catherine Middleton's family were based for the Royal Wedding in 2011 was opened by Otto Goring in 1910. It was THE FIRST HOTEL IN THE WORLD WITH A PRIVATE BATHROOM AND CENTRAL HEATING IN EVERY ROOM. During the First World War the Goring became the command centre for the Chief of Allied Forces. The hotel was also a favourite venue for the Queen Mother.

The church of ST JOHN'S SMITH SQUARE, built for Queen Anne in 1714 by Thomas Archer, is affectionately known as 'Queen Anne's footstool'. When Archer told the crotchety Anne that he was seeking ideas for the design, she angrily kicked over her footstool and told him to take his inspiration from that. Hence the square shape and four corner towers.

CHAPTER FOUR

ROYAL ST JAMES'S
& WHITEHALL

BUCKINGHAM PALACE ✦ ST JAMES'S PALACE
✦ CLARENCE HOUSE ✦ MARLBOROUGH HOUSE
✦ BANQUETING HOUSE

When the Queen is in London, she resides in BUCKINGHAM PALACE, the official London residence of the British monarch since 1837.

Buckingham Palace

BUCKINGHAM PALACE is built on the site of a mulberry garden, planted by James I in order to establish an English silk industry. James's predecessor Queen Elizabeth I had made SILK STOCKINGS fashionable when she wore THE FIRST PAIR SEEN IN ENGLAND (now on display at Hatfield House), and James I decided to cash in by planting 100,000 mulberry trees to feed the silkworms, on land acquired by Henry VIII next to St James's Palace. James's

scheme unfortunately didn't work, largely because he planted the wrong type of mulberry tree.

Tea Time

The keeper of the mulberry garden, Lord Goring, built himself a house in the south of the garden which eventually passed to the Earl of Arlington and was rebuilt as Arlington House. In 1665, the year of the Great Plague, the Earl imported from Holland THE FIRST 'POUND OF TEA' TO FIND ITS WAY TO ENGLAND, and it seems reasonable to assume that it was in Arlington House, where Buckingham Palace now stands, that THE FIRST POT OF TEA IN ENGLAND WAS BREWED.

Buckingham House

In 1703 John Sheffield, Duke of Buckingham, bought the land, demolished Arlington House and built himself a palatial pile, a step to the north, calling it BUCKINGHAM HOUSE. The Duke's third wife, an illegitimate daughter of James II, lived there in grand style until she died in 1742, and eventually the house was bought by George III as a private residence for his wife, Queen Charlotte. All but one of King George and Queen Charlotte's 15 children were born in the Queen's House, as it was then known.

In June 1780, during the anti-Catholic Gordon Riots, the picturesque guardsmen in their red coats were actually called upon to defend their sovereign when a group of agitators entered St James's Park and advanced on the Queen's House. Ordered by the King not to open fire, the guards saw off the mob with fixed bayonets.

From a House to a Palace

On his accession, George IV asked JOHN NASH to transform the Queen's House into a palace, so that he could move there from nearby Carlton House. Nash enlarged the house, adding two wings to make a three-sided courtyard, and created MARBLE ARCH, based on the Arch of Constantine, as a triumphal entrance between the arms of the wings.

George IV died before the palace was finished, and his successor, William IV, hated the place, even offering it to the government after fire destroyed the Palace of Westminster in 1834. William did commission EDWARD BLORE to complete the palace, however, and so it was almost ready when Queen Victoria moved there from Kensington Palace two weeks after her accession in 1837. Queen Victoria was thus THE FIRST MONARCH TO USE BUCKINGHAM PALACE AS AN OFFICIAL RESIDENCE.

In 1847 Edward Blore enclosed the courtyard with the east front, with a wide balcony facing the Mall from which the monarch and the Royal Family could greet the crowds on state occasions. The first occasion when the balcony was used was for Queen Victoria to watch the Scots and Coldstream Guards parade before marching off to the Crimea. George VI appeared on the balcony to celebrate VE Day at the end of the Second World War, and the Royal Family now assemble on the balcony for all royal celebrations such as jubilees and weddings.

The redundant Marble Arch was moved to the former site of the Tyburn Gallows, where it now stands as the centrepiece of a traffic island and gives its name to an underground station.

In 1852 John Nash's nephew, SIR JAMES PENNETHORNE, added the south wing to Buckingham Palace, which included the massive ballroom, 123 ft (37 m) long and 60 ft (18 m) wide, not

only THE LARGEST ROOM IN BUCKINGHAM PALACE, but THE LARGEST ROOM IN LONDON at the time it was built. The first ball held in the new ballroom was in 1856 to celebrate the end of the Crimean War. Today the ballroom is used for state banquets and investitures, where the Queen stands under a giant canopy designed by Sir Edwin Lutyens from the shamiana (a kind of Indian tent) used at George V's Delhi Durbar in 1911.

After the death of Prince Albert in 1861, Queen Victoria hardly used Buckingham Palace, preferring to live at Windsor or Balmoral, and the palace was left shuttered, with with the furniture under dust sheets. In 1873 the Queen lent the palace to the SHAH OF PERSIA during his state visit and he rather made himself at home – eating his meals off the floor, organising a prize fight in the courtyard and strangling one of his staff with a bowstring, before burning the corpse and burying it in the garden.

Edward VII, who was born and died at Buckingham Palace, loved it there and redecorated and refurbished the palace, bringing it alive with a series of glittering receptions and balls.

In 1911, as a tribute to the memory of Queen Victoria, SIR ASTON WEBB erected the huge VICTORIA MEMORIAL STATUE in front of the palace and, in order to make a processional route from Admiralty Arch, widened the Mall, which had originally been laid out by Charles II as somewhere he could play 'paille maille', an expansive game not unlike croquet.

In 1913 George V had the crumbling east front refaced in Portland Stone, creating the famous view of Buckingham Palace we recognise today.

The modern palace has 775 rooms, including 19 State Rooms, 240 bedrooms for the Royal Family, guests and staff, 78 bathrooms, a cinema and a swimming pool. Today the State Rooms in Buckingham Palace are open to the public in the summer months while the Queen is away.

Queen's Gallery

The Duke of Edinburgh came up with the idea of building a gallery on the site of the royal chapel that had been destroyed by bombing in the Second World War, where works of art from the Royal Collection could be exhibited. THE QUEEN'S GALLERY was opened in 1962 and was THE FIRST PART OF BUCKINGHAM PALACE EVER TO BE OPENED TO THE PUBLIC.

Royal Mews

THE ROYAL MEWS was moved from Charing Cross to its present location

by George III in 1760, when he purchased Buckingham House. In 1764 he added a riding school and this was enlarged by John Nash for George IV in 1825.

Today the Queen's motor-cars and state carriages, as used for state visits, royal weddings and the Opening of Parliament, are kept there. Perhaps the grandest of these is the GOLD STATE COACH, which was built for George III in 1762 and has been used for jubilee celebrations and for every coronation since that of George IV.

The carriages are also used for conveying newly appointed ambassadors and high commissioners between their official residences and Buckingham Palace for their audiences with the Queen.

A daily occurrence since 1843 is the departure from the Royal Mews of a Brougham carriage to collect and deliver mail between St James's Palace and Buckingham Palace.

Buckingham Palace Gardens

BUCKINGHAM PALACE GARDENS, which still contain a descendant of one of James I's mulberry trees, were designed by William Aiton of Kew Gardens in 1828. The gardens are tended by eight full-time gardeners, cover some 42 acres (17 ha) and form THE LARGEST PRIVATE GARDEN IN LONDON. The lake is supplied by water from the Serpentine in Hyde Park.

The gardens also include a summer-house designed by William Kent, a helicopter pad and a tennis court.

A focal point of the garden is the WATERLOO VASE, an enormous urn commissioned by the Emperor Napoleon to commemorate his expected triumphs, and then given to the Prince Regent after Napoleon's defeat at the Battle of Waterloo in 1815. It was intended to place the vase in the Waterloo Chamber at Windsor Castle, but it proved too heavy for the floor and was placed in the Buckingham Palace gardens instead.

Every year the Queen holds a number of garden parties at Buckingham Palace for people who have achieved something of worth in the public arena. Tea and sandwiches are provided in marquees while, to the strains of the National Anthem, the Queen walks from the Bow Room to her own private tea tent, greeting the assembled guests as she goes.

The gardens also hosted a Children's Party at the Palace in 2006, when 2,000 children were invited to help celebrate the Queen's 80th birthday.

St James's Palace

Red-brick ST JAMES'S PALACE, lying to the north-east of Buckingham Palace,

is the senior official palace of the sovereign.

The great Tudor gatehouse of St James's Palace is one of London's most distinctive landmarks, and proudly sports the 'HR' of Henry VIII, who built the famous palace between 1531 and 1536 on the site of a leper hospital dedicated to St James. Inside, the initials 'HA' entwined in a lover's knot on two of the old fireplaces recall that Anne Boleyn spent the night at St James's after her coronation. Quite a lot of Henry's original palace, which was built around four courtyards, survives, including two State Rooms, some turrets and, the Chapel Royal.

After Whitehall Palace was destroyed in a fire in 1698, St James's Palace became the sovereign's official residence, which it remains to this day, even though no monarch has lived there since WILLIAM IV. That is why foreign ambassadors and high commissioners are still formally accredited to the Court of St James's.

Today St James's Palace is used for the offices of members of the Royal Family and as the London residence for PRINCESS ANNE, PRINCESS BEATRICE OF YORK and PRINCESS ALEXANDRA.

Chapel Royal

The CHAPEL ROYAL was decorated by HANS HOLBEIN to commemorate HENRY VIII's marriage to ANNE OF CLEVES – the marriage was over before the paint was dry, but they did set a trend for royal marriages in the chapel.

Princess Mary, later QUEEN MARY II, was married to WILLIAM OF ORANGE in the chapel in 1677. Her sister Princess Anne, later QUEEN ANNE, married

GEORGE OF DENMARK there in 1683; GEORGE III married PRINCESS CHARLOTTE in 1761; and Prince George, later GEORGE IV, married CAROLINE OF BRUNSWICK in 1795.

QUEEN VICTORIA was married to PRINCE ALBERT in the chapel in 1840 and her marriage certificate hangs in the vestry. In 1893 her grandson Prince George (later GEORGE V) married PRINCESS MARY OF TECK there.

The heart of Henry's eldest daughter QUEEN MARY I is buried beneath the choir stalls – she died in the palace in 1558. ELIZABETH I knelt in the chapel to pray for deliverance from the Spanish Armada and rode out from St James's to give her famous speech to her troops at Tilbury. And CHARLES I took Communion in the chapel before he was escorted across St James's Park to the scaffold.

In 1997 family and friends paid their private respects to DIANA, PRINCESS OF WALES, as she lay in her coffin before the altar of the Chapel Royal, prior to her funeral in Westminster Abbey.

CHARLES II and JAMES II were both born at St James's Palace and baptised in the Chapel Royal, as were MARY II and QUEEN ANNE, the latter giving birth to the majority of her 17 children at St James's. Sadly only five lived, and none survived childhood – hence the Hanoverian succession.

Queen's Chapel, St James's
In 1623 JAMES I commissioned INIGO JONES to build the QUEEN'S CHAPEL at St James's Palace for the wedding of his son Prince Charles to the Spanish Infanta. Work stopped when the

marriage didn't happen, but was resumed in time for Charles (by now CHARLES I) to marry HENRIETTA MARIA there in 1627.

The Queen's Chapel was THE FIRST CLASSICAL CHURCH IN BRITAIN. Reached from St James's Palace by crossing Marlborough Road, the chapel is occasionally open to the public.

Clarence House

CLARENCE HOUSE is the OFFICIAL RESIDENCE OF THE PRINCE OF WALES AND THE DUCHESS OF CORNWALL, as well as PRINCE HARRY.

The house was built between 1825 and 1827 by John Nash for the DUKE OF CLARENCE, later William IV, and his wife Princess Adelaide, who found William's bachelor apartment in

St James's Palace somewhat cramped. When William became King the improvements to Buckingham Palace, begun by George IV, had yet to be completed, and William found Clarence House more comfortable so he continued to live there throughout his short reign, from 1830 to 1837.

Clarence House incorporates the Tudor buildings at the south-west corner of St James's Palace and is connected to the old palace's state apartments by a first-floor corridor. It also shares the palace gardens.

When William IV died in 1837 his sister PRINCESS AUGUSTA took over Clarence House, followed by Queen Victoria's mother, the Duchess of Kent, who lived there from 1841 until she died in 1861.

In 1866 Queen Victoria's second son ALFRED, DUKE OF EDINBURGH took up residence, and after his marriage to MARIE ALEXANDROVA, the daughter of Tsar Alexander II, in St Petersburg in 1874, he began to enlarge and redecorate Clarence House, adding a new south entrance with cast-iron Doric columns. On the first floor he created a Russian Orthodox chapel for his wife, which was dismantled after his death.

After the Duke of Edinburgh died in 1900, Clarence House went to his younger brother ARTHUR, DUKE OF CONNAUGHT, and then, during the Second World War, it was used as a headquarters for the British Red Cross and St John's Ambulance. The house was badly damaged in the Blitz.

In 1947 PRINCESS ELIZABETH, eldest daughter of George VI, the future Elizabeth II, married PHILIP MOUNTBATTEN and they moved into Clarence House two years later in 1949 as the Duke and Duchess of Edinburgh. In 1950 PRINCESS ANNE was born in Clarence House.

After Princess Elizabeth became Queen in 1952 she and Philip moved into Buckingham Palace, and the following year QUEEN ELIZABETH THE QUEEN MOTHER became Clarence House's most celebrated occupant. Initially PRINCESS MARGARET lived there with her mother but she later moved on to Kensington Palace.

Queen Mother at Clarence House

It became customary for all Foreign Heads of State to visit the Queen Mother at Clarence House for afternoon tea on the first day of a State Visit.

On her 70th birthday on 4 August in 1970, the Queen Mother made a special appearance at the entrance to

Clarence House, flanked by the whole Royal Family, to greet well-wishers gathered outside on Stable Yard Road, a birthday tradition that continued until her death in 2002.

The ground floor of Clarence House is open to the public between August and October, and visitors can see the Queen Mother's extensive collection of 20th-century British art, with works by Graham Sutherland, Walter Sickert, Augustus John and John Piper.

Marlborough House

Today MARLBOROUGH HOUSE serves as the headquarters of the COMMON-WEALTH SECRETARIAT, but over the years it has been home to many members of the Royal Family.

Marlborough House was built on Crown land in 1710 for SARAH, DUCHESS OF MARLBOROUGH, a close friend of Queen Anne. The design was by Sir Christopher Wren's son, also Christopher, no doubt drawn up under his father's watchful eye, and the house is built with Dutch red bricks brought over from Holland as ballast for the troop ships that carried the Duke of Marlborough's soldiers to the Continent.

Inside, the walls are covered with remarkable murals portraying Marlborough's battles.

Sarah continued to live there after she was widowed in 1722 and planned to open up a new driveway from her front door into Pall Mall. However, she had so annoyed the Prime Minister, Sir Robert Walpole, by interfering in affairs of state, that he bought up the houses standing in her way and foiled her plan. The blocked-up archway can still be seen from Pall Mall.

In 1817 the house reverted to the Crown and was given to George IV's daughter PRINCESS CHARLOTTE and her husband LEOPOLD. Charlotte died in childbirth that year, but Leopold retained Marlborough House until he became King of the Belgians in 1831.

William IV's widow QUEEN ADELAIDE moved in after her husband's death in 1837 and gave a much talked-about wedding banquet for Queen Victoria and Prince Albert there in 1840.

In 1849 Marlborough House was enlarged by Sir James Pennethorne to make it suitable as the official residence of Edward, Prince of Wales (later EDWARD VII) once he reached 18. Edward would eventually live there with his wife ALEXANDRA for 40 years, during which time Marlborough House became the centre of London's social life, with the royal couple and their friends becoming known as the 'Marlborough House Set'.

Edward's second son Prince George, later GEORGE V, was born in Marlborough House in 1865, and when Edward became King in 1901 he gave

Marlborough House to Prince George.

When Edward VII died in 1910, his widow Queen Alexandra moved back into Marlborough House. The small tombstones of her dogs and pet rabbit, Benny, can still be found in the garden, while set into the garden wall on Marlborough Road is an art nouveau memorial to the popular Queen Alexandra, the last great work of SIR ALFRED GILBERT, who designed the statue of Eros in Piccadilly Circus.

George V's widow QUEEN MARY moved into Marlborough House in 1936 and died there in 1953.

Group tours of Marlborough House take place on Tuesday mornings or during London's Open House Weekend.

Carlton House

CARLTON HOUSE, now replaced by CARLTON HOUSE TERRACE, was sandwiched between Pall Mall and St James's Park, and was built in 1714 for HENRY BOYLE, BARON CARLETON and in 1732 was purchased by George II's son FREDERICK, PRINCE OF WALES, who asked WILLIAM KENT to lay out the gardens.

Between 1783 and 1796 the house was substantially remodelled by HENRY HOLLAND for George, Prince of Wales, later GEORGE IV. He filled the house with a multitude of paintings by the great artists of the day including Joshua Reynolds, Thomas Gainsborough and George Stubbs, and many of the finest paintings in today's ROYAL COLLECTION came from Carlton House.

Carlton House became the centre of a new rage in dancing, THE WALTZ, which had been introduced to England at Brocket Hall in Hertfordshire by the dazzling Lady Caroline Lamb. In 1815 the Prince hosted the TSAR OF RUSSIA and the KING OF PRUSSIA at Carlton House for a glittering banquet to celebrate victory at Waterloo, and in 1816 his only child by Caroline of Brunswick, PRINCESS CHARLOTTE, was married to PRINCE LEOPOLD OF SAXE-COBURG in the Crimson Drawing Room.

In 1825, five years after George became King George IV, Carlton House was demolished and replaced with two white stuccoed terraces of grand houses, designed by John Nash and known as Carlton House Terrace.

Duke of York Column

Located between the east and west terraces is the DUKE OF YORK COLUMN, designed by Benjamin Wyatt. It was erected in 1833 as a monument to George III's second son, the 'Grand Old Duke of York' who, as Commander-in-Chief, reorganised the British army into a professional force and founded Sandhurst Royal Military Academy. The column is plain as it was paid for by stopping a day's wages from every soldier in the army and there was not sufficient money for decorating it with relief carvings. Indeed, it was suggested that the column was made so tall, 124 feet high, so that the Duke was put out of reach of his creditors.

Inside the column is a spiral staircase of 168 steps leading to a viewing platform, which was enclosed in iron after a French musician, Henri Stephan, committed suicide by jumping off the gallery, in May 1850. The gallery was closed permanently at the beginning of the 20th century.

Whitehall Palace

In 1530 Henry VIII acquired York Place, just north of the Palace of Westminster, from the disgraced Cardinal Wolsey. York Place had been built in the 13th century for Walter de Grey, Archbishop of York, and expanded by Wolsey into a sumptuous residence for himself. Henry further extended the house into THE LARGEST PALACE IN EUROPE, bigger than Versailles or the Vatican, with over 1,500 rooms.

The palace was soon named WHITEHALL after the white stone from which it was constructed. Henry moved the royal court out of the Palace of Westminster and made Whitehall the official residence of the monarch in London. He celebrated marriage to Anne Boleyn and to Jane Seymour there, and died in Whitehall Palace in 1547.

The site of Henry's cockpit is now occupied by the CABINET OFFICE, while the tiltyard for jousting is now HORSE GUARDS PARADE. Henry built up an impressive wine cellar, which still exists beneath the Ministry of Defence.

Scotland Yard

The palace was built around a series of courtyards, one of which was named SCOTLAND YARD, where the Kings of Scotland would stay when visiting London. The first headquarters of Sir Robert Peel's newly formed Metropolitan Police Force was located in Scotland Yard in 1829 and the name has been kept for all their subsequent headquarters.

JAMES I drew up plans with INIGO JONES for a huge new palace, but the only part that got built was the Banqueting House. The rest of Henry's palace was destroyed in a fire in 1698 and the monarch's official residence was moved to St James's Palace.

Whitehall Palace is commemorated by Whitehall, the main thoroughfare from Trafalgar Square to the Houses of Parliament. It is lined on either side by Government departments, making the name Whitehall synonymous with Government administration and the Civil Service.

Banqueting House

The BANQUETING HOUSE is the only part of the huge royal Palace of Whitehall that survives above ground today. It was commissioned by James

While the main hall of the Banqueting House was used for receptions, ceremonies and theatrical performances, the vaulted undercroft was designed as a discreet drinking den for James I and his friends.

The famous painted ceiling of the main hall at the Banqueting House was commissioned by CHARLES I in 1636 from the Flemish painter PETER PAUL RUBENS and is the only painted ceiling by Rubens that survives in situ. The three main canvases depict the Union of Crowns and the wise rule of James I, and Charles should have perhaps studied the message a bit more closely, for it was his own unwise rule that led to his execution here in 1649. The ceiling was the last thing Charles saw before he stepped out of the window on to the scaffolding outside.

I to replace an earlier banqueting hall that burned down in 1619 and was designed by Inigo Jones as THE FIRST COMPLETE PALLADIAN BUILDING IN BRITAIN – the Queen's House at Greenwich, also by Jones, was started earlier but not completed until 1635.

Well, I never knew this
about
ROYAL ST JAMES'S AND WHITEHALL

When the Queen is in residence at Buckingham Palace the Royal Standard is flown above the palace. Before 1997 no flag flew above Buckingham Palace when the Queen was absent, but after the death of Diana, Princess of Wales, the fact that there was no flag flying at half-mast above the palace caused considerable controversy, and eventually it was agreed that a Union Jack should be flown there at half-mast. Since that time the Union Jack has been

flown above the palace when the Queen is not present, and this is now lowered to half-mast in times of national mourning, such as after the death of the Queen Mother, the 9/11 attacks in New York or the London bombings of 7 July in 2005.

The Church of ST MARTIN-IN-THE-FIELDS, at the northeastern corner of Trafalgar Square, is THE PARISH CHURCH OF BUCKINGHAM PALACE and any baby born in the palace is entered into the St Martin's church register. The present church was built by JAMES GIBBS in 1726 and has been the inspiration for the design of many an American church with its rectangular shape, portico and high steeple. CHARLES II was christened in a previous church on the site in 1630, and his mistress NELL GWYN was buried there in 1687.

Standing alone on its own island off Trafalgar Square is a statue of CHARLES I gazing down Whitehall to the Banqueting House, where the King met his end. Cast in 1633, it is THE OLDEST BRONZE STATUE IN BRITAIN and THE FIRST EQUESTRIAN STATUE OF A KING. Every year on 30 January the Royal Stuart Society lays a wreath at the foot of the statue in memory of THE ONLY KING OF ENGLAND TO BE BEHEADED.

CONSTITUTION HILL was so named because this is where CHARLES II used to take his daily 'constitutional', or walk.

In 1811 George III was considered so ill that Parliament passed the Regency Act giving the Prince of Wales (later George IV) 'full power and authority in the name of His Majesty' as Prince Regent and this gave rise to the period known as the Regency. In 1825 the Prince Regent asked John Nash to create a ceremonial route, now called Regent Street, from Carlton House to a new area of parkland in Marylebone that would be known as The Regent's Park.

THE PRINCE REGENT was a great fan of JANE AUSTEN and kept her books at all of his many houses. In 1815 he graciously invited her to CARLTON HOUSE, and in return she dedicated her next book, *Emma*, to the Prince: 'To His Royal Highness the Prince Regent, this work is, by His Royal Highness's permission, most respectfully dedicated to His Royal Highness by his Royal Highness's dutiful and obedient humble servant, the Author.'

CHAPTER FIVE

Royal London

St Paul's ✦ Tower of London ✦ Kensington Palace ✦ Royal Albert Hall ✦ Albert Memorial ✦ Royal Hospital ✦ Smithfield

While Westminster may be considered to be the heart of Royal London, containing the greatest number of royal homes and offices, there are nonetheless plenty of royal locations to be found elsewhere in London.

St Paul's Cathedral

In July 1981, over half a million people thronged the streets of London and 750 million people tuned into the television to watch PRINCE CHARLES and LADY DIANA SPENCER marry in ST PAUL'S CATHEDRAL. St Paul's was chosen over Westminster Abbey, where Charles's parents had been married, because it was larger, with a capacity of 3,500 compared to the abbey's 2,000. The wedding attracted THE LARGEST EVER TELEVISION AUDIENCE UP TO THAT TIME.

QUEEN ELIZABETH II celebrated both her Golden Jubilee and her 80th birthday with services in St Paul's in 2002 and 2006, respectively.

Old St Paul's

The St Paul's Cathedral in which Charles and Diana were married is the fifth place of worship to stand on the site since ENGLAND'S FIRST CHRISTIAN KING, ETHELBERT OF KENT, dedicated the first small wooden church there to St Paul in 604. This was rebuilt in stone but burned down by the Vikings in 962. The third church, built by the Saxons, was destroyed by fire in 1087 and was replaced by the Normans over a 200-year period. They built a huge cathedral, over 600 ft (180 m) in length, THE LONGEST AND LARGEST CATHEDRAL IN ENGLAND. The spire, completed in 1315, reached a height of 489 ft (149 m), THE SECOND HIGHEST IN ENGLAND after that of Lincoln Cathedral, which was 525 ft (160 m) high.

Two Saxon kings were buried in Old Saint Paul's: KING SEBBI, King of Essex, in 695 and ETHELRED THE UNREADY in 1016.

JOHN OF GAUNT, third son of Edward III and founder of the Royal Houses

of York and Lancaster, was buried in Old St Paul's in 1399.

RICHARD II lay in state in Old St Paul's, displayed there for all to see by the man who had deposed him, Henry IV, to prove that Richard was indeed dead. HENRY VI and HENRY VII also lay in state in Old St Paul's.

HENRY V prayed at the high altar before going to France in 1415, and on his return came back and gave thanks for his famous victory at the Battle of Agincourt.

In 1501 St Paul's saw its first royal wedding when ARTHUR, PRINCE OF WALES, the eldest son of Henry VII, married CATHERINE OF ARAGON there, amid much pomp and ceremony. The wedding was the first act in a tumultuous chain of events that would eventually lead to the Reformation; for Arthur died less than five months later, aged just 15, and seven years after that his younger brother, by then Henry VIII, married Catherine in a private ceremony at Greenwich. When Catherine failed to give Henry a male heir, he sought to blame it on the fact that Arthur and Catherine's marriage must have been consummated and that therefore his own marriage to his brother's wife was illegitimate.

Old St Paul's burned down during the Great Fire of London in 1666 and was replaced by Sir Christopher Wren's Renaissance masterpiece, which took 35 years to build and is still THE ONLY DOMED CATHEDRAL IN ENGLAND.

A statue of QUEEN ANNE stands outside the west end of the cathedral and celebrates the completion of the new St Paul's in 1710. Queen Anne had earlier held a service of thanksgiving in the almost complete cathedral for the Duke of Marlborough's victories in the War of the Spanish Succession.

GEORGE III held a thanksgiving service in St Paul's after his recovery from illness in 1789.

In 1897 QUEEN VICTORIA sat in her open carriage outside St Paul's to listen to a service of celebration for her Diamond Jubilee. She was too frail to mount the steps into the cathedral.

Tower of London
A Palace and a Prison

White Tower

'In truth, there is no
sadder spot on the earth'
Thomas Babington Macaulay

The Tower of London, known simply as the Tower, was built by William the Conqueror to strike awe and fear into the hearts of the people, not just of London, but of all England, and for many centuries after the Normans it continued to cast its daunting shadow across English history.

The Tower has grown into a vast complex of fortifications since William started it in 1078, but the Conqueror's central keep (known as the WHITE TOWER since it was whitewashed in 1240) still dominates the setting and is virtually unchanged since it was built almost 1,000 years ago. With walls 15 ft (4.6 m) thick and reaching a height of 90 ft (27 m), it was easily THE TALLEST BUILDING IN LONDON when it was built and was quite unlike anything ever seen in England before.

Spiral Staircase

Of the Tower's four turrets only the one in the north-east corner is round (the other three are square) and this is to accommodate a spiral staircase that gave access to BRITAIN'S FIRST ROYAL OBSERVATORY (although maybe this claim could be made for Stonehenge). This staircase established the custom of building staircases that spiralled upwards in a clockwise direction allowing the defender to keep his sword arm free – provided he was right-handed.

[48]

It is now THE OLDEST AND MOST COMPLETE NORMAN CASTLE KEEP IN BRITAIN. Inside is THE OLDEST UNALTERED CHURCH IN LONDON, ST JOHN'S CHAPEL, and THE FIRST LATRINES TO BE SEEN IN ANY BUILDING IN BRITAIN.

The man who designed and constructed this extraordinary fortress was GUNDULF, BISHOP OF ROCHESTER, a monk who had come over from Normandy with Lanfranc, William's newly appointed Archbishop of Canterbury. Gundulf went on to oversee a number of huge military projects, including the castles at Colchester and Rochester, and is considered to be THE FIRST 'ROYAL ENGINEER'. Gundulf is buried in another of his triumphs, Rochester Cathedral.

HENRY III converted the Tower into a fortress by encircling the keep with a curtain wall studded with 13 bastion towers and dug a moat on the outside filled with water from the Thames. This was probably just as much to keep in his menagerie of animals as his human prisoners.

EDWARD I then extended the site to its present 18 acres (7.3 ha) by constructing a second curtain wall and a number of further towers. He also built the infamous TRAITORS' GATE, through which prisoners entered the Tower, having been brought along the river. Few such prisoners ever left the Tower again.

The monarch who made most use of Traitors' Gate was HENRY VIII, who much enjoyed staying at the Tower and made major improvements to the royal lodgings there. It was during his reign that the Tower acquired its reputation for brutality, and a period of just seven years from 1535 to 1542 saw the imprisonment and execution of SIR THOMAS MORE, CARDINAL JOHN FISHER, ANNE BOLEYN, THOMAS CROMWELL and CATHERINE HOWARD.

Inmates and Executions

The FIRST NOTABLE PRISONER IN THE TOWER was RANULF FLAMBARD, BISHOP OF DURHAM, who was sent there by Henry I for financial mismanagement

Ceremony of the Bath

On the eve of his coronation Henry IV initiated the Ceremony of the Bath at the Tower, choosing 40 of his followers to become Knights of the Bath. Each was spiritually cleansed and purified in the baths adjoining St John's Chapel, and as they bathed Henry made the Sign of the Cross on each man's back. They then spent a night of prayer and meditation in the chapel and in the morning each was granted the 'accolade' – a ritual with which Henry conferred knighthood upon them by striking them on the shoulder with his sword. This last gesture is still used by the monarch today, while the official Order of the Bath was founded by George I in 1725.

during William II's reign. Flambard was also the first prisoner known to have escaped from the Tower – shinning down a rope apparently smuggled to him in a cask of wine.

In 1381 RICHARD II took refuge in the Tower during the Peasants' Revolt. Eighteen years later, in 1399, he was held prisoner and forced to abdicate there in favour of his cousin Henry Bolingbroke, later Henry IV.

In 1471 HENRY VI was found dead in the WAKEFIELD TOWER, most probably murdered by Edward IV's brother Richard of Gloucester, the future Richard III.

In 1483 RICHARD III celebrated at the tower after his coronation, despite knowing full well that his nephews Edward V and Richard, Duke of York, had been murdered there to clear his own way to the throne. The deed most likely took place in a tower near to Traitors' Gate, built by Richard II over a gateway of Henry III, which became known as the BLOODY TOWER after the Earl of Northumberland committed suicide there in 1585. SIR WALTER RALEIGH was incarcerated in the same tower by James I for 13 years at the beginning of the 17th century.

The future Elizabeth I stayed in the Bell Tower in the south-west corner of the curtain wall while she was being held prisoner at the Tower by her sister, the Catholic Queen Mary, who suspected Elizabeth of being involved in a Protestant plot against her. Elizabeth would take a daily constitutional along the ramparts, and this section of the wall is now called Elizabeth Walk. Charles II's illegitimate son the Duke of Monmouth was later incarcerated in the Bell Tower after his unsuccessful uprising against his uncle James II.

Tower Green

While high-profile executions took place in public on Tower Hill, beheadings that were unpopular and likely to incite a riot, particularly those of women, were performed inside the Tower walls on Tower Green, using a scaffold erected specifically for the purpose.

ANNE BOLEYN was executed there in 1536, three years to the day after her coronation, and CATHERINE HOWARD in 1542. LADY JANE GREY was executed on Tower Green in 1554 and then buried, like her fellow royal victims, next door in the CHAPEL ROYAL OF ST PETER AD VINCULA.

In 1601 Elizabeth I's fallen favourite ROBERT DEVEREUX, EARL OF ESSEX, BECAME THE LAST PERSON TO BE EXECUTED ON TOWER GREEN.

The LAST MAN TO BE EXECUTED ON TOWER HILL was the Jacobite peer LORD LOVAT, in 1747. He too was buried in the Chapel Royal of St Peter ad Vincula.

THE LAST MONARCH TO SLEEP IN THE TOWER was JAMES I.

The LAST PRISONERS TO BE HELD AT THE TOWER were Hitler's deputy RUDOLPH HESS, detained there for four days in 1941, and the KRAY TWINS, Ronnie and Reggie, who were held at the Tower in the early 1950s before being sent to Shepton Mallet military prison for deserting their National Service.

Today, people come willingly to the Tower to see the ravens and the Yeoman Warders, as well as the Crown Jewels, which are housed in the Waterloo Block.

Ravens

In 1804 the Royal Menagerie, started by Henry III in 1252, was opened for the public to come and see, and this is where William Blake saw his 'Tyger, Tyger, burning bright'. In 1835 one of the lions attacked a member of the garrison and the animals were moved to the new zoo in Regent's Park – all except for the ravens, for legend has it that if the ravens ever leave the Tower of London the Kingdom will collapse. They are carefully watched over and fed with raw meat from Smithfield by the Yeoman Warder Ravenmaster.

Yeoman Warders

The Yeoman Warders were formed out of the Yeoman of the Guard by Henry VIII in 1509 specifically to guard the Tower. While there are no more prisoners for them to guard, the Yeoman are responsible for watching over the Crown Jewels, although their role today is mainly ceremonial and to act as tour guides. Their uniform sports a Tudor Rose, in honour of their founder, to which was added a thistle, in honour of Scotland after the Act of Union in 1707, and a shamrock, in honour of the union with Ireland in 1801.

Ceremony of the Keys

The main ceremonial duty of the Yeoman Warders is the Ceremony of the Keys, which has taken place daily at the Tower for over 700 years.

At 9.40 p.m. every night the Chief Yeoman Warder, escorted by four armed guards, goes round and locks all the main gates of the Tower. He is then challenged by a sentry and is allowed to pass only on speaking the password 'The Queen's Keys!'

The Chief Yeoman Warder is then met by a ceremonial guard who present arms on the Broad Steps in front of the White Tower. The Chief Warder proclaims 'God preserve Queen Elizabeth', to which everyone present replies 'Amen' and the Last Post is sounded.

It is possible to attend the ceremony by applying to the Tower of London in writing, at least two months in advance.

Kensington Palace

KENSINGTON PALACE came to prominence in August 1997 when it was the focus of one of the most extraordinary and spontaneous exhibitions of public mourning ever witnessed in Britain, as thousands of people laid flowers at the south gates of the palace in memory of DIANA, PRINCESS OF WALES, who had died in a car crash in Paris. Kensington

tower, which still survives today. Work proceeded with such haste that part of the new king's state rooms collapsed, killing eight labourers, but the work was completed swiftly and William and Mary were able to take up residence in time for Christmas.

had been her principal residence since her separation from Prince Charles in 1992, and it was here that she brought up her two sons William and Harry. Many people felt that they could best express their respects for the 'People's Princess' by coming in person to Kensington Palace, the backdrop to so many news bulletins and photographs that had become a regular feature of people's daily lives, not just in Britain but around the world.

Before that, Kensington Palace had been a relatively unobtrusive feature of Royal London. Its royal story begins with WILLIAM AND MARY in the late 17th century.

William III suffered badly from asthma, and his wife Queen Mary II was keen to find somewhere for them to live away from the smog and damp of their principal London royal residence at Whitehall Palace. So, in the summer of 1689, they purchased Nottingham House, in the village of Kensington, a modest Jacobean mansion built in 1605 and owned by the Earl of Nottingham. They then asked CHRISTOPHER WREN to enlarge the house as quickly as he could, which he did by retaining the original house and adding a three-storey pavilion to each corner and designing a new entrance on the west front, through an archway surmounted by a clock

First Light

The following year a broad avenue was laid out along the south side of Hyde Park to create a safe highway for the King and Queen to get to Kensington from St James's Palace and Whitehall. The RUE DU ROI, or ROTTEN ROW as it became known, was lit at night by 300 oil lamps, making Rotten Row THE FIRST ARTIFICIALLY LIT ROAD IN BRITAIN. Rotten Row survives as a sandy bridleway through Hyde Park and is used by the Household Cavalry, based at Hyde Park Barracks, to exercise their horses.

Queen Anne

Mary's sister ANNE moved into Kensington Palace on becoming Queen in 1702. Like William III, Anne's husband PRINCE GEORGE OF DENMARK suffered from asthma. In 1704 Anne commissioned SIR JOHN VANBRUGH to build her a large baroque Orangery or 'Summer Supper House', where she would take tea, or dine amongst the lemon trees and exotic plants, while an orchestra, hidden behind the foliage, played in the background.

Anne was devastated when her husband Prince George died at Kensington in 1708 and refused to visit the palace for many months. Six years later she died there herself.

George I

GEORGE I had the core of the palace remodelled to make it more regal with three new state rooms, the finest of which was the Cupola Room. The interiors were designed by William Kent, who also transformed Wren's King's Staircase into the Grand Staircase.

Looking down over the balustrade on the walls are some of the more extraordinary members of George's household, painted by William Kent, including the court comedian, a dwarf named ULRICH JORRY, two Turks, MEHEMET and MUSTAPHA, who had been with George at the Siege of Vienna in 1685 and were rewarded with paid employment at George's court for life, and PETER THE WILD BOY, who had been found living like a wild animal in the woods near Hanover and brought to England as a pet.

George II

GEORGE II was the LAST REIGNING MONARCH TO LIVE IN KENSINGTON PALACE. He made Kensington one of his principal homes and spent up to six months of the year there. He also had the gardens laid out in the form we know them today, creating the ROUND POND and the SERPENTINE as a water vista for his adored wife Caroline. When she died at Kensington in 1737 a distraught George shut up most of the palace, and after he died there himself in 1760 Kensington became a home for minor royals or – as Edward VIII would later so delicately put it – an aunt heap.

Princess Victoria

One such 'aunt' was QUEEN VICTORIA, who was born at Kensington Palace in 1819 and was christened in the Cupola Room.

Princess Victoria continued to live at Kensington Palace with her mother, the Duchess of Kent, until the morning of 20 June 1837 when she was awoken early in her bedroom at Kensington and informed that she was now Queen of England. That very day she moved out and took up residence in Buckingham Palace.

Duke Heap

Kensington Palace was the official residence of Princess Margaret until her death in 2002 and today is the official London residence of the Duke and Duchess of Gloucester, the Duke and Duchess of Kent, Prince and Princess Michael of Kent and the newly married Duke and Duchess of Cambridge.

Royal Albert Hall

In September every year, enthusiastic crowds fill the ROYAL ALBERT HALL to wave the Union Jack and celebrate the Last Night of the Proms. Founded by SIR HENRY WOOD in 1894 and hosted by the Royal Albert Hall since 1941,

the Proms make up THE LARGEST FESTIVAL OF CLASSICAL MUSIC IN THE WORLD.

The Royal Albert Hall was named in honour of Queen Victoria's husband PRINCE ALBERT, who died in 1861. Victoria herself laid the foundation stone in 1867 and the hall was opened in 1871 by Edward, Prince of Wales, with the words, 'The Queen declares this Hall is now open.' Victoria was too overcome with grief to speak.

In 1918 Sir Hubert Parry's choral version of 'Jerusalem' was performed for the first time in the Royal Albert Hall, in celebration of the granting of the vote to women. Jerusalem is now a favourite at the Last Night of the Proms.

Royal Albert Memorial

Facing the Royal Albert Hall from across the road is the ROYAL ALBERT MEMORIAL, Victorian England's answer to the Taj Mahal, an elaborate statement of Queen Victoria's undying love for Prince Albert. The structure of the memorial was designed by GEORGE GILBERT SCOTT, who was knighted by Queen Victoria for his work. At the centre is a statue of Prince Albert, seated and holding a catalogue of the Great Exhibition, sculpted by J.H. Foley.

Royal Hospital, Chelsea

In 1682 CHARLES II laid the foundation stone of the ROYAL HOSPITAL in Chelsea, which he had commissioned from CHRISTOPHER WREN for the 'succour and relief of veterans broken by age and war'. The story goes that Charles was encouraged in the enterprise by his mistress NELL GWYN, whose own father had been made destitute in the Civil War. In 1692 the hospital opened with a full complement of 476 Chelsea Pensioners in residence, and there has been very little change to the building since, except for some remodelling of the interior by Robert Adam in 1776.

In 1852 the DUKE OF WELLINGTON lay in state in the Great Hall at Chelsea, drawing thousands of mourners, and in 1949 BRITAIN'S FIRST TELEVISED CHURCH SERVICE was broadcast from the hospital's chapel.

Each year on the Royal Hospital Founder's Day, which is OAK APPLE DAY, 29 May, the Grinling

Oak Apple Day

After being defeated at the Battle of Worcester by Oliver Cromwell in 1651, Charles II spent six weeks on the run, disguised variously as a woodcutter and a manservant, as he made his way down to the south coast, where he was able to charter a coal boat out of Shoreham to transport him to France and safety.

At one point, in order to evade pursuers, Charles had to spend the night hiding in an oak tree, in the middle of a field beside BOSCOBEL HOUSE in Shropshire. The tree became known as the Royal Oak and has given its name to countless inns and Royal Navy ships. The actual oak tree was vandalised by souvenir hunters but a descendant, grown from an acorn of the original, stands in its place.

Charles passed the following night in a priest hole in Boscobel House itself, reached via a trapdoor on the landing outside what was then the cheese room – the hidden room was so small that Charles could not lie down.

When Charles returned to claim his throne in 1660, he arrived in London on his 30th birthday, 29 May, to find everyone wearing a sprig of oak in their hats in celebration of the Royal Oak, and since then 29 May has been known as Oak Apple Day – until 1859 it was a public holiday.

Boscobel House and the Royal Oak are now
in the care of English Heritage and can be visited.

Gibbons bronze of Charles II in Roman costume, situated in the south court, is garlanded with oak leaves.

The Royal Hospital, Chelsea, is still home to some 400 Chelsea Pensioners, each of whom receives board and lodging, a uniform and nursing care. Everyday uniform is navy blue, the famous red coat being kept for ceremonial occasions or for when acting as a guide for visitors to the hospital.

Set well back from the busy Embankment road the hospital is often overlooked, but Christopher Wren's glorious red-brick building is, after Greenwich, the loveliest façade on the River Thames, and the grounds are amongst the most delightful in London. Since 1913 the Royal Horticultural Society's Chelsea Flower Show has been held in the grounds during May.

Smithfield

In June 1381 the 14-year-old Richard II proved his mettle when he stood up to an angry crowd at SMITHFIELD, outside the city walls. Led by WAT TYLER and JACK STRAW, the labourers of Kent and Essex had marched on London to protest about an unfair poll tax that was levied on everyone, regardless of whether they were rich or poor. When they arrived in London the men rioted, sacking John of Gaunt's Savoy Palace, storming the Tower of London and executing the Archbishop of Canterbury, SIMON OF SUDBURY, on Tower Hill.

Richard agreed to meet the men's leaders on neutral ground at Smithfield,

but as the two parties were lining up to face each other Wat Tyler approached the King insolently, as if spoiling for a fight. The Lord Mayor of London, WILLIAM WALWORTH intervened, drew his dagger and plunged it into Tyler's neck. The King's knights then surrounded Tyler and finished him off. Seeing this, the crowd surged towards the royal party, but Richard rode forward alone and shouted, 'Sirs, will you kill your king? I am your king, I am your captain, your leader!' He then rode out of the square, followed by the crowd, who quietly dispersed, and the revolt was over.

Later on, when it was safe, Richard let his true feelings be known, declaring, 'Serfs you are and serfs you will remain.'

Smithfield, a 'smooth field' outside the walls of London, had long been famous for its horse market and, as a convenient open space near the city, was much used for tournaments and sporting events. Edward III held a royal tournament there for the King of France in 1357 and another, lasting a whole week, for his mistress Alice Perrers, in 1384.

Reflecting its roots as the home of ENGLAND'S LARGEST MEDIEVAL HORSE MARKET, Smithfield is now the location for BRITAIN'S LARGEST WHOLESALE MEAT MARKET.

Place of Execution

Smithfield was also a place of execution. In 1305, during the reign of Edward I, the Scottish rebel leader WILLIAM WALLACE was executed there, after which his head was removed, boiled in tar and displayed on a stake on London Bridge.

In 1330 Edward III had his mother's lover ROGER MORTIMER hanged and quartered at Smithfield. His body was left hanging there for two days, as a warning to others.

A stone near the gateway to St Bartholomew's church commemorates JOHN BRADFORD and JOHN PHILPOT, two of the Protestant martyrs burned at the stake while Queen Mary I sat watching from the room above the gate, drinking wine and eating roast chicken.

Well, I never knew this
about
ROYAL LONDON

As the birthplace of QUEEN VICTORIA, Kensington is known as ROYAL KENSINGTON.

The ROYAL ALBERT HALL boasts THE LARGEST PIPE ORGAN IN BRITAIN.

The DIANA PRINCESS OF WALES MEMORIAL FOUNTAIN, beside the Serpentine in Hyde Park, was closed before it even opened in 2004 because it was deemed too slippery, several people having fallen over while paddling in the water. Today it is monitored by attendants and is actually a delightful place to sit and cool your feet on hot summer days. Watching the water bubbling and tumbling past at varying speeds along a variety of channels is surprisingly therapeutic.

Opened in 1879, the elaborate ROYAL ARCADE, which runs between Old Bond Street and Albemarle Street, was regularly visited by Queen Victoria, which is how it earned its 'royal' name.

In 1757 GEORGE II presented the ROYAL LIBRARY COLLECTION, begun by Edward IV in the 1470s, to the newly founded British Museum, located in Old Montague House. When George IV later gave over 65,000 books collected by George III to the museum, it had to be rebuilt and enlarged by SIR ROBERT SMIRKE into the building we see today. The museum collection is known as the KING'S LIBRARY.

British Museum

The dagger with which William Walworth felled Wat Tyler during the confrontation at Smithfield is on show in the FISHMONGER'S HALL by London Bridge.

Fishmonger's Hall

The ROYAL ACADEMY OF ARTS was founded by KING GEORGE III in 1768 to promote art in Britain through education and exhibition. The king appointed SIR JOSHUA REYNOLDS as the first president. The first exhibition of contemporary art open to all artists, now called the Royal Academy Summer Exhibition,

was held in 1769. The Academy moved to its present location in Burlington House on Piccadilly in 1868.

The church of ST CLEMENT DANES in the Strand is so named because it is the burial place of the Danish King of England, HAROLD HAREFOOT, son of King Canute.

At the London premiere of HANDEL'S MESSIAH at Covent Garden in 1743, George II led the audience in a standing ovation for the Hallelujah Chorus, starting a tradition carried on to this day.

The NATIONAL ANTHEM was first played in public in 1745, at the Theatre Royal, Drury Lane, in London, after a performance of *The Alchemist* by Ben Jonson. Hanoverian London was feeling nervous after the Jacobite victory at the Battle of Prestonpans and it was hoped that the patriotic words of the song, which are by an unknown author, would inspire people to rally round King George II.

CHAPTER SIX

ROYAL THAMES

RIVER PAGEANTS ✦ KINGSTON
✦ HAMPTON COURT PALACE ✦ RICHMOND PALACE
✦ KEW PALACE ✦ GREENWICH PALACE

A spectacular river pageant on the River Thames was chosen for the climax of Queen Elizabeth II's Diamond Jubilee celebrations, upholding a royal tradition that goes back centuries.

Royal River Pageants

RICHARD III IN 1483 WAS THE FIRST ENGLISH MONARCH TO PROCESS TO HIS CORONATION ALONG THE THAMES BY BOAT.

In 1487 Henry VII's queen, ELIZABETH OF YORK, processed from Greenwich to the Tower of London accompanied by an assortment of livery barges in 'a Barge garnysshed and apparellede, passing al other, wherin was ordeynede a great red Dragon spowting Flamys of Fyer into Temmys'.

HENRY VIII loved to travel in splendour along the Thames as he moved between his various Thames-side royal palaces, from Greenwich to Windsor. He owned two royal barges, the *Lion* and the *Greyhound*, which were kept in the Royal Bargehouse at Lambeth.

In 1533 Henry's second wife ANNE BOLEYN travelled from Greenwich to the Tower of London for her coronation in the most spectacular river procession ever seen on the Thames, accompanied by more than 300 boats ablaze with banners and draped in gold cloth. The Queen's barge was preceded by two special barges, one carrying wild, fire-breathing monsters, the other sporting Anne's emblem, a crowned white falcon on a rose, encircled by 'virgyns singyng and plaiyng swetely'. Three years later she was taken along the same route to her execution.

In 1553 Edward VI's chosen heir LADY JANE GREY was transported down the Thames in a grand procession from Syon House in Brentford, where she had been proclaimed Queen, to the Tower of London, to await her coronation. This would be the only state pageantry Lady Jane would ever experience, for nine days afterwards she was removed from the throne by Mary I and later executed.

In 1610 JAMES I held a three-day river pageant on the Thames, with music and a mock sea battle, to celebrate his son PRINCE HENRY becoming Prince of Wales.

In 1662 Samuel Pepys described the sumptuous pageantry that accompanied the arrival of CHARLES II and his queen CATHERINE OF BRAGANZA at Whitehall from Hampton Court, as 'the most magnificent triumph that ever floated on the Thames, considering the innumerable boates and vessells dress'd and adorn'd with all imaginable pomp, but above all the thrones, arches, pageants, and other representations, stately barges of the Lord Maior and Companies with various inventions, musiq and peals of ordnance both from ye vessels and the shore'.

In the summer of 1717 GEORGE I sailed up the River Thames with his mistress, Sophia Charlotte von Kielmansegg, to picnic in the secluded private gardens of Lady Ranelagh, next to the Royal Hospital in Chelsea. Accompanying them were 50 musicians playing a new suite by George's favourite composer and protégé, GEORGE FRIDERIC HANDEL. The suite, which became known as the WATER MUSIC, so impressed the King that he ordered it to be played three times.

In 1749 George II commissioned Handel again, this time to compose a piece to celebrate the end of the War of Austrian Succession. Handel's composition was accompanied by a spectacular display of fireworks from barges floating on the Thames and became known as THE MUSIC FOR THE ROYAL FIREWORKS.

In 1831 WILLIAM IV and his wife QUEEN ADELAIDE sailed down the Thames from Somerset House to open the new London Bridge, built to replace the famous bridge lined with buildings that had been begun over 600 years before by Henry II in 1176.

Royal river pageants were also held to celebrate Elizabeth II's coronation in 1953 and Silver Jubilee in 1977.

Royal River

The River Thames has long been associated with royalty. In 890 KING ALFRED THE GREAT held what is regarded as THE FIRST ENGLISH PARLIAMENT in a field beside the River Thames at SHIFFORD, in Oxfordshire. In the words of an Anglo-Saxon poem, 'There sat at Shifford many thanes, many bishops and many learned men, wise earls and awful knights . . . and Alfred, England's herdsman, England's darling; he was King of England; he taught them that could hear how they should live.'

Magdalen College, Oxford

around 1130. Nothing remains of Beaumont except a plaque set into a pillar at the end of Beaumont Street, near the Ashmolean Museum. The palace was handed over to the Carmelites in 1318 and demolished at the Dissolution of the Monasteries.

Oxford

In 872, King Alfred stopped for refreshment at a little priory founded in the previous century by Princess Frideswalde, beside a ford on the River Thames, where farmers crossed the river with their oxen. He began talking with the monks and got into a spirited debate that lasted for several days. And so began the reputation for learned conversation of OXFORD.

Oxford has many royal connections. KING RICHARD I and KING JOHN were born there in 1157 and 1167 respectively, in BEAUMONT PALACE, built by Henry I outside the north gate of Oxford

Christ Church Cathedral, Oxford

CHARLES I set up the royal court at Oxford in 1642 and it remained there for the duration of the Civil War. Charles resided in Christ Church and established a royal mint there. His stay in Oxford is commemorated by two bronze statues of Charles and his wife Henrietta Maria in the quadrangle of St John's College.

Royal Kingston-upon-Thames

In 838 the Saxon KING EGBERT OF WESSEX held a Grand Council under the trees at the 'king's tun' or 'king's estate' on the Thames, at the first fording place above the London reaches of the river, which here formed the border between Wessex and Mercia.

Seven Saxon kings were subsequently crowned here and, as an important coronation site, Kingston-upon-Thames is entitled to call itself ROYAL KINGSTON-UPON-THAMES.

Royal Palaces on the River Thames

Since the Thames provided a safe highway, a number of monarchs built country palaces along its banks, where they could go and escape from the pollution and politics of London. The Tudors were foremost amongst them.

Hampton Court Tudor Palace

HAMPTON COURT, the ultimate expression of Tudor grandeur, was not begun by a king but by the son of an Ipswich butcher – Thomas, later CARDINAL, WOLSEY. Wolsey acquired the site in 1514 and determined to build himself the finest house in England, a Renaissance palace such as cardinals in Rome might occupy. The result was THE LARGEST HOUSE IN ENGLAND, boasting over 1,000 rooms.

Wolsey's first guests when the house had been completed in 1517 were Henry VIII and his wife Catherine of Aragon, who were aghast at, and not a little envious of, such splendour. A decade later, when Wolsey had failed to procure Henry a divorce from Catherine of Aragon and had begun to fall from favour, he gave Hampton Court to Henry – the greatest gift ever given voluntarily by a subject to his king. It did him no good. Two years later Wolsey died on his way to the Tower, charged with high treason.

Henry immediately set about enlarging and improving the house, and by the time he had finished it was THE LARGEST ROYAL RESIDENCE IN BRITAIN. The first priority was the Great Hall with its mighty hammer-beam roof and minstrel's gallery, which was completed in 1535, THE LAST GREAT HALL OF ITS KIND EVER BUILT FOR AN ENGLISH MONARCH. Henry was so impatient for the hall to be done that the craftsmen had to work in shifts for 24 hours a day, at night by candlelight.

To service the Great Hall, enormous kitchens were built where food could be prepared for the King, his guests and his retinue of 500 servants. Fresh water was carried down from the springs at Coombe Hill and under the Thames through 3 miles (4.8 km) of lead pipe.

One of Henry's favourite features was the tennis court, begun by Wolsey in 1526. Henry was playing tennis there when he heard the news of Anne Boleyn's execution in 1536. He didn't drop a point. THE ROYAL TENNIS COURT IS NOW THE OLDEST SURVIVING REAL TENNIS COURT IN BRITAIN and is still used today by the 500 members of the Hampton Court Real Tennis Club.

In 1537 JANE SEYMOUR, Henry's third wife, gave birth to EDWARD, his longed for son and heir, at Hampton Court. Edward was baptised in the Chapel Royal, but Jane sadly died of complications not long afterwards. In 1540 Henry signed the divorce papers ending his marriage to ANNE OF CLEVES at Hampton Court and three weeks later secretly married CATHERINE HOWARD upriver at Oatlands Palace, proclaiming her Queen in the Great Hall at Hampton Court.

Later that year Henry was attending mass in the chapel at Hampton Court when he was informed by Archbishop Cranmer of Catherine's infidelity. When Catherine heard what was happening she ran screaming down the corridor from her apartments and beat in vain on the locked chapel doors, before being dragged away by the King's servants. Her wailing ghost still haunts the palace today.

In 1543 Henry married his sixth and final wife, CATHERINE PARR, at Hampton Court. She made the mistake of arguing with Henry about religion, and in a fit of rage he called for her to be tried and executed. He soon calmed down and forgot about it, but next day when they were walking together in the palace gardens an armed guard arrived to arrest Catherine – much to Henry's bemusement.

In 1540 ENGLAND'S FIRST ASTRONOMICAL CLOCK was installed on the gatehouse to the inner court, still known as Anne Boleyn's gate. The clock was essential as a means of calculating the times of high and low water on the Thames, for those travelling to and from the palace by boat – which is, of course, the only way to arrive at Hampton Court.

In 1554 MARY I and KING PHILIP OF SPAIN spent part of their honeymoon at Hampton Court after their marriage in Winchester Cathedral. These were perhaps the happiest days of Mary's unhappy life, and when she thought she was pregnant she set up a nursery at Hampton Court in anticipation – but it turned out to be a phantom pregnancy, the first of two.

The Stuart kings added very little to Hampton Court architecturally, but culturally they were very active. In 1603 JAMES I was entertained by William Shakespeare and his company of 'King's Men' in the Great Hall, and the following year James hosted a Grand Conference in the Great Hall which resulted in one of the most important and influential English language books of all time – the KING JAMES BIBLE.

In 1625 CHARLES I honeymooned at Hampton Court with HENRIETTA MARIA, but 22 years later was held prisoner there. He escaped from the palace and made his way to Carisbrooke Castle on the Isle of Wight, but was recaptured and eventually executed.

In 1662 CHARLES II brought his unpopular new bride CATHERINE OF BRAGANZA to honeymoon at Hampton Court, where she was compared most unfavourably with his many mistresses. Some good did come out of the marriage, though. Her dowry was Bombay.

Renaissance Palace

Shortly after their coronation in 1689 WILLIAM AND MARY commissioned CHRISTOPHER WREN to rebuild Hampton Court for them. The plan was to demolish the old Tudor buildings of Henry VIII, except for the Great Hall, and create a Renaissance palace to rival Versailles. In the end time and money only allowed for two new sets of baroque royal apartments, one for the Queen and one for the King, both equally grand as they were joint monarchs, arranged around a new courtyard, the FOUNTAIN COURT. Inside there were intricate mouldings and fireplaces carved by GRINLING GIBBONS, while the Italian ANTONIO VERRIO created some of the first baroque murals and ceilings seen in Britain.

The gardens were relandscaped in the style of the gardens at Versailles and planted with exotic flowers from around the world from Mary's own collection, while a Privy Garden was created for William, bounded by iron gates and railings designed by French Huguenot ironworker JEAN TIJOU.

William also ordered Hampton Court's famous hedge maze, which was planted in 1690, mainly of hornbeam, and is THE OLDEST HEDGE MAZE IN BRITAIN. It covers a third of an acre (0.13 ha) and has over half a mile (0.8 km) of paths.

Work stopped on the new palace when Queen Mary died in 1694, but resumed three years later after Whitehall Palace burned down. In 1702 William fell from his horse, Sorrel, in the park at Hampton Court and died not long afterwards in Kensington Palace.

QUEEN ANNE carried on the work of William and Mary and added a small banqueting house overlooking the river. SIR JOHN VANBRUGH completed the circuit of royal apartments for GEORGE I, whose son Prince George later had WILLIAM KENT and SIR JAMES THORNHILL add their own decorations to the interior.

GEORGE II was the last monarch to reside at Hampton Court, in 1737. GEORGE III had bad memories of being bullied there by his father and never set foot in the palace once he was King.

QUEEN VICTORIA opened Hampton Court Palace to the public in 1838.

Richmond Palace

HENRY I was the first to occupy a residence at Richmond (then called Sheen) when he lived for a while in the King's House, Sheen. It became a royal residence when EDWARD I moved there

with his court in 1299. After the Scottish resistance leader William Wallace was executed in London, the Scottish commissioners came to Sheen to ask Edward to choose between the Scottish contenders for the throne.

EDWARD III died at Sheen in 1377, alone except for his mistress, who stole the rings from his dead fingers.

RICHARD II made Sheen his main residence in 1383 and honeymooned there with his beloved wife ANNE OF BOHEMIA. When she died there of the plague, aged just 28, Richard was so distraught that he ordered Sheen to be demolished.

Henry VII rebuilt the palace after a fire had destroyed what was left in 1497 and renamed it Richmond, after the North Yorkshire town of which he was Earl. He described his new palace as 'this earthly paradise of our realm in England'. In 1502 Henry's daughter PRINCESS MARGARET was betrothed to KING JAMES IV OF SCOTLAND at Richmond. Their descendants would

come to rule England and Scotland as the Royal House of Stuart. In 1509 HENRY VII died in Richmond Palace of tuberculosis.

In 1513 the body of James IV of Scotland was brought to Richmond from Flodden battlefield and lay unburied in Sheen Priory, next door to the palace, for a number of years. The body disappeared when the priory was dissolved in 1539.

HENRY VIII gave Richmond to Cardinal Wolsey in return for Hampton Court, but soon took it back when Wolsey fell from grace and gave it to Anne of Cleves. In 1554 Henry's daughter Mary spent part of her honeymoon there with her new husband King Philip of Spain.

ELIZABETH I had THE WORLD'S FIRST FLUSH WATER CLOSET installed at Richmond. It was invented by her godson SIR JOHN HARINGTON and, to avoid embarrassment, they agreed to refer to the device as her 'throne', or sometimes her 'John'. Elizabeth died at Richmond in 1603.

JAMES I stayed at Richmond to hunt stags in what is now called the Old Deer Park beside the Thames, and in 1637 created the much larger Richmond Park for the purpose.

In 1650, during the Commonwealth period, Richmond Palace was demolished on the orders of Oliver Cromwell. All that remains of it today is the Wardrobe, the Trumpeter's House and the Gatehouse, which together make up a delightful area of cobbled lanes and narrow passageways down by the river, on the south-west side of Richmond Green.

Kew Palace

KEW PALACE, THE SMALLEST AND MOST INTIMATE OF ALL THE ROYAL PALACES, was built in 1631 by a Dutch merchant called Samuel Fortrey and was originally called the Dutch House. In 1729 it was purchased by GEORGE II as a country home for his daughters Anne, Caroline and Amelia. Their brother, Frederick, Prince of Wales, who lived opposite in Kew House, eventually moved his young son George into Kew Palace and it became known as the Prince of Wales's House.

George, when he became King George III, gave Kew Palace to his wife Charlotte. She died there in 1818 and lay in state in the Dining Room before being buried at Windsor. It was while CHARLOTTE was lying ill at Kew Palace that the significant double marriage of George's two younger brothers took place there: William, Duke of Clarence (later William IV), married Princess Adelaide of Saxe-Meiningen, and Edward, Duke of Kent, married Princess Victoria of Saxe-Coburg – the latter couple would be Queen Victoria's parents.

After this Kew Palace was rather neglected, and Queen Victoria ordered it to be opened to the public in 1898.

In the 1990s the palace underwent restoration and in 2006 PRINCE CHARLES was able to host a dinner there to celebrate the 80th birthday of his mother, Elizabeth II.

Kew Gardens

GEORGE II and his wife CAROLINE OF ANSBACH had been the first royals to move to Kew when they bought a small summer hideaway in the Old Deer Park at Richmond and rebuilt it as RICHMOND LODGE. George was at Richmond Lodge in 1727 when he was informed that his father had died and he was now King.

Caroline laid out the first royal gardens at Richmond Lodge on the site of what is now part of Kew Gardens. They were pleasure gardens rather than botanic gardens and included two follies, the Hermitage, complete with a real hermit, and Merlin's Cave, in which she kept her library.

In 1730 FREDERICK, PRINCE OF WALES and his wife AUGUSTA took out a lease on a house about a mile away toward the river, Kew House, nicknamed the White House because of its elegant white stucco façade. Here they began to establish a botanic garden. When Frederick died in 1759, Augusta consoled herself by expanding the garden, laying the foundations for what would become the ROYAL BOTANIC GARDENS. In 1759 she appointed the botanist WILLIAM

AITON, a former director of Chelsea Physic Garden, as the first director of her botanic garden at Kew.

George III at Kew

The octagonal ten-storey PAGODA in Kew Gardens was built in 1761 by Sir William Chambers as a gift for Augusta from her son George III. At the same time George put up a small cottage in the gardens as a wedding present for his wife Charlotte. QUEEN CHARLOTTE'S COTTAGE is still standing.

George III later combined the grounds of Richmond Lodge and the White House, creating one vast royal botanic garden, which he asked Capability Brown to redesign. He later opened the garden to the public.

In 1768 George encouraged the botanist JOSEPH BANKS to sail to the South Seas with Captain Cook and bring back any new specimens he might find to Kew.

In later years George was brought to the White House at Kew to recover from his bouts of insanity, and in 1800 he had the White House demolished as it held such dreadful memories for him.

In 1840 the gardens were presented to the nation and became a national botanic garden. The Royal Botanic

Gardens, Kew, as they are now known, are today responsible for THE WORLD'S LARGEST COLLECTION OF LIVING PLANTS.

Greenwich Palace

Birthplace of Tudor Monarchs

HENRY VII established GREENWICH as a royal palace and as the birthplace of the Tudor monarchs.

Henry V's brother HUMPHREY, DUKE OF GLOUCESTER had been the first to build a home beside the river at Greenwich, in 1427, which he called Bella Court, described as 'one of the finest houses in England'. He also built a watch-tower at the top of the hill where the Royal Observatory now stands, to guard the approach to London along the road from Dover.

Humphrey was something of a scholar and accumulated ENGLAND'S FIRST LARGE PRIVATE LIBRARY at Bella Court. He left it to Oxford University, where it formed the nucleus of the Bodleian Library.

Henry VI and his wife Margaret of Anjou honeymooned at Bella Court, and she was so taken with the place that she had Humphrey arrested for high treason and he conveniently died in prison. She was then able to have Bella Court for herself which she renamed the Palace of Placentia, the pleasant place.

Tudor Palace

Henry VII changed the name to Greenwich Palace, and in 1491 his wife

ELIZABETH OF YORK gave birth there to Henry VIII.

In 1516 Henry VIII's first wife CATHERINE OF ARAGON gave birth to his first daughter, MARY, at Greenwich, with Cardinal Wolsey acting as godfather. That same year Henry took a leading part in THE FIRST MASQUERADE SEEN IN ENGLAND, performed in the park surrounding the palace.

In 1536, three years after the great river procession from Greenwich that marked her coronation, Henry's second wife ANNE BOLEYN gave birth there to his second daughter, ELIZABETH. It was during a jousting tournament at Greenwich that Anne supposedly dropped her handkerchief as a signal to her lover, a gesture that ultimately led to her appointment with the executioner's axe on Tower Green.

In 1540 Henry married his fourth wife ANNE OF CLEVES, the Mare of Flanders, at Greenwich.

Henry VIII set up an armoury at Greenwich, which produced armour to rival the best in Europe, some examples of which can be seen in the Tower of London. He also built two royal dockyards on either side of Greenwich, at DEPTFORD and WOOLWICH. Henry's daughter Mary had a narrow escape while watching from the palace windows as a ship sailed past on its way to the dockyard at Deptford. The ship fired a salute in recognition of the Royal Standard flying from the roof, but the gun was loaded and the cannon ball smashed through Mary's quarters, frightening the life out of the Princess and her ladies.

In 1553 Henry's longed-for son and heir, EDWARD VI, died at Greenwich just six years after his father had passed away upriver at Whitehall Palace.

ELIZABETH I loved Greenwich as a summer residence, and it was at Greenwich that the gallant SIR WALTER RALEIGH placed his cape over a puddle so that his queen wouldn't get her feet wet. And it was at Greenwich that Elizabeth reluctantly signed the death warrant of Mary, Queen of Scots.

In 1581 Elizabeth I knighted SIR FRANCIS DRAKE aboard his ship the *Golden Hind* at Deptford in recognition of Drake becoming THE FIRST ENGLISHMAN TO CIRCUMNAVIGATE THE GLOBE.

Nearly 400 years later, in 1967, ELIZABETH II used the same sword to knight SIR FRANCIS CHICHESTER, in recognition of his becoming THE FIRST MAN EVER TO CIRCUMNAVIGATE THE GLOBE SINGLE-HANDEDLY VIA THE GREAT CAPES.

The Queen's House

In 1616 JAMES I asked his court architect INIGO JONES to build a new pavilion at the old Tudor palace in Greenwich as

a gift for his queen, ANNE OF DENMARK, by way of apology for swearing at her in public when she shot one of his dogs while out hunting.

Jones had just been on a tour of Italy, and so he came up with a classical design inspired by the Medici villa at Poggio a Calano by Giuliano Sangallo. The house that emerged was THE FIRST CLASSICAL PALLADIAN BUILDING IN BRITAIN. It contained two parts, one standing within the old palace and the other within the park, linked by a bridge across the road from Greenwich to Woolwich so that the Queen could pass over without having to use the public thoroughfare. The colonnaded walks added later by Jones to east and west follow the line of the road and, as the road did, run under the house.

Work stopped in 1618 when Queen Anne died but was completed in 1635 for Charles I's wife HENRIETTA MARIA. Jones created a number of 'cubes', following the principles of symmetry, proportion and harmony as espoused by the Italian classical architect Andrea Palladio. He also introduced a number of innovations, including THE FIRST UNSUPPORTED SPIRAL STAIRCASE IN BRITAIN, THE TULIP STAIRCASE, and THE FIRST EXAMPLE IN AN ENGLISH HOUSE OF AN ENTRANCE HALL ALSO USED AS A RECEPTION ROOM.

The Queen's House, which represents the birth of classical architecture in Britain, was the only part of the old Greenwich Palace to escape the rebuilding of Greenwich begun by Charles II and completed by Sir Christopher Wren and Nicolas Hawksmoor for William and Mary.

Royal Hospital

In 1692 QUEEN MARY II commissioned SIR CHRISTOPHER WREN to design a hospital for seamen, the naval equivalent of the soldier's hospital at Chelsea, on the site of the old Tudor palace at Greenwich, which had been demolished by Charles II in preparation for a brand new palace that never got built. Mary's one request was that the view from the Queen's House to the river should not be obstructed, and so Wren and his assistant Nicholas Hawksmoor designed pairs of separate

buildings that left the Queen's House as the centrepiece. The result is one of Britain's great architectural panoramas.

Painted Hall

The highlight of the west wing is the PAINTED HALL, once described as 'the finest dining hall in the western world'. The painting on the ceiling is a tribute to William and Mary and shows them bestowing 'Peace' and 'Liberty' on Europe, while elsewhere George I is seen making his historic arrival at Greenwich and Queen Anne gazes in a motherly fashion at the continents of the world.

The decoration, which is THE LARGEST PAINTING IN BRITAIN, took SIR JAMES THORNHILL 19 years to complete. He finished it in 1727 and got a knighthood, as well as nearly £7,000 – three-quarters of a million pounds in today's currency.

Queen's Chapel

The Painted Hall is balanced across the courtyard by the ornate QUEEN'S CHAPEL, originally designed by Wren and then redesigned by JAMES 'ATHENIAN' STUART after a fire. The chapel was used as the setting for one of the weddings in the film *Four Weddings and a Funeral*.

Both hall and chapel are now open to the public, while the rest of the Greenwich complex is occupied by the University of Greenwich and the National Maritime Museum.

Well, I never knew this
about
ROYAL THAMES

The LAST PURPOSE-BUILT ROYAL BARGE, built for Frederick, Prince of Wales in 1731, is on show in the National Maritime Museum in Greenwich. It was last used in 1849 to convey Prince Albert and two of his children to the opening of the Coal Exchange in the City.

In 2010 ELIZABETH II broadcast her Christmas address from Hampton Court Palace, the first time Hampton Court had been used for this event.

RICHMOND in Surrey, named by Henry VII after his Earldom in North Yorkshire, is the second of 46 Richmonds around the world, all of which take their name from Richmond in Yorkshire.

CAPABILITY BROWN planted the GREAT VINE at Hampton Court during the reign of George III. Today the vine has a trunk 85 inches (216 cm) thick and branches up to 115 ft (35 m) long, and is THE BIGGEST AND OLDEST VINE IN BRITAIN. It still produces a good crop of black grapes every year.

Designed as a dining room, the PAINTED HALL at Greenwich was deemed too grand for the poor sailors to eat in, and it lay empty until 1806, when ADMIRAL LORD NELSON was brought to the hall to lie in state for three days before his funeral in St Paul's Cathedral.

THOMAS TALLIS, known as the 'Father of English church music', is buried in the church of ST ALFEGE in Greenwich, where you can see the original organ keyboard on which he taught a young Elizabeth I to play while she was living in Greenwich Palace. The wooden keys show signs of wear caused by Elizabeth's constant playing.

To mark Queen Elizabeth's 2012 Diamond Jubilee, Greenwich was granted the right to call itself ROYAL GREENWICH.

CHAPTER SEVEN

ROYAL WINDSOR

WINDSOR CASTLE ✦ HOME PARK ✦ FROGMORE
✦ FORT BELVEDERE ✦ WHAT'S IN A NAME?

WINDSOR CASTLE, standing on a chalk bluff above the River Thames, is THE LARGEST INHABITED CASTLE IN THE WORLD and THE LONGEST-OCCUPIED ROYAL CASTLE IN EUROPE. It is where Queen Elizabeth and the Duke of Edinburgh spend most of their weekends when they are based in London. Although they hold occasional banquets and state occasions there, Windsor is much more their home, while Buckingham Palace is their office. At Windsor the Royal Family can relax, walk or ride in the Home Park or Great Park and generally recover from the stresses of the week.

As well as the castle there are a number of royal homes dotted around Windsor Great Park where different members of the Royal Family can stay separate from the castle.

Windsor Castle

'The Most Romantique
Castle in the World'
Samuel Pepys

Windsor Castle was begun by WILLIAM THE CONQUEROR in 1070, as one of a defensive circle of fortresses built around London. On top of the motte William erected a round wooden keep, the shape designed to feed into the local belief that this was the site of King Arthur's Round Table. The present Round Tower, whose shape gives Windsor Castle its distinctive silhouette, is built on the foundations of the original 12th-century stone keep and was heightened by Sir James Wyattville in the 19th century to give it a more imposing appearance.

William the Conqueror did not use the castle as a residence, preferring to use Edward the Confessor's palace of Kingsbury, 2 miles (3.2 km) down river at Old Windsor.

William's grandson HENRY II rebuilt the wooden castle and halls in stone and began to put up the ring of curtain walls. These were completed by HENRY III, who added a number of rounded D-shaped towers, inspired by ideas brought back from the Crusades.

Edward III

EDWARD III, who was born in Windsor Castle in 1312, transformed what was already a substantial palace into a castle fit for the Golden Age of Chivalry, and to this purpose he ended up spending more money on Windsor than any medieval monarch had ever spent on one palace, much of it eventually raised from ransoms earned by his victories over the French at the Battles of Crecy and Poitiers during the Hundred Years War.

Edward's dream was to recreate the court of King Arthur at Windsor, and he began work on a round banqueting hall designed to hold a new round table for his knights. The hall never got finished but the table was built and now hangs in the Great Hall at Winchester.

Instead, in 1348, Edward established the ORDER OF THE GARTER at Windsor and declared Henry III's old chapel its spiritual home, rededicating the chapel to St George, the Order's patron saint.

St George's Chapel

The superb ST GEORGE'S CHAPEL at Windsor was Edward IV's great contribution to architecture. Edward saw himself as a warrior king and he decided

to build a glorious new chapel worthy of the Knights of the Garter, whose home up until then was a rather dingy chapel built back in the 13th century by Henry III. Edward also wanted a building that would outshine his rival Henry VI's great chapel across the river in Eton.

Work began in 1472 but Edward died long before it was finished. Henry VII and Henry VIII completed the task, just as they had done for Henry VI's chapel at King's College in Cambridge.

St George's Chapel is now considered to be one of the finest medieval churches in Europe, so Edward's wishes eventually came true. Edward IV was THE FIRST MONARCH TO BE BURIED IN ST GEORGE'S CHAPEL, in March 1483. In his latter years he had become something of a glutton and he died of a stroke caused by indigestion.

Ironically, the next monarch to be buried in Edward IV's new chapel was Henry VI, whose body was removed there from Chertsey Abbey by Richard III in 1484, in an attempt to stop Henry's tomb becoming a place of pilgrimage.

St George's Chapel eventually took over from Westminster Abbey as the royal burial place of choice and there are now ten monarchs buried there.

Albert Memorial Chapel

Separated by a passageway from St George's Chapel, Windsor, is the ALBERT MEMORIAL CHAPEL, built by Henry VII as his original burial place, before he settled on his new chapel at Westminster Abbey. Henry VIII bestowed it upon Cardinal Wolsey, for whom a magnificent tomb was prepared, before he fell from favour. The empty tomb was wrecked during the Civil War, all except for the black and white marble sarcophagus, which was later used to enclose Lord Nelson's tomb at St Paul's Cathedral.

Queen Victoria had the chapel converted into a memorial for Prince Albert. Two members of the Royal Family lie there, Victoria's youngest son PRINCE LEOPOLD, and Edward VII's eldest son PRINCE ALBERT VICTOR, whose tomb, sculpted by the designer of Eros at Piccadilly Circus, SIR ALFRED

Monarchs Buried in St George's Chapel

EDWARD IV, HENRY VI, HENRY VIII, who lies with his third and favourite wife JANE SEYMOUR, mother of his only son Edward, CHARLES I, brought here in a snowstorm after his execution, GEORGE III, GEORGE IV, WILLIAM IV, EDWARD VII, GEORGE V and GEORGE VI.

Gilbert, is considered one of the finest examples of 19th-century sculpture in Britain.

Henry VIII and Windsor Castle

Henry VIII rebuilt the main gateway into Windsor Castle, which is now known appropriately enough as King Henry VIII's Gateway, and added a new wooden north terrace overlooking what is now the Home Park. Henry loved Windsor, but he loved fine living too, and in his final years he had to be hoisted up the stairs to his 11 ft (3.4 m) square bed by a system of ropes and pulleys.

Elizabeth I rebuilt her father's north terrace in stone and created a long gallery above it where she could stroll and look out over the garden when the weather was cold.

A Long Walk

At the Restoration Charles II set about refurbishing the by now almost ruinous castle, and decorated the interior with carvings by Grinling Gibbons and murals by his court painter Antonio Verrio. He then created the Long Walk, a wide avenue of elm trees stretching for 3 miles (4.8 km) from the castle to Snow Hill in the Great Park, along which he could process in grand style to go out hunting. He also built a house for his

mistress Nell Gwyn just outside the walls, connected to his apartments in the castle by a secret tunnel.

George III

George III loved Windsor and would spend every summer there with his family. He enjoyed strolling over the bridge to Eton to watch the cricket or talk to the college pupils and enquire about their studies. To this day George III's birthday, the Fourth of June, is celebrated by Eton College as a holiday, with speeches and a procession of boats on the river.

It was while out driving in Windsor Great Park that George III suffered the first manifestation of the madness that would so sorely afflict him in his latter years. He alighted from his carriage, approached an oak tree, shook it warmly by one of its lower branches and proceeded to engage it in conversation, apparently under the impression that the tree was the King of Prussia.

George III was the first monarch to die in Windsor Castle.

Waterloo Chamber

It was under George IV that Windsor took the shape we see today. He commissioned Jeffry Wyattville to refashion the castle in Gothic style and redecorate his private apartments in the east front at a cost of over one million pounds.

The grandest of all the State Rooms

built by Wyatville is the enormous WATERLOO CHAMBER, created in 1830 to house the portraits of all the leaders who had combined to defeat Napoleon, which had been painted by Sir Thomas Lawrence after the Battle of Waterloo in 1815, at the request of George IV. Since 1914 the annual Waterloo Banquet has been held in the chamber, which also hosts the annual Garter Luncheon.

The walls of the Waterloo Chamber are lined with panelling carved by Grinling Gibbons in the 1680s and salvaged by Wyatville from the Royal Chapel when he was demolishing it in the 1820s.

The Indian carpet, laid down in 1894, was woven for Queen Victoria's Golden Jubilee by inmates of the prison in Agra. It weighs two tons and is THE LARGEST SEAMLESS CARPET IN THE WORLD. It took 50 soldiers to roll the carpet up and move it during the fire of 1992.

Queen Victoria

QUEEN VICTORIA enjoyed life at Windsor with her family, but after Prince Albert died there in 1861, she turned the castle into a shrine. The room where Albert expired was left untouched, including even the glass from which he had drunk his medicine, and a freshly pressed suit was laid out on the bed every day.

20th Century

When EDWARD VII came to the throne in 1901 he revitalised Windsor, clearing out the clutter from many of the rooms and installing electric lights, central heating, telephones and garages for his fleet of limousines. GEORGE V kept life formal at Windsor and adopted the name Windsor for the Royal Family during the First World War. After GEORGE VI moved in, reluctantly, from the Royal Lodge in the Great Park, he revived the annual Garter Service in St George's Chapel, which had been discontinued in 1805.

In 1992 a devastating fire ripped through the State Rooms, destroying nine of them and damaging many others, although most of the artworks were rescued. The castle was restored to its former state by skilled modern craftsmen, and the repairs were paid for by opening Buckingham Palace during the summer months when the Queen is at Balmoral.

The Home Park

The HOME PARK, which lies within Windsor Great Park to the north and east of the castle, is the Queen's private back garden, and is rarely open to the public. It is a garden of extraordinary beauty with spreading lawns and avenues of noble beech trees, and has that unmistakable feel of an English country park. It is easy to understand why the Queen loves Home Park so much, and it is also easy to picture her tramping through the fallen leaves in her very English head-scarf and wellingtons, with her dogs scampering beside her.

As well as gardens the Home Park

features farmland, a golf course, a bowling green, a cricket field, tennis courts, butts for archery and Frogmore House.

Frogmore House

FROGMORE HOUSE in the Home Park was a favourite retreat of Queen Victoria. It was built in 1680 and lived in from 1709 to 1738 by the DUKE OF NORTHUMBERLAND, one of Charles II's illegitimate sons by his mistress Barbara Villiers. In 1790 the house was enlarged by James Wyatt for George III, who gave it to his wife Queen Charlotte.

Queen Victoria gave Frogmore House to her mother, the DUCHESS OF KENT, in 1841. After the Duchess died in 1861, not long before Prince Albert, Victoria had a small mausoleum built for her to lie in by the lake in the garden.

Edward VII's eldest son PRINCE ALBERT VICTOR was born at Frogmore in 1864, and in 1900 Queen Victoria's great-grandson and the present Duke of Edinburgh's uncle, EARL MOUNTBATTEN OF BURMA, was born there.

The Royal Mausoleum

The magnificent ROYAL MAUSOLEUM standing in the grounds of Frogmore House was built by Queen Victoria as a grand resting place for Prince Albert after he died in 1861. Victoria was inspired by the mausoleum that her Uncle Leopold had built for his wife Princess Charlotte at Claremont in

Surrey. The Royal Mausoleum was completed in 1871 and Victoria was laid to rest there alongside Albert in 1901.

The mausoleum is constructed in the shape of a Greek cross, and the Romanesque exterior is made of Aberdeen granite and Portland stone with a copper roof. The opulent interior is decorated with paintings by Raphael, who was regarded by Prince Albert as the greatest of all painters, the sarcophagus is of Aberdeen granite, and there are splendid effigies of Victoria and Albert in marble.

In 1972 the DUKE OF WINDSOR (formerly Edward VIII) was buried in the mausoleum, and his wife WALLIS was buried next to him there in 1986.

The Royal Mausoleum is only open to the public on rare occasions, usually bank holidays.

Fort Belvedere

EDWARD, PRINCE OF WALES (briefly Edward VIII), lived at FORT BELVEDERE in Windsor Great Park, near Sunningdale, from 1930 until 1936, and

it was here that the Abdication Crisis was played out.

Fort Belvedere was built in 1755 as an exotic, turreted summer house for George II's son the DUKE OF CUMBERLAND, known as 'Butcher' Cumberland, victor of the Battle of Culloden. The view from the top of the turret takes in seven counties and VIRGINIA WATER, an artificial lake laid out by the Duke in 1746 using the labour of Jacobite prisoners captured at Culloden.

In 1828 the summer-house was enlarged and turned into a battery for royal salutes by SIR JEFFRY WYATTVILLE, who was at the time remodelling Windsor Castle for George IV. The fort continued to be used for salutes until 1907, when the building was converted into a seven-bedroom residence and given to Queen Victoria's third son PRINCE ARTHUR, DUKE OF CONNAUGHT.

In 1929 George V gave Fort Belvedere to Edward, Prince of Wales, who took up residence in 1930. Edward used the Fort for country entertaining and from 1935 the house was lavishly redecorated by HERMAN SCHRIJVER, a decorator used by Edward's intended fiancée Wallis Simpson.

Edward stayed on at Fort Belvedere when he became King in 1936 and held meetings there with Prime Minister Stanley Baldwin to discuss his abdication. On 10 December 1936, as Edward VIII he signed the Instrument of Abdication at Fort Belvedere in the presence of his three brothers, Albert, Duke of York (who was about to become George VI), Henry, Duke of Gloucester and George, Duke of Kent. The next day Edward made his infamous abdication broadcast from Windsor Castle. 'I have found it impossible to carry the heavy burden of responsibility and to discharge my duties as King as I would wish to do without the help and support of the woman I love.'

What's in a Name?

Normally, monarchs give their names to places, but in 1917, in the midst of anti-German sentiment during the First World War, George V decided to change his family name from the Germanic Saxe-Coburg-Gotha to something more British, and he chose the name of his favourite home – Windsor.

Royal House Names

Each royal dynasty since William the Conqueror has been given a name. The NORMANS took their name from their homeland of Normandy. The PLANTAGENETS were named after the sprig of broom, or planta genesta, that Henry II's father, Geoffrey, Count of Anjou, wore in his hat. The TUDOR name comes from the Welsh Ty Dur, which means House of Steel. The STUARTS were originally STEWARTS, a derivation of Steward – the family were appointed High Stewards of Scotland by David I. Mary, Queen of Scots changed the spelling to Stuart when she became Queen of France – there is no 'w' in French. The HANOVERIANS took their name from their German homeland of Hanover.

What's in a Number?

It was the Normans who introduced surnames into England, which is why kings are numbered from William the Conqueror. The Saxon kings were given names that reflected their character such as 'the Peaceable', 'the Unready' or 'the Magnificent'. Thus, although there were three Saxon Edwards, it is a later Plantagenet king who is called Edward I – he should by rights be Edward IV.

Royal Nicknames

WILLIAM II was known as 'Rufus' because of his red hair and face.

HENRY I was 'Beauclerc', meaning 'well read' – as a younger son he was not expected to become King and so was educated to go into the Church.

RICHARD I was 'Coeur de Lion' or 'Lionheart' for his exploits on crusade.

JOHN was 'Lackland', because he was the youngest son and there was no land left for him to inherit.

EDWARD I was 'Longshanks', because of his long legs.

QUEEN MARY I was 'Bloody Mary', because she had nearly 300 Protestants burned at the stake.

ELIZABETH I was the 'Virgin Queen', because she never married.

CHARLES II was the 'Merrie Monarch', because of his fun-loving character, which was in such contrast to the dour Commonwealth of Oliver Cromwell.

Unlucky Royal Names

John

In Scotland, John, Earl of Carrick, changed his name to Robert III when he became King because John was considered unlucky after the disastrous reign of John Balliol, puppet King to Edward I of England.

In England, ever since the days of 'Bad' King John in the early 13th century, the name John has been considered unlucky in royal circles. George V's fifth son Prince John suffered from epilepsy and for most of his short life was kept out of the public eye. When he was 12, John's condition got worse and he was given his own home at Wood Farm on the Sandringham estate, where he had his own household with tutor, cook and live-in maid. He died there, aged 13, in 1919 and was buried in the churchyard of St Mary Magdalene, Sandringham.

Arthur

The name of the legendary King Arthur's court, Camelot, came to symbolise a golden age cut short by tragedy, and was most famously applied to the presidency of John F. Kennedy which was brought to an end by assassination in 1963.

Prince Arthur of Brittany was murdered by his uncle King John, while Prince Arthur, eldest son of Henry VIII, died at the age of 15.

Albert

On his accession to the throne Edward VII chose to use Edward rather than his first name Albert in deference to his father Albert, who Edward felt should be remembered as the only Albert of the Royal Family.

James

Every king named James has come to a bad end, except for James VI of Scotland and I of England, who himself narrowly escaped death in the Gunpowder Plot.

James I of Scotland was murdered.

James II of Scotland was blown up by an exploding cannon.

James III of Scotland was murdered on the orders of his son.

James IV of Scotland died at the Battle of Flodden Field.

James V of Scotland died of despair after his army was defeated by the English at the Battle of Solway Moss and two weeks later his wife gave birth to a daughter.

James VII of Scotland and II of England was forced to abdicate after he produced a Catholic heir, threatening the Protestant Succession.

Star Struck

George III was fascinated by science and he paid for William Herschel's 40-ft (12 m) telescope, THE BIGGEST TELESCOPE EVER BUILT AT THE TIME. When Herschel discovered the planet Uranus he named his discovery Georgium Sidus, meaning George's Star. The following year George appointed Herschel 'King's Astronomer'.

The First Victoria

Queen Victoria was not, in fact, the very first Queen Victoria. The first was the very first British Queen – Boudicca. The name Boudicca comes from the Celtic word 'bouda' meaning 'victory' and as a

Places in America named after British Monarchs

VIRGINIA was named after the Virgin Queen, Elizabeth I.

NORTH AND SOUTH CAROLINA were named after Charles I (Latinised as Carola).

MARYLAND was named after Henrietta Maria, Queen of Charles I.

JAMESTOWN, THE FIRST PERMANENT ENGLISH SETTLEMENT IN AMERICA, was named after James I, as were the JAMES RIVER. CAPE HENRY and CAPE CHARLES were named after his sons.

NEW YORK was named after James, the Duke of York and Albany, later James II, as was ALBANY, the state capital.

WILLIAMSBURG was named after William of Orange (William III).

ANNAPOLIS, the state capital of Maryland, was named after the future Queen Anne, then Princess Anne, in 1694.

GEORGIA, founded by social reformer James Oglethorpe as a new colony where Britain's poor, particularly those in debtors' prisons, could start a new life, was named after George II.

---

heroic warrior and resistance leader against the Romans, Boudicca was an inspiration to her namesake Victoria. In 1902, a statue by THOMAS THORNYCROFT of a resplendent Boudicca commanding her chariot was unveiled by Westminster Bridge, as a glorious tribute to Queen Victoria, who had died the year before.

Legend has it that Boudicca is buried beneath Platform 9 at King's Cross station – not far, of course, from Platform 9¾, the departure point for Harry Potter's Hogwarts Express.

Wessex

In 1999 Queen Elizabeth II's youngest son EDWARD became the first EARL OF WESSEX since the Norman Conquest. Elizabeth II can trace her ancestors back to the House of Wessex, the first of whom, CERDIC, found the Kingdom of the West Saxons, or Wessex, in the 6th century.

In fact Cerdic has bequeathed us something more than just a kingdom and a royal family – he unwittingly left us with the excellent name of CEDRIC. Sir Walter Scott, writing his 1819 novel *Ivanhoe*, wanted to use Cerdic's name for one of his characters but misspelt it as Cedric – and the name stuck.

Perhaps the most celebrated member of the House of Wessex, and the only English monarch ever to have been given the epithet 'the Great', was

Places named after Queen Victoria

There are more places around the world named after Queen Victoria than any other British monarch. Here are just some of them

The States of QUEENSLAND and VICTORIA in Australia

VICTORIA, capital of the Canadian province of British Columbia

REGINA, capital of the Canadian province of Saskatchewan

LAKE VICTORIA in East Africa, Africa's largest lake and the second largest freshwater lake in the world (after Lake Superior in Canada)

VICTORIA FALLS, between Zambia and Zimbabwe,
THE LARGEST FALLS IN THE WORLD.

QUEENSTOWN in the Eastern Cape of South Africa

PORT VICTORIA, capital of the Seychelles

VICTORIA, VIRGINIA, USA, a railway town named by railroad financier Henry Rogers, who admired Queen Victoria

ALFRED THE GREAT, who reigned as King of Wessex from 871 to 899. In order to fortify his kingdom against the Vikings, Alfred established THE FIRST ROYAL NAVY, with which to fend off the Viking longboats. Alfred's navy was the inspiration for all future national navies, and in the 18th century the new UNITED STATES NAVY commemorated Alfred's achievement by naming ITS FIRST FLAGSHIP USS *ALFRED.*

The FIRST EVER BAN ON SUNDAY TRADING in England was ordered by King Alfred's grandson ATHELSTAN OF WESSEX, a staunch Christian.

Well, I never knew this
about
ROYAL WINDSOR

Because Windsor Castle lies within its boundaries, the county of Berkshire is known as ROYAL BERKSHIRE. The nickname for the football team of Reading, Berkshire's county town, is THE ROYALS.

OLIVER CROMWELL used Windsor Castle as the headquarters for his army throughout the duration of the Civil War and even imprisoned Charles I there. When Charles eventually returned to Windsor it was in a coffin, his severed head restitched on to his body, which was buried under the floor of the chapel.

George III's wife QUEEN CHARLOTTE introduced THE FIRST CHRISTMAS TREE INTO ENGLAND at Windsor Castle in 1800, and it was made popular by Victoria and Albert, who posed for the *Illustrated London News* in front of a decorated tree at Windsor in 1846.

The marathon in the 1908 Olympics was started at Windsor Castle so that the Royal Family could get a good view, and the distance from below their viewing position at the castle to the finishing line at White City, 26 miles, 385 yards, became the standard distance for the modern marathon.

QUEEN MARY'S DOLL'S HOUSE, which is housed at Windsor Castle, was designed in 1924 by SIR EDWIN LUTYENS for George V's wife. The interior furnishings were made by the top craftsmen of the time, and the house serves as a unique historical document of how the Royal Family lived in that period. The lights all work, the baths are plumbed,

the lavatories flush and the wine bottles are filled with real wine. Contemporary writers such as J.M. Barrie, Sir Arthur Conan Doyle, Rudyard Kipling, Thomas Hardy and W. Somerset Maugham all wrote stories for special books that were made to scale.

Windsor Castle is right under the flight path of the world's busiest international airport at Heathrow, and the present occupant of the castle, Queen Elizabeth II, has learned to tell the make of each aircraft passing overhead from its engine noise.

ADELAIDE, capital of South Australia, was named in honour of Queen Adelaide, wife of William IV.

CHAPTER EIGHT

Royal England
Homes and Palaces

Sandringham ✦ Highgrove ✦ Osborne House
✦ Brighton Pavilion ✦ Hatfield Palace
✦ Clarendon Palace ✦ Claremont ✦ Eltham Palace
✦ Cliveden ✦ Park Place

While later monarchs have tended to spend their time mostly in London or Windsor where their principal residences are located, there are plenty of former royal homes and palaces to be found all over England. Some are still royal homes.

Sandringham

Just before he died in 1861, Queen Victoria's husband Prince Albert decided to look for a country house for their eldest son Edward, somewhere away from the fleshpots of London, where the Prince of Wales could indulge in more healthy outdoor pursuits. Albert alighted on Sandringham, in Norfolk, the home of Lord Palmerston's stepson Charles Spencer Cowper, but died before he could complete the deal. Edward, who visited for the first time in 1862, liked it right away and concluded the purchase, moving in the following year with his new bride Alexandra.

It soon became clear that the house, a simple Georgian villa built in 1771, was too small for Edward's growing family, let alone partying, so the old house was demolished and replaced in 1870 with a grand 'Jacobethan' style edifice with gables and turrets designed by A.J. HUMBERT, and described by one visitor as 'looking like a Harrogate hotel'. Above the door was inscribed 'This house was built by Albert Edward and Alexandra his wife in the year of our Lord, 1870'.

In 1881 a ballroom was added and further guest accommodation ten years later after a fire that broke out during preparations for Edward's 50th birthday.

Sandringham became for Edward 'the house I like best', where he could enjoy hunting and shooting and where he kept his racehorse stud. In order to spend as much time as possible outdoors Edward devised SANDRINGHAM TIME, whereby the clocks at Sandringham were all set half an hour fast to make the most of the short winter days. Edward's nephew Kaiser Wilhelm stayed three times.

When Queen Victoria paid her first visit in 1871, Edward went down with typhoid, the illness that had killed his father ten years before, but Edward recovered. In 1892 Edward's eldest son PRINCE ALBERT VICTOR, DUKE OF CLARENCE, died of pneumonia at Sandringham.

GEORGE V established the custom of spending Christmas and New Year at Sandringham, a tradition still followed by the Royal Family today. On Christmas Day in 1932 he made THE FIRST CHRISTMAS BROADCAST ON LIVE RADIO from Sandringham's business room. The speech was drafted by RUDYARD KIPLING.

George V died at 'dear old Sandringham, the place I love better than anywhere in the world' in 1936.

EDWARD VIII only spent one day at Sandringham and swore he would 'fix those bloody clocks' on his accession, duly abolishing Sandringham Time in 1936.

Like his father, GEORGE VI, who was born on the Sandringham Estate, in York Cottage, loved Sandringham, writing to his mother, 'I have always been so happy here, I love the place.' He died there in 1952.

ELIZABETH II continues to enjoy Sandringham and in 1957 made THE FIRST TELEVISED CHRISTMAS BROAD-CAST live from the library at Sandringham.

The gardens at Sandringham were first opened to the public by Edward VII in 1908, and Elizabeth II opened up the house to the public in 1977, the year of her Silver Jubilee. Sandringham House can now be visited in the summer months.

Highgrove

The Prince of Wales's principal private residence is HIGHGROVE, near Tetbury in Gloucestershire, which he purchased in 1980 from Maurice Macmillan, son of the former Prime Minister Harold Macmillan. Prince Charles and his new bride Diana moved in together in 1981 following their marriage in St Paul's Cathedral and used Highgrove as a weekend retreat.

The royal couple's children, Princes William and Harry, spent a lot of time at Highgrove during their early years and still visit their father there when time allows.

Prince Charles laid out the gardens to his own design and farms the 900-acre (364 ha) estate organically, selling produce from the estate under the name Duchy Originals.

Highgrove is a classical Georgian house built in 1798 by a local Huguenot family called Paul. In 1988 Prince Charles embellished the plain exterior with a new balustrade and pediment.

Osborne House

When Queen Victoria and Prince Albert were looking for a country retreat for their growing family in the 1840s, Victoria remembered happy times spent as a child on the Isle of Wight, and decided that was where they should look. When they saw OSBORNE HOUSE just outside East Cowes, overlooking the Solent, Victoria declared it 'impossible to imagine a prettier spot' and they purchased the house with 342 acres (138 ha) in 1845.

The Georgian house already there was not nearly big enough to accommodate the Royal Family, and so it was pulled down and replaced with a vast Italian Renaissance-style villa, designed that way by Prince Albert to complement the view, which reminded him of the Bay of Naples. The builder was THOMAS CUBITT, who was responsible for the

famous façade of Buckingham Palace. Much of the cost was met by the sale of the Prince Regent's Royal Pavilion in Brighton.

The house consisted of two main wings connected by a Grand Corridor which the royal couple filled with a parade of statues and which made for a fine undercover promenade in bad weather. The whole house was filled with gifts presented to the Queen from around the world and exhibits from the Great Exhibition.

The gardens were laid out in terraces, also in the Italian style, and included the FIRST PALM TREE PLANTED IN A PRIVATE GARDEN IN ENGLAND, a gift from King Ferdinand of Portugal. A 'Swiss Cottage', dismantled and brought piece by piece from Switzerland, was set up in the garden as a place for the royal children to learn domestic and gardening skills.

On 26 May 1857, Queen Victoria and her family posed for THE FIRST EVER OFFICIAL ROYAL FAMILY PHOTOGRAPH, at Osborne House.

After Prince Albert died in 1861, Victoria kept Osborne House as a shrine to his memory and spent much of her long period of mourning there. Affairs of state still had to be seen to, however, and in 1890 a new wing was added with a huge banqueting hall designed and decorated in Indian style to reflect Victoria's position as the Empress of India. Rudyard Kipling's father, Lockwood, director of the Lahore Central Museum, was consulted about the design. The room contained items given to the Queen on her Golden and Diamond Jubilees and included large blue Indian vases that concealed the electric lights.

After the death of Queen Victoria at Osborne in 1901, her successor Edward VII presented Osborne House to the nation. For a while it was used as a Royal Naval College, and during the First World War as an officers' convalescent home, with poet Robert Graves and *Winnie the Pooh* author A.A. Milne amongst the patients.

Osborne House is now in the care of English Heritage, and house and garden have been restored as closely as possible to how they were in Queen Victoria's time.

Brighton Pavilion

In 1783 GEORGE, PRINCE OF WALES (later George IV) went to stay with his uncle the Duke of Cumberland in the little fishing village of BRIGHTHELMSTONE on the Sussex coast. The trip was on the orders of his doctor, who thought that sea bathing might help ease the Prince's embarrassing swollen neck glands, which George tried to conceal by wearing high collars.

Marine Pavilion

George was much taken with Brighton and returned the following year, leasing a house on the Steine, an area of grassland east of the village that overlooked the promenade, and then in 1786 he took out a lease on a nearby farmhouse. In 1787 the Prince had the architect HENRY HOLLAND transform the farmhouse into a modest neo-classical villa with a domed saloon and extending wings north and south, which was named the Marine Pavilion.

George set up his 'wife' MARIA FITZHERBERT in a rented house next door and for the next few years the couple held court in Brighton as man and wife. After dinner George liked to practise with his firearms and more than once, after a mite too much claret, sent the orchestra diving for cover as he fired at the chandeliers. His guests were invited to join in – and one, Lady Downshire, actually winged the lead violin.

During the French Revolution the Prince and Mrs Fitzherbert would stand on the beach and welcome the small boats filled with bedraggled aristocrats fleeing the guillotine. Many were put up in the Pavilion, given supper and then sent on their way to London.

In 1804 Prince George commissioned WILLIAM PORDEN to extend the pavilion by building an indoor riding school and stable for 62 horses. The riding school has since been transformed into a concert hall and conference centre known as the Dome.

Mrs Fitzherbert's House

At the same time Mrs Fitzherbert had a new house built for her on what is now the Old Steine, and she continued to live there even after she and George moved apart when he became Prince Regent in 1811. She lived there until her death in 1837 and is buried in the Roman Catholic church of St John the Baptist in Bristol Road, her effigy showing her wearing three rings. Her house is now a YMCA hostel.

Eastern Promise

William Porden's vast new stable block, designed in the Indian style and the most opulent stable block ever built in Britain, completely dwarfed the pavilion.

So, in 1815, once George had become Prince Regent and come into a lot more money, much of it from his indulgent mother Queen Caroline, he commissioned JOHN NASH to outshine the stables and transform the pavilion into an exotic pleasure palace. Nash, inspired by studying books about India's Mogul emperors, combined Indian, Islamic and Chinese architectural elements to create a strikingly romantic ensemble, with distinctive onion domes and an abundance of minarets, pinnacles and cupolas. Two new wings were added containing two state rooms, the Music Room and the Banqueting Hall, and the whole exterior was rendered to look like Bath stone.

No expense was spared on the interior which was filled with the finest furniture and a riot of dragons and serpents, lacquer and gilt, mirrors and crystal chandeliers – the chandelier in the Banqueting Hall, lit by gas, had a lotus flower motif and weighed over a ton. The roofs of the Banqueting Hall and Music Room were designed to resemble Saracen tents, while the iron pillars of the Great Kitchen, THE FIRST IRON PILLARS TO BE USED IN THE CONSTRUCTION OF A HOUSE ANYWHERE, were made to look like palm trees. The kitchen was supplied with running water direct from local springs, while the Prince's bath, 16 ft (4.9 m) long, 10 ft (3 m) wide and 6 ft (1.8 m) deep, was filled with salt water pumped in from the sea.

Banquets at Brighton usually consisted of over 100 dishes and afterwards the Prince Regent often entertained his guests by singing to them in a pleasing baritone, which apparently impressed even the Italian composer Rossini when he was a guest.

When George became King in 1820, he lost interest in Brighton, preferring the delights of Windsor Castle, then being refurbished by James Wyatt, or Buckingham Palace, which John Nash was working on.

William IV is Amused

George's brother, WILLIAM IV, loved Brighton and spent part of every summer at the Pavilion. He particularly enjoyed tramping up and down Brighton's new CHAIN PIER, THE WORLD'S FIRST SEASIDE PLEASURE PIER, built by SIR SAMUEL BROWN in 1823 along the lines of his pioneering Union Chain suspension bridge over the Tweed in Northumberland. William thought the pier 'the most delightful place in the world'.

Victoria is Not

QUEEN VICTORIA on the other hand, disliked the Pavilion, calling it 'an odd Chinese looking thing' and found it too public, surrounded as it now was by the rapidly expanding town of Brighton. She eventually bought Osborne House on the Isle of Wight as her seaside retreat, and in 1850 the

Pavilion was sold to Brighton Council, since when it has been gradually restored to its original splendour and is now open to the public.

Hatfield Palace

ELIZABETH I was sent to live in the royal palace at HATFIELD in Hertfordshire when she was a three-month-old princess. The palace was built by Henry VII's minister Cardinal Morton in 1497 and was seized by Henry VIII at the Dissolution of the Monasteries and made into a home for his daughters.

In 1558 Elizabeth was sitting reading under an oak tree in the park at Hatfield when the news was brought to her that her sister Mary had died and she was now Queen of England. She is reported to have said, 'This is the Lord's doing, and it is marvellous in our eyes.' The spot is marked by a plaque, and a young oak tree.

Elizabeth held her first Great Council in the Great Hall at Hatfield, which is the only part of the Old Palace to survive. It is now used for banquets.

Elizabeth's successor JAMES I didn't like Hatfield and swapped it with his Chief Minister Robert Cecil, the Earl of Salisbury, for THEOBALDS, the Cecils' house near Cheshunt. Cecil tore down three wings of the Old Palace and used the bricks to build the present Hatfield House, which is constructed in a combination of Elizabethan and Jacobean styles.

Hatfield House contains two famous portraits of Elizabeth I, the Ermine Portrait by Nicholas Hilliard and, in the Marble Hall, the Rainbow Portrait

thought to be by Isaac Oliver. Also in the house are a pair of Elizabeth's silk stockings, THE FIRST SILK STOCKINGS SEEN IN ENGLAND.

The Cecil family still own Hatfield House and today it is the home of the 7th Marquess of Salisbury.

Clarendon Palace

In 1164 HENRY II issued from CLARENDON PALACE what some regard as ENGLAND'S FIRST CONSTITUTION, the CONSTITUTIONS OF CLARENDON, which brought the Church under the authority of the Crown and English law.

Clarendon Palace, set on a green hilltop overlooking Salisbury from the east, began life as a hunting lodge for the Norman kings, and was extended into a palace with a vast wooden hall, to become one of Henry II's favourite country homes. This was THE FIRST ROYAL PALACE NOT TO BE FORTIFIED, ENGLAND'S FIRST DOMESTIC MANOR HOUSE. It covered some 5 acres (2 ha) and included terraced gardens.

HENRY III made Clarendon into a sumptuous place, decorating many of the rooms with tiles fired in the FIRST TILE KILN KNOWN OF IN ENGLAND OUTSIDE A MONASTERY (now in the British Museum). A quite beautiful floor of medieval tiles made in this kiln, some showing Richard I on crusade, was found on the site and is thought to have been from the chambers of Henry III's queen, Eleanor of Provence. Also found was THE EARLIEST KNOWN EXAMPLE OF A BRADAWL and THE EARLIEST KNOWN PIECE OF GLASS WITHIN A LEAD FRAME.

King David of Scotland and King John of France were held captive here by Edward III.

It was at Clarendon, in 1453, that HENRY VI had the first attack of the madness that would afflict him.

Clarendon began to deteriorate in the time of Henry VIII, and the last recorded royal visit was from ELIZABETH I in 1574.

Although there is now very little left of the palace, the site is being slowly rescued from beneath the encroaching vegetation and there is a lovely walk to the ruins from Salisbury, through the grounds of CLARENDON PARK, once THE LARGEST DEER PARK IN ENGLAND. The views from here of the spire of Salisbury Cathedral are sublime.

Claremont

In about 1700 SIR JOHN VANBRUGH, the architect of Blenheim Palace and Castle Howard in Yorkshire, built himself a small brick house at the bottom of a gentle hill near Esher in Surrey.

Some years later he sold it to Thomas Pelham-Holles, the EARL OF CLARE. The Earl put up a tall ornamental tower on top of the hill, from where he could survey the Surrey countryside and views stretching from Windsor Castle to St Paul's Cathedral. He named the property CLARE MOUNT.

The Earl went on to become the Duke of Newcastle and to serve as Prime Minister. When he died in 1768, CLIVE OF INDIA bought the house and completely rebuilt it as it stands today. The new house was designed by the

landscape gardener CAPABILITY BROWN, AND IS THE ONLY HOUSE HE EVER DESIGNED THAT STILL STANDS.

Clive died before the house was finished and the house then passed through a number of hands before it was bought by the nation as a wedding gift for George IV's daughter PRINCESS CHARLOTTE and her husband Prince Leopold in 1816. Charlotte died there the following year after giving birth to a still-born son, and the doctor who saw to her, Sir Richard Croft, was so overcome by shame and remorse he shot himself.

Leopold's niece Princess Victoria was a frequent visitor to Claremont and spent her first ten birthdays there. When her uncle left to become King of the Belgians, Victoria bought the house as a gift for her own son PRINCE LEOPOLD, THE DUKE OF ALBANY. His son Charles should later have inherited the house, but he had served in the German army in the First World War and the inheritance was disallowed.

The house is now a school, while the gardens are run by the National Trust. They contain the work of many of the top 18th-century garden designers including Sir John Vanbrugh, Charles Bridgeman, William Kent and Capability Brown and are regarded as THE FINEST 18TH-CENTURY LANDSCAPED GARDENS IN BRITAIN.

Eltham Palace

ELTHAM PALACE in south-east London was given to Edward II by Anthony Beck, the Bishop of Durham in 1305.

Used as a hunting lodge, it continued to be a popular royal residence until the Tudors expanded nearby Greenwich Palace. In 1470 EDWARD IV added a magnificent Great Hall, giving Eltham THE THIRD LARGEST HAMMERBEAM ROOF IN ENGLAND. The palace was neglected after the Civil War and except for the Great Hall became ruinous. In the 1930s it was rebuilt by the COURTAULD family and decorated in spectacular art deco style, while incorporating the medieval Great Hall. The Courtaulds also restored the picturesque gardens, from which there are amazing views across London, awash with trees, to St Paul's Cathedral. Today Eltham Palace is in the hands of English Heritage.

Cliveden House

In 1737 FREDERICK, PRINCE OF WALES, oldest son of George II, took out a lease on CLIVEDEN HOUSE, standing high above the River Thames near Maidenhead. It had been built in 1666 for the Duke of Buckingham, who later killed his mistress's husband there in a duel and frolicked with his lover in the poor man's fresh blood, thus establishing Cliveden's reputation for high society high jinks, which it has maintained ever since.

It was at Cliveden in 1740, during a party thrown by Prince Frederick, that 'RULE BRITANNIA' WAS PERFORMED FOR THE FIRST TIME as part of a masque. The words were written by the Scottish poet JAMES THOMSON (while he was staying at the Dove pub by the river in Hammersmith) and the music was composed by Prince Frederick's favourite English composer THOMAS ARNE.

Prince Frederick was also a keen cricketer, and while playing a game of cricket in the garden at Cliveden he was fatally struck on the chest by the ball (*see* Royal Wales).

The present house was built by Sir CHARLES BARRY for the DUKE OF SUTHERLAND, and later became the country home of the Astors, who threw wild parties there in the 1930s for their friends in the 'Cliveden Set'.

In 1961, the Secretary of State for War JOHN PROFUMO met call-girl CHRISTINE KEELER in the swimming pool at Cliveden, and began a scandalous relationship that did much to bring down Harold Macmillan's government.

The Duke of Buckingham would have been proud.

Park Place

Not content with Cliveden, in 1738 Prince Frederick bought PARK PLACE, a large French Renaissance style house set in extensive grounds near Henley in Oxfordshire that had been built a few years earlier by the Duke of Hamilton. The Prince wanted it as a private country estate of his own where he could bring up his children, including the future George III. Prince Frederick planted three cedar trees at the front of the house, which are still standing there today.

When Prince Frederick died suddenly in 1751, his wife Augusta retreated to their house at Kew and sold Park Place to the eccentric GENERAL HENRY SEYMOUR CONWAY, who made improvements to the gardens, planting ENGLAND'S FIRST LOMBARDY POPLARS and erecting in the grounds a prehistoric Druid's Circle from Jersey.

A later owner managed to acquire the top portion of Christopher Wren's wedding cake steeple from St Bride's, Fleet Street, in London, which had been broken off by a lightning strike. He placed it in the garden in celebration of Queen Victoria's coronation in 1838.

In 1865 Queen Victoria herself visited Park Place incognito, with an eye to buying it, but decided not to.

Even she might have been stretched to buy Park Place today. In August 2011 Park Place became BRITAIN'S MOST EXPENSIVE HOUSE when it was sold to a Russian buyer for £140 million.

Bagshot Park

BAGSHOT PARK, on the borders of Surrey and Berkshire, is the official residence of the Earl and Countess of Wessex.

The original building at Bagshot, known as Bagshot Lodge, was a small hunting lodge built by Inigo Jones for Charles I in 1631. This was enlarged in the 1770s by James Paine for George Keppel, the 3rd Earl of Albemarle, an ancestor of Edward VII's mistress Alice Keppel and the present Duchess of Cornwall.

In 1798 Sir John Soane remodelled the house for the Duke of Clarence (later William IV) and he lived there until 1816, when it became the home of Prince Frederick, Duke of Gloucester, and his new wife Princess Mary, daughter of George III.

In the 1870s Queen Victoria had the house demolished and a vast new red-brick mansion constructed as a wedding present for her third son Prince Arthur, Duke of Connaught.

During a later tour of India, the Duke met Lockwood Kipling, father of Rudyard Kipling and a well-known designer, and asked him to design a billiard room for Bagshot Park in the Indian style. The room, which includes some beautiful carvings, was constructed in India and then installed at Bagshot over two years by two Indian craftsmen who slept in a tent in the grounds.

Well, I never knew this
about

ROYAL ENGLAND'S HOMES AND PALACES

BRITAIN'S VERY FIRST ROYAL PALACE was FISHBOURNE PALACE, 2 miles (3.2 km) west of Chichester. It was built for KING COGIDUBNUS (r. AD 60–80) a Celtic client-king who paid homage to Rome and adopted Roman ways. Fishbourne, THE LARGEST ROMAN BUILDING EVER DISCOVERED IN BRITAIN, was begun some 30 years after the Roman invasion of AD 42 on the site of a small Roman supply station and grew into THE LARGEST ROMAN RESIDENCE IN NORTHERN EUROPE, covering an area of some 500 square feet, which is bigger than Buckingham Palace. It contains THE LARGEST COLLECTION OF MOSAICS EVER FOUND ON THEIR ORIGINAL SITE IN BRITAIN, including perhaps the most famous Roman mosaic in Britain, CUPID ON A DOLPHIN. Fishbourne Palace burned down in AD 280 and wasn't rediscovered for nearly 1700 years, until 1960.

Over Christmas and New Year 1400–01, King Henry IV entertained THE ONLY BYZANTINE EMPEROR EVER TO VISIT ENGLAND, MANUEL II PALAIOLOGOS, at ELTHAM PALACE. Henry arranged a joust in the emperor's honour, and the jousting yard can still be seen at Eltham.

DIANA, PRINCESS OF WALES, was born at PARK HOUSE, on the edge of the Sandringham estate, in 1961. The house was leased by the Queen to Diana's parents Viscount and Viscountess Althorp. It is now run as the Park House Hotel.

Diana is buried on an island in the grounds of ALTHORP, her family's ancestral home in Northamptonshire.

Prince Charles's home at Highgrove stands at one corner of what was once known as THE GOLDEN TRIANGLE, made up of three royal houses in Gloucestershire: HIGHGROVE, Princess Anne's GATCOMBE PARK near Minchinhampton, and NETHER LYPIATT, once the home of Prince and Princess Michael of Kent.

Gatcombe Park was bought by the Queen in 1976 as a belated wedding present for Princess Anne after her marriage to Captain Mark Phillips in 1973. It was built in the 1740s and previous owners included Samuel Courtauld and the Conservative politician RAB Butler.

NETHER LYPIATT is an exquisite small classical manor house built in 1698, hidden along a small twisting Cotswold Lane 500 ft (152 m) above Stroud. The house has been described as 'perfect in every way' and was perhaps the inspiration for the Governor's Mansion in Colonial Williamsburg, Virginia. It was built for 'Hanging Judge' Cox, whose son, ironically, hanged himself in one of the rooms and is supposed to haunt the place. In 2006 Prince and Princess Michael of Kent sold Nether Lypiatt to Labour politician Lord Drayson.

OSBORNE HOUSE contains one of the oldest working water closets in Britain, an original Joseph Bramah model built in the late 18th century.

While he was recuperating at Weymouth in Dorset, GEORGE III became THE FIRST MONARCH TO USE A BATHING MACHINE, of which a replica can be seen on the sea front at Weymouth. As George entered the water for the first time a band, hidden in another machine, struck up 'God Save the King'.

The FIRST KNOWN ENGLISH LETTER was sent from PEVENSEY in 1399 by LADY JOAN PELHAM to her husband, Sir John Pelham. Lady Pelham was defending PEVENSEY CASTLE against the forces of RICHARD II while her husband was absent in exile with Henry Bolingbroke (Henry IV). In the letter she hopes he is safe and signs off, 'Written at Pevensey in the Castle by your own poor J. Pelham.'

CHAPTER NINE

ROYAL ENGLAND BIRTHS, BURIALS & BETWEEN

CANTERBURY ✦ WINCHESTER ✦ WORCESTER
✦ GLOUCESTER ✦ KING'S LANGLEY ✦ TEWKESBURY
✦ FOTHERINGHAY ✦ GRAFTON REGIS ✦ HEVER CASTLE
✦ LEEDS CASTLE ✦ QUEEN ELIZABETH'S HUNTING LODGE
✦ KING'S COLLEGE CHAPEL

As well as royal homes and palaces there are a host of royal birthplaces, burial sites, castles and cathedrals throughout England that have special royal connections.

Canterbury

ST AUGUSTINE'S ABBEY in Canterbury is THE EARLIEST BURIAL PLACE OF ENGLISH KINGS. It was founded by ST AUGUSTINE, THE FIRST ARCHBISHOP OF CANTERBURY, outside the eastern walls of the city on land given by KING ETHELBERT, THE FIRST CHRISTIAN ENGLISH KING.

St Augustine died in 604 and was buried in the abbey. Many of the early archbishops were buried there, on one side of the abbey, while the Kings of Kent were buried on the other side, starting with King Ethelbert, who was laid to rest there in 616. In this way St Augustine's Abbey became the FIRST BURIAL PLACE OF ENGLISH KINGS, and a powerful symbol of the alliance of Church and Crown that would play such a significant part in Britain's royal history.

The abbey was demolished at the Dissolution of the Monasteries and the ruins now form part of the Canterbury World Heritage Site, along with St Martin's Church, the earliest Christian church, and the cathedral.

Canterbury Cathedral is the burial place of HENRY IV and his QUEEN JOAN OF NAVARRE and also of the BLACK PRINCE, eldest son of Edward III.

Winchester

WINCHESTER WAS THE FIRST ROYAL CAPITAL OF ENGLAND, the burial place of many of the Saxon kings and the birthplace of HENRY III.

In 871 Alfred the Great was crowned in the Old Minster at Winchester, founded in 648 by King Cenwahl. He made Winchester his capital, establishing a Royal Mint and storing his Treasury there. He also laid out the grid system of streets that are still in use today and rebuilt the walls of the old Roman town – the surviving city walls we see today are largely the work of his Saxon builders.

Alfred was King of Wessex, the most powerful of the Saxon kingdoms, and when the Kings of Wessex united England Winchester became the capital of the whole country. It remained the capital for 20 years after the Norman invasion, sharing the honours with London.

When Alfred died he was buried in the Old Minster beside his grandfather King Egbert. His remains were moved in 1109 when the monks of the Old Minster were transferred to a larger abbey in Hyde, just outside the city walls.

HYDE ABBEY was completely demolished at the Dissolution of the Monasteries and Alfred's remains were lost, although what is thought to be Alfred's grave was excavated in 1999 in the grounds of what is now the River Park Recreation Centre, and a memorial garden was created to mark the spot.

A statue of King Alfred the Great, sculpted by HAMO THORNYCROFT, brother of the founder of the Thornycroft shipbuilding firm, stands near the River Itchen and gazes down the high street towards old Westgate. It was unveiled in 1901.

Winchester Cathedral

The present WINCHESTER CATHEDRAL, THE LONGEST MEDIEVAL CATHEDRAL IN

EUROPE, was largely constructed during the reign of William the Conqueror using stones from the Old Minster. The remains of the Saxon kings, and King Canute, who was also buried in the Old Minster, were placed in mortuary chests and placed on top of the choir screen in the new cathedral.

The coronation of William the Conqueror's wife MATILDA was held in Winchester Cathedral in May 1068; and in 1100 the body of William's son WILLIAM RUFUS was brought from the New Forest and laid to rest under the cathedral tower – which promptly fell down. Another of William's four sons, RICHARD, DUKE OF BERNAY, who had also died in a hunting accident in the New Forest, in 1081, is buried some-where in the cathedral.

QUEEN MARY I married PHILIP OF SPAIN in Winchester Cathedral in 1554 and they spent the first night of their honeymoon in Wolvesey Palace next door.

Great Hall

In 1067 William the Conqueror began a castle at Winchester and, in 1207, Henry III was born there. In 1222 Henry erected a large, elegant Great Hall for the castle, considered to be THE FINEST 13TH-CENTURY HALL IN ENGLAND. It is the only part of Winchester Castle that survives. The Hall has an interesting 'double cube' design, with the height and width, 55 ft (17 m), being exactly half the length, 110 ft (34 m).

At one end of the Hall hangs what was at one time thought to be KING ARTHUR'S ROUND TABLE from Camelot. It was actually constructed in the late 13th century for Edward III. The table was repainted for Henry VIII, with the portrait of King Arthur bearing an extraordinary likeness to Henry.

Worcester Cathedral

KING JOHN was buried, at his own request, in WORCESTER CATHEDRAL, near the shrines of his two favourite Anglo-Saxon saints, St Wulfstan and St Oswald. His tomb rests in the chancel and is crowned with THE OLDEST ROYAL EFFIGY IN BRITAIN, created in 1232.

Nearby, in a plain tomb set at the centre of his own ethereal chantry, lies PRINCE ARTHUR, elder brother of Henry VIII, who died at Ludlow Castle in 1502, aged 15. The chantry, carved out of creamy white stone and richly ornamented, is a peerless example of Tudor craftsmanship, almost a miniature version of Henry VII's chapel in Westminster Abbey. It seems likely that the cathedral was spared by Henry VIII at the Dissolution of the Monasteries because of the presence of Arthur's chantry.

All that remains of the cathedral built by St Wulfstan in 1084 is the Norman crypt, one of the most breathtaking rooms in England. A forest of slender pillars, 150 of them each with a differently carved capital, it is THE SECOND OLDEST CATHEDRAL CRYPT IN ENGLAND and, in many people's eyes, the finest.

Worcester Cathedral also possesses ENGLAND'S ONLY ROUND CHAPTER HOUSE, the FIRST ROOM BUILT IN ENGLAND WITH A CENTRAL PILLAR SUPPORTING A VAULTED ROOF and the blueprint for all subsequent medieval chapter houses. The original Norman pillar is still standing but the walls were restored in 1400.

Seen from the county cricket ground across the River Severn, Worcester Cathedral, which contains work of every century from the 11th to the 16th, is a perfect picture of England, and provides almost too serene a setting for the resting place of such a tumultuous monarch.

Gloucester

GLOUCESTER, burial place of Edward II, has an ancient royal history. Standing on the lowest crossing point of the River Severn, the area was occupied long before the Romans built the fortified city of Glevum, whose street plan is still exactly followed by the modern city.

In 681 Ethelred, King of Mercia, founded St Peter's Abbey in Gloucester, and in the 9th century Gloucester was refortified as a burgh by Alfred the Great's daughter ETHELFLEDA, who also founded a priory where she herself was buried in 918. In the 10th century the remains of St Oswald, King of Northumbria, were brought to the priory, which was renamed St Oswald's in his honour and which became a place of pilgrimage, greatly enriching the town of Gloucester. There is very little left of St Oswald's today.

There was also a Saxon palace at Gloucester where Edward the Confessor would spend every Christmas, a custom that was followed by William the Conqueror.

The Dukedom of Gloucester is a royal title and was first conferred on Thomas of Woodstock, one of the sons of King Edward III. Perhaps the most famous, or infamous, Duke of Gloucester to date is Richard III.

armour, a map of England on his lap, in what is now the cathedral's chapter house.

Gloucester's Norman nave is one of the most impressive examples in England, while the Norman crypt is ONE OF ONLY FOUR APSIDAL CRYPTS IN THE COUNTRY.

Gloucester Cathedral

GLOUCESTER CATHEDRAL was originally built as a minster on the orders of William the Conqueror in 1072, and a few years later William came to Gloucester to hold the Grand Council in which he gave the order for the preparation of the Domesday Book. The King addressed the Council in full

Robert of Curthose

In 1134 William the Conqueror's oldest son ROBERT OF CURTHOSE was buried in the minster at his own request,

On Christmas Day 1085 William the Conqueror convened a Great Council at Gloucester, where he ordered a comprehensive survey of England to determine, county by county, what land was held by whom and how much each holding was worth in terms of livestock and tenants. This was THE FIRST AUDIT EVER MADE OF AN ENTIRE COUNTRY and was called the DOMESDAY BOOK because, as was said at the time, 'its decisions, like the Day of Judgement, are unalterable'.

having been held prisoner in Cardiff Castle by his younger brother Henry I for nearly 30 years. His monument is ONE OF THE OLDEST WOODEN MONUMENTS IN ENGLAND.

In 1216 Henry III was crowned in the minster, while London was in the hands of the French.

Edward II

In 1327 Edward II was buried in the minister at Gloucester amid great pomp and ceremony, in a magnificent tomb built by his son Edward III, guilt ridden at his role in his father's tragic end. The tomb became a place of pilgrimage and brought great wealth to the minster, which was remodelled around the Norman nave into the very FIRST MAJOR BUILDING OF THE ENGLISH PERPENDICULAR STYLE. The north transept of Gloucester Cathedral, begun in 1329, is regarded as THE BIRTHPLACE OF ENGLISH PERPENDICULAR.

First Fan Vaulting

The incomparably beautiful cathedral cloisters, built between 1360 and 1370, are THE EARLIEST EXAMPLE OF FAN VAULTING IN THE WORLD. This was THE FIRST FAN TRACERY THE WORLD HAD EVER SEEN and inspired the marvellous roof of Henry VII's chapel at Westminster Abbey and that of St George's Chapel at Windsor.

These cloisters were used as the setting for Hogwarts School in the Harry Potter films.

Crecy Window

Gloucester's east window was built in 1349 to commemorate the local knights who had fought at the Battle of Crecy in 1346. THE CRECY WINDOW, as it is known, is THE LARGEST MEDIEVAL STAINED-GLASS WINDOW IN BRITAIN, 72 ft (22 m) high and 38 ft (11.5 m) across. One of the panels shows a figure holding a club and addressing a ball in what is thought to be THE EARLIEST EVER PICTURE OF GOLF.

Tower

In 1450 the foundation stones of the cathedral tower were laid. It stands 225 ft (69 m) high and is regarded as THE FINEST PERPENDICULAR TOWER IN THE WORLD.

The minster was refounded as a cathedral by Henry VIII in 1541 after the Dissolution of the Monasteries.

King's Langley

KING'S LANGLEY, in Hertfordshire, was the original burial place of Richard II. After his body had lain in state in Old St Paul's Cathedral, Richard was buried in the friary beside the royal palace at King's Langley, the home of his uncle, Edmund of Langley. As one contemporary chronicler put it, 'The great ones were not there, neither was there any crowd of common people.' However, in 1414, Henry V had Richard's body moved to Westminster Abbey and placed beside his wife Anne of Bohemia in the tomb Richard had prepared for them both in 1394.

The earliest known royal residence in Langley was a hunting lodge belonging to Henry III. This was later developed into a comfortable palace for EDWARD I, and included refinements such as carpets and baths, introduced by Edward's Spanish wife ELEANOR OF CASTILE.

Langley became a favourite residence of EDWARD II, who rode out from there for the wedding of his friend PIERS GAVESTON at Berkhamsted. After Gaveston's execution at Warwick in 1312, Edward had his friend's bones brought to Langley, where they were buried with great reverence in the friary that Edward had himself established in the park in 1308.

EDWARD III often stayed at Langley and ruled from there during the Black Death when it was unsafe to stay in London. His fifth son, Edmund, was born at Langley in 1341, and grew up to become THE 1ST DUKE OF YORK, and founder of the ROYAL HOUSE OF YORK.

Edmund of Langley and his wife were buried in the friary, and their grand tomb, flaunting the royal arms, was

later moved into All Saints Church where it rests today.

There is nothing left to see of the friary or Piers Gaveston's grave, which has vanished. The site of the great palace of King's Langley is now occupied by the Rudolph Steiner School.

Tewkesbury Abbey

TEWKESBURY ABBEY is the burial place of Henry VI's son PRINCE EDWARD, the last Lancastrian pretender and THE ONLY PRINCE OF WALES TO DIE IN BATTLE. He was brought to the abbey in 1471 after the Battle of Tewkesbury, during the Wars of the Roses. Victory gave Edward IV of York the throne, and Prince Edward lies beneath a simple brass plate on the floor of the

RICHARD, 3RD DUKE OF YORK, father of Edward IV, was slain at the Battle of Wakefield in 1460, during the Wars of the Roses, and this event is thought to be the origin of the mnemonic for remembering the colours of the rainbow: Richard Of York Gave Battle In Vain (red, orange, yellow, green, blue, indigo, violet).

sanctuary. Behind the high altar lies Edward IV's brother GEORGE, DUKE OF CLARENCE, who had been imprisoned in the Tower of London in 1478 for plotting against his brother, and was found drowned in a butt of malmsey (Madeira) wine.

Tewkesbury Abbey, begun in 1102, is a former Benedictine abbey and now one of the largest parish churches in England, with THE LARGEST NORMAN TOWER IN THE WORLD. The abbey was reconsecrated following the Battle of Tewkesbury after Yorkist soldiers slaughtered a number of defeated Lancastrians who had sought sanctuary in the abbey.

Fotheringhay

FOTHERINGHAY CASTLE in Northamptonshire was the birthplace of Edward IV's brother, the future Richard III, in 1452.

As the ancestral home of the Dukes of York, the little village of Fotheringhay has played a prominent role in the story of Royal Britain.

The castle at Fotheringhay was originally a Norman motte and bailey affair, with a stone keep, built by Simon de Senlis, who married William the Conqueror's daughter Judith. In the 13th century it was purchased by Henry III and eventually found its way down to Edmund of Langley, fifth son of Edward III and founder of the House of York, who rebuilt the castle into a noble palace for his son Edward.

Edward, who became 2nd Duke of York, began the building of the remarkable church next door to the castle, and this became the burial place of the Dukes of York from this time on. Edward was the first to be laid to rest there after being killed at the Battle of Agincourt in 1415.

His son Richard, 3rd Duke of York, father of Edward IV and Richard III, was brought to Fotheringhay after his death at the Battle of Wakefield in 1460, during the Wars of the Roses. Edward IV led the funeral procession, having rescued his father's head from York, where it had been stuck on a spike on Micklegate Bar with the message 'Let York overlook York'.

Henry VIII gave the castle to Catherine of Aragon, and in 1587 Mary, Queen of Scots, was brought to Fotheringhay to await her execution – she was beheaded in the banqueting hall on 8 February. Her body lay at Fotheringhay for six months before it was taken by night to Peterborough Cathedral for burial.

In 1627 Charles I ordered the castle, so full of wretched memories for the Stuarts, to be pulled down and the building where such historic events

took place has almost vanished, although you can still climb the mound where the great hall stood and gaze down at the River Nene as it winds placidly through fields filled with patches of tall purple thistles – planted by the tragic Scottish Queen and nick-named 'QUEEN MARY'S TEARS'. Two hundred years after she died, a gold ring, decorated with a lover's knot entwined around the initials of Mary and Darnley was found among the castle ruins.

Fotheringhay today is a peaceful place of woodlands and green meadows. The huge majestic church, almost a cathedral even though much reduced, dominates the village, its noble tower rising in stages and crowned with pinnacles decorated with the falcon of the House of York. The tombs of the Dukes of York were moved to the sanctuary on the orders of Elizabeth I.

Lancastrian soldier killed at the Battle of St Albans in 1461, who had petitioned him for the return of her late husband's estates. Edward fell desperately in love with Elizabeth, but she refused to submit to his advances until he agreed to marry her.

They were eventually married at THE HERMITAGE in GRAFTON in Northamptonshire, the home of Elizabeth's father, Sir Richard Woodville. In 1524 their grandson Henry VIII built a manor house in Grafton and used it to woo Anne Boleyn. He later bestowed the village with the suffix Regis, in recognition of Grafton's contribution to royal marriages.

In 1675 Charles II created the dukedom of Grafton for his natural son Henry by Barbara Villiers.

Hever Castle

Labours of Love

Grafton Regis

In 1464 Edward IV secretly married Lady Elizabeth Grey, the widow of a

The moated 13th-century HEVER CASTLE in Kent was Anne Boleyn's childhood home, and possibly her birthplace. Henry VIII came here many times while he was pursuing Anne, and also her sister Mary, who was Henry's mistress before he became obsessed with Anne. Mary gave in to the King too easily and he tired of her. Anne, however, refused the King's advances until he made her his queen and it drove him wild with desire. Both sisters were ladies-in-waiting to Henry's first wife Catherine of Aragon.

The first castle was built at Hever in 1270 and the sturdy three-storey gatehouse survives from that building. The moat and battlements were added by Sir John de Cobham, and then Anne's family converted the castle into a comfortable home.

After Anne's execution and the death of her father, Henry took over Hever and gave it to his fourth wife Anne of Cleves as part of his divorce settlement. It eventually came to Catherine of Aragon's daughter Mary I, but she wanted rid of the place where her father had cavorted with the woman who had destroyed her own mother's marriage, so she gave it to a courtier, Sir Edward Waldegrave.

Hever then fell out of sight until the 1930s, when it was bought and restored by the American financier WILLIAM WALDORF ASTOR. Amongst the refurbishments, fitted to the dining room door, is the lock with which Henry VIII secured his bedchamber when he was travelling.

Hever Castle, which is open to the public, looks today much as it must have looked when Henry and Anne were courting there, and has a magical atmosphere.

Leeds Castle

The romantically situated island castle at Leeds in Kent, described as 'the loveliest castle in the world', has been the much loved home of many of England's

Queens since Edward I honeymooned there with his second wife in 1299 and gave the castle to her as a wedding gift.

Leeds began life as a Saxon manor house called Esledes. The first stone castle was built on two islands by a Norman knight called Robert de Crevecoeur, whose family held it until they sided with Simon de Montfort in 1265 and the castle was subsequently confiscated by Henry III.

EDWARD I and his first wife ELEANOR OF CASTILE loved Leeds and stayed there often, during which time Edward put up a fortified gatehouse and curtain wall. When Eleanor died in 1290 Edward had a chapel added to the Gloriette, a small building containing apartments which was situated on the tiny north island, and ordained that a mass should be said there every day for her soul. In 1978 the chapel was reconsecrated and made a Chapel Royal by the Archbishop of Canterbury, Donald Coggan.

EDWARD II slightly spoiled the romance of Leeds by giving it to one of his male favourites, Bartholomew de Badlesmere, but when Bartholomew refused entry to Edward's wife Isabella, Edward took the castle back by siege and had Bartholomew executed.

EDWARD III sumptuously upgraded the apartments in the Gloriette and then RICHARD II hired Henry Yevele, architect of the nave at Canterbury Cathedral, to create a palace worthy of his wife ANNE OF BOHEMIA.

After deposing Richard, HENRY IV gave Leeds to his wife JOAN OF NAVARRE, and their son Henry V gave it to his wife CATHERINE DE VALOIS.

HENRY VIII transformed Leeds from a castle into a lavish fortified palace. He stayed there with his whole court while on the way to the Field of the Cloth of Gold in France in 1520. He also sometimes stayed there, as well as at Grafton, while visiting Anne Boleyn at Hever.

EDWARD VI gave Leeds away to a courtier, and since then it has been in private hands. Much restored in the 19th century, today it is owned by a trust and is open to the public.

Queen Elizabeth's Hunting Lodge, Chingford, Essex

QUEEN ELIZABETH'S HUNTING LODGE stands on the edge of Epping Forest north of Chingford. Originally known as the Great Standing, it was built in 1543 by Henry VIII as a grandstand from where guests could observe the hunt. On hearing of the defeat of the Spanish Armada in 1588, Elizabeth rode her white horse up the shallow steps of the staircase inside and on to the platform so that she could wave to the celebrating crowd. The lodge, which offers wonderful views across Epping Forest, now houses a museum.

King's College Chapel

HENRY VI himself laid the foundation stone of KING'S COLLEGE CHAPEL in Cambridge on 25 July 1446, thus putting in place the first piece of what he hoped would be a church without equal in size and beauty.

Henry would not live to see his dream realised, but the building completed by HENRY VIII in the 1530s was even then recognised as possibly 'the most beautiful building in the world'. Numerous carvings of the initials of Henry VIII and Anne Boleyn found throughout the building are a rarity and help to date the completion of the chapel with great accuracy – they were only married for three years between 1533 and 1536.

King's College Chapel is 289 ft (88 m) long and the ceiling, once described as 'the noblest stone ceiling in existence', is THE LARGEST FAN VAULT CEILING IN THE WORLD, 40 ft (12 m) in width and 80 ft (24 m) above the floor. It was built in just three years between 1512 and 1515 by master mason John Wastell. The sense of light and space inside the chapel under that ceiling is awe-inspiring, and the exceptional acoustics it provides have helped KING'S COLLEGE CHOIR to become one of the finest and most famous choirs in the world.

Well, I never knew this
about

ROYAL ENGLAND BIRTHS, BURIALS & BETWEEN

Treasures from the SUTTON HOO burial chamber in Suffolk, the final resting place of the 7th-century Saxon king RAEDWALD of East Anglia, and THE LAST PAGAN ROYAL BURIAL SITE IN ENGLAND, are housed in the British Museum.

KING EGBERT, the founder of the kingdom of Wessex, was THE FIRST KING TO BE BURIED IN THE SAXON MINSTER AT WINCHESTER.

The room in the old manor house at SUTTON COURTENAY by the River Thames in the Vale of the White Horse, where the EMPRESS MATILDA daughter of Henry I was born in 1101, overlooks the churchyard where GEORGE ORWELL, author of *Animal Farm* and *1984*, is buried.

Associated with royalty since a visit by Henrietta Maria, the wife of Charles I, in 1630, and popular with Queen Victoria and Prince Albert, TUNBRIDGE WELLS was granted the right to call itself ROYAL TUNBRIDGE WELLS by Edward VII.

Prince Frederick, Duke of York and Albany, son of George III, occupied No. 1 in THE WORLD'S FIRST CRESCENT in Bath. The Crescent was subsequently renamed the ROYAL CRESCENT.

Following a visit from Queen Victoria in 1875, LEAMINGTON SPA in Warwickshire was granted the title of ROYAL LEAMINGTON SPA.

The suffix Regis, meaning 'of the king', usually indicates that the manor once belonged to a king. However, it can be granted as a special accolade by a king if he feels the honour is warranted. For instance, Lyme Regis in Dorset, an important medieval port, was granted the suffix 'Regis' by Edward I in 1284. Bognor Regis was so honoured in 1929 by George V, who spent several months there convalescing after a serious illness.

In 1043 Edward the Confessor founded a college of secular canons at WIMBORNE MINSTER in Dorset, where KING

ETHELRED, older brother of Alfred the Great, is buried beneath THE ONLY BRASS TO MARK THE BURIAL SITE OF AN ENGLISH KING. Also buried in the minster are JOHN BEAUFORT, DUKE OF SOMERSET and his wife, maternal grandparents of Henry VII. Wimborne Minster possesses ONE OF ONLY FOUR SURVIVING CHAINED LIBRARIES IN THE WORLD.

ALLERTON CASTLE in North Yorkshire was the home of PRINCE FREDERICK AUGUSTUS, DUKE OF YORK, second son of George III. As a means of keeping his estate workers gainfully employed he ordered them to construct a Temple of Victory on top of Allerton Hill, on the estate, and the ceaseless activity of the men as they tramped up and down the hill gave rise to the nursery rhyme: 'The Grand Old Duke of York, he had ten thousand men. He marched them up to the top of the hill and he marched them down again.'

Among the ruins of St Mary's church at EASTWELL near Ashford in Kent is a rough stone tomb containing the remains of RICHARD PLANTAGENET, illegitimate son of Richard III, who was forced after his father's death at the

Battle of Bosworth to live out his life in disguise as a labourer. The nearby PLANTAGENET COTTAGE now occupies the site of the small stone house Richard built for himself with his own hands.

Buried in the church of Holy Trinity Church, in BOSHAM in Sussex, is King Canute's daughter, who drowned in the local millstream. It was at Bosham that Canute tried to turn back the waves. Bosham was also the birthplace (and possible burial place) of KING HAROLD, the last Saxon King of England.

In the church at STANTON HARCOURT in Oxfordshire hangs the very flag that Robert Harcourt, Standard Bearer to Henry Tudor, carried into the Battle of Bosworth Field in 1485 and waved in triumph over the dead body of Richard III, ushering in the Tudor era.

The body of OLIVER CROMWELL, who was offered the Crown but refused it, is said to be buried in a secret room of his daughter's home at NEWBURGH PRIORY in Yorkshire. Edward, Prince of Wales, later Edward VII, made a failed attempt to break into the wooden coffin to see what was there, leaving a ragged hole in the side.

In 1588 ELIZABETH I travelled from St James's Palace to the fort her father had constructed at TILBURY on the north bank of the River Thames in Essex. She had come to review her troops, who were encamped at West Tilbury on the hillside above the fort, awaiting the arrival of the Spanish Armada. There she delivered perhaps the most famous inspirational speech to the troops by any English monarch: 'I know I have the body of a weak and feeble woman, but I have the heart of a king, and a King of England, too, and think foul scorn that any Prince of Europe should dare to invade the borders of my realm.'

Queen Elizabeth I also paid a visit to England's newest royal place of interest, BUCKLEBURY, in Berkshire, the childhood home of KATE MIDDLETON, a future Queen, and now the DUCHESS OF CAMBRIDGE. Elizabeth came to see John Winchcombe, grandson of the famous local wool merchant Jack O'Newbury, who lived in the Manor House (of which only one wing remains, after a fire in 1830). An avenue of oak trees was planted to celebrate Elizabeth's visit and this can still be seen

on the Common today. A Winchcombe descendant, Frances, married the politician Lord Bolingbroke (who was later exiled for supporting the Jacobite Rebellion of 1715) and they entertained QUEEN ANNE at the Manor House. The avenue of oak trees was added to in celebration of Wellington's victory at the Battle of Waterloo in 1815, and in 1972 some of the ancient oaks were replaced with young trees to celebrate a visit by QUEEN ELIZABETH II. In 1980 PRINCESS ANNE planted a tree to mark the 80th birthday of the Queen Mother. In Bucklebury church is THE ONLY CHURCH WINDOW IN ENGLAND DECORATED WITH A FLY – painted in the 17th century with the wings on one side of the glass and the body and legs on the other, it is so realistic that people are often seen trying to flick it away.

CHAPTER TEN

ROYAL SCOTLAND – PRESENT

HOLYROOD ✦ BALMORAL ✦ BIRKHALL
✦ CASTLE OF MEY ✦ ST ANDREWS

Queen Elizabeth and her family usually spend several months of the year in Scotland. She has Scottish blood, being descended from the Scottish Stuart monarchs through her Hanoverian ancestors – George I, the first Hanoverian King, was the great grandson of James VI of Scotland (James I of England). And Prince William met his bride, Kate Middleton, while studying at St Andrews University in Scotland.

After the Hanoverian victory over the Jacobites at Culloden in 1746, Scottish highland culture, kilts, clan chiefs, bagpipes and Highland dancing, was suppressed, but in 1822 George IV made a royal visit to Edinburgh, where Sir Walter Scott organised a ceremony in his honour packed with symbols of the old traditional Scottish ways. The King himself even wore a kilt and processed from Holyrood to Edinburgh Castle amongst a throng of clansmen, and so was reborn the royal love affair with all things Scottish that persists to this day.

The Queen and the Duke of

Edinburgh usually spend late June and early July on official duty at the Palace of Holyroodhouse, while their summer holidays are spent at Balmoral, their private residence on Deeside, during August and September.

Official Residences

Palace of Holyroodhouse

The PALACE OF HOLYROODHOUSE in Edinburgh is the Queen's official residence in Scotland and she stays here when performing official duties in Scotland. During HOLYROOD WEEK, which is at the end of June and the beginning of July, the Queen carries out official engagements such as investitures and garden parties. Queen Elizabeth's grandparents George V and Queen Mary began the tradition of holding garden parties during Holyrood Week.

Holyrood Abbey

The Palace of Holyroodhouse began life as a monastery, founded by KING DAVID I of Scotland in 1128.

While out hunting near Arthur's Seat one day David was thrown from his horse and attacked by a stag, but was saved from being gored by a shining cross, which appeared in the sky and frightened the beast away. In gratitude David founded the Abbey of the Holy Rood, or Cross, on the site, a simple Norman building that was reconstructed in fine Gothic style in 1195. Three kings were married in the abbey, JAMES II in 1449, JAMES III in 1469 and

JAMES IV in 1503; and James II was crowned King of Scotland there in 1437, as was CHARLES I in 1633.

The abbey was plundered by the Earl of Hertford's men in 1544, but the east gable was refurbished as a chapel royal for the coronation of Charles I, and again in 1687 by James VII as a home for the Catholic Royal Order of the Thistle. In 1688 a Protestant mob celebrating the accession of William of Orange ransacked the royal vaults and removed the head of Mary, Queen of Scots' second husband Lord Darnley, who was buried there alongside David II, James II and James V – all their ashes were scattered to the winds.

All that remains of the medieval abbey is the roofless nave of the church and some foundations of the transept.

Palace of Holyroodhouse

In 1501 JAMES IV determined to make Edinburgh the undisputed capital of Scotland and to build a lavish royal palace for himself and his new wife Margaret Tudor, the sister of Henry VIII of England, so that they could move out of the draughty and uncomfortable old Edinburgh castle. Only fragments of the gatehouse to this grand palace survive, but the Great Tower built by JAMES V in 1529 is still there, as is the west front he added in 1535.

MARY, QUEEN OF SCOTS, spent much of her life in Scotland at Holyrood and married two of her husbands there, LORD DARNLEY and the EARL OF BOTHWELL. For her marriage to Darnley in 1565 there were two days of celebrations, with fanfares greeting the bride and groom as they entered the Great Hall to feast each night.

Mary's joy was to be short-lived, however. The following year, in the Queen's apartments at Holyrood, located in the wing to the left of the front door, Mary's Italian secretary DAVID RIZZIO was murdered. Darnley, a bully and a drunk, suspected Rizzio of being Mary's lover. On the evening of 9 March, Mary and Rizzio were having supper together in her rooms when Darnley and his henchmen burst in, dragged Rizzio away – he was crying 'Save my life, Madame, save my life!' – and stabbed him horribly to death in the Queen's outer chamber. The bloodstains are still there to be seen.

Darnley himself was found murdered not long afterwards, strangled in the garden of the nearby Kirk o' Fields as he fled from the burning building.

Mary and Darnley's son JAMES VI lived at Holyrood from the age of 12 until he went to England to accept the English crown as James I in 1603.

James's grandson CHARLES II is responsible for how the palace looks today. He commissioned the most fashionable Scottish architect of the time, SIR WILLIAM BRUCE, to extend the palace around a courtyard and smarten up the royal apartments. THE GALLERY, THE LONGEST AND LARGEST ROOM IN THE PALACE, was adorned with 110 portraits by JACOB DE WITT of Scottish kings from Fergus I to Charles II, 89 of which still hang in the Gallery today.

In 1745 BONNIE PRINCE CHARLIE held court at Holyrood for five weeks, throwing a state ball in the Gallery and healing people with his touch to prove that he was the rightful king.

Grand Visits

After this the palace was rather neglected and was kept ticking over by the Hereditary Keepers of Holyroodhouse, the DUKES OF HAMILTON. That was until the grand visit of GEORGE IV to Scotland, organised by SIR WALTER SCOTT in 1822, when the palace was sumptuously refurbished, all except for the apartments of Mary, Queen of Scots, which George ordered to be 'preserved sacred from every alteration'. George became so elated by the gorgeousness of the celebrations that he fell down the stairs, his landing being cushioned by a heroic Scottish baronet who flung himself to the floor to break the King's fall.

QUEEN VICTORIA started the custom of HOLYROOD WEEK, during which the monarch stays for a week at Holyrood and entertains guests from all over Scotland. Victoria used to enjoy driving round Arthur's Seat, taking a route now known as the Queen's Drive.

Private Residences

Balmoral

England, thy beauties are tame and
    domestic,
To one who has roamed over
    mountains afar
Oh! for the crags that are wild and
    majestic
The steep frowning glories of dark
    Lochnagar

These words, written by LORD BYRON in 1807, reportedly inspired Queen Victoria to visit Deeside when she and Prince Albert came to Scotland in 1842, to see for themselves the romantic land of tartans and clans as described by Sir Walter Scott. She thought about buying ARDVERIKIE CASTLE, on the shores of Loch Laggan in Inverness-shire (Glenbogle in the BBC television series *Monarch of the Glen*), but when the lessee of BALMORAL CASTLE on the banks of the River Dee, Sir Robert Gordon, brother of the Prime Minister Lord Aberdeen, choked to death on a fish bone, the Queen moved fast and took up the lease straight away.

'A pretty little castle in the old Scotch style' is how Queen Victoria described the old Balmoral, which was situated on the site of a hunting lodge belonging to Robert II of Scotland, but when she and Albert purchased the 20,000-acre (8,000 ha) estate outright in 1852 with their own private money, they decided to build a new castle next to it, more in keeping with the needs of the burgeoning Royal Family.

Queen Victoria laid the foundation stone of the new Balmoral Castle on 28 September 1853. Before the stone was put in position she signed a parchment with the date on it, and placed this, along with examples of each of the current coins of the realm, into a bottle and then inserted the bottle into a cavity beneath where the stone was about to go.

Once the new castle had been completed, in 1856, the old castle was demolished. The position of the front door of the old castle is marked by a stone located on the front lawn opposite the tower and about 300 ft (90 m) from the garden path.

Constructed out of grey granite from the nearby quarries at Glen Gelder, largely to Prince Albert's own design, Balmoral Castle is a splendid example of Scottish Baronial style. Albert had the interior decorated with an abundance of thistle motifs and a special black, red and lavender Balmoral tartan pattern concocted by Prince Albert himself which, according to one of Queen Victoria's granddaughters, 'had a way of flickering before your eyes and confusing your brain'. At that time Balmoral also had MORE WATER CLOSETS THAN ANY OTHER HOUSE IN BRITAIN – 14.

Victoria and Albert would visit Balmoral at the end of every summer, and throw themselves into the Highland life, stalking, fishing, mountain climbing, and attending the Braemar Games.

After Prince Albert died in 1861, Victoria spent many months of the year in mourning at Balmoral and erected a granite pyramid to 'Albert the Great and Good' on the spot where he had shot his last stag.

EDWARD VII continued to spend some time at Balmoral every summer, but it was GEORGE V who really loved the place, a love he passed on to his son GEORGE VI and his granddaughter QUEEN ELIZABETH II, who spends the months of August and September there every year, and continues the tradition set by Queen Victoria of attending the Braemar Games.

Braemar Games

Braemar lies 1,000 ft (305 m) up in the Grampian Mountains at the centre of THE HIGHEST PARISH IN BRITAIN, about 10 miles (16 km) west of Balmoral.

By tradition, the BRAEMAR GAMES were started in 1057 by MALCOLM III (Canmore), who camped at Braemar before meeting Macbeth in battle at Lumphanan. Here he held THE FIRST BRAEMAR GAMES as a means of identifying his most accomplished soldiers.

In 1715 the Braemar Gathering was used as a front by the 6TH EARL OF MAR to assemble his troops and raise the standard for the first Jacobite Rising. The spot where the standard was actually raised is now occupied by the INVERCAULD ARMS HOTEL.

After the Battle of Culloden in 1746 such gatherings were banned, along with other Highland customs such as the speaking of Gaelic and the wearing of kilts. The Games were revived in 1832 and gained royal approval in 1848 when Queen Victoria attended, while staying at Balmoral.

Birkhall

When PRINCE CHARLES remarried in 2005, he and his new bride, the DUCHESS OF CORNWALL, honeymooned

---

John Brown

The Queen came to rely heavily on the strength and sound common sense of her ghillie, JOHN BROWN, a relationship that upset both her courtiers and other members of the Royal Family. After Victoria's death, her son Edward VII expunged all memory of Brown from Balmoral, destroying any trinkets and photographs he could find. The statue of Brown that the Queen had put up outside the garden cottage where she would retire to write was smuggled out of harm's way to a remote part of the estate behind the dairy, where the King was unlikely to come across it. A pleasant hour or two can be had exploring the grounds of Balmoral trying to find it.

at BIRKHALL, his country house on the edge of the Balmoral estate in Aberdeenshire. While in Scotland the royal couple are known as the DUKE AND DUCHESS OF ROTHESAY, a title held by the eldest sons of the Kings of Scotland since 1398, when Robert I made his son David SCOTLAND'S FIRST DUKE.

Birkhall was built in 1715 and was bought by Prince Albert in 1849 as a place for the Prince of Wales (later Edward VII) to stay away from his parents at Balmoral. Before Edward moved in, the house was let to the Queen's physician SIR JAMES CLARK, who invited FLORENCE NIGHTINGALE to stay. It was while she was staying at Birkhall that Florence was encouraged by Queen Victoria in her plans to go and nurse the soldiers on the front line in the Crimea.

The QUEEN MOTHER, who could never decide if Birkhall was a 'small big house' or a 'big small house', occupied Birkhall as her Deeside home from 1952 until her death in 2002.

Castle of Mey

The only home ever owned personally by QUEEN ELIZABETH, THE QUEEN MOTHER, was the exquisite little CASTLE OF MEY in Caithness, THE MOST NORTHERLY CASTLE ON THE BRITISH MAINLAND. She bought the castle in 1952, having come across it while staying in Caithness, in mourning for her husband George VI. Curiosity took her down the drive, and there she found the castle in a state of dereliction – the family living in one room and their sheep in another.

The Castle of Mey was built in 1572 by the 4TH EARL OF CAITHNESS for his second son WILLIAM. The following year William was murdered by his older brother JOHN, who was murdered then in his turn. John's father kept him in jail, fed him with nothing but salt beef and, 'withholding all drink from him, left him to die of a raging thirst'. And so the castle went to the third son GEORGE, who became 5th Earl of Caithness.

The 5th Earl locked his daughter up in the attic for daring to fall in love with a local ploughman. Driven mad by her confinement, the poor girl flung herself out of the window, plunging to her death on the stones below. She is reputed to haunt the castle to this day, in the guise of the 'Green Lady'.

From this time the castle passed through a number of hands and gradually slipped into disrepair until rescued and restored by the Queen Mother in 1952.

It is a magical place, a miniature grey stone castle embowered in virtually the only trees in Caithness and set against a backdrop of wide green fields and impossibly blue, foam-flecked sea.

The Queen Mother came to stay twice every year until her death in 2002, for three weeks in August and a week in October. In 1996 she put the castle in trust to secure its future, and today it is open for visitors, except for one week in August when Prince Charles and the Duchess of Cornwall stay.

The joy of the Castle of Mey is that it was the Queen Mother's private home and is still full of her personal belongings and effects, such as jigsaw puzzles and her favourite *Dad's Army* videos, which are strewn about as if she has just popped out for a walk. A visit here feels more like being a guest than a tourist.

The walled garden is planted with old-fashioned British favourites such as blackcurrants, gooseberries and rhubarb, and if you walk up to the end of the tiny front garden you can gaze upon the Queen Mother's award-winning herd of black Aberdeen Angus cattle, THE MOST NORTHERLY HERD OF ABERDEEN ANGUS CATTLE IN THE WORLD.

St Andrews University

It was while studying at ST ANDREWS UNIVERSITY between 2001 and 2004 that PRINCE WILLIAM met his future bride, CATHERINE 'KATE' MIDDLETON. As well as finding a wife, the Prince earned a Scottish Master of Arts degree with upper second class honours in geography, THE BEST DEGREE EVER ACHIEVED BY AN HEIR TO THE BRITISH THRONE.

Founded in 1413, St Andrews is SCOTLAND'S OLDEST UNIVERSITY and the third oldest in the English-speaking world, behind Oxford and Cambridge. It was also the home of BRITAIN'S FIRST FEMALE STUDENT IN 1862, THE FIRST STUDENT UNION IN 1864, and BRITAIN'S FIRST MARINE LABORATORY in 1882. In 1858 SIR DAVID BREWSTER, inventor of the telescope, became Principal of the University. Famous teachers and alumni include Benjamin Franklin, Doctor of Laws in 1759, Edward Jenner, pioneer of vaccinations, writers Rudyard Kipling, J.M. Barrie and Fay Weldon, and John Napier, the inventor of logarithms. The students still sport red gowns, as worn by their medieval predecessors, so that the university provosts can spot them when they are out on the town.

St Andrews

ST ANDREWS gets its name from Scotland's patron saint, whose relics,

now lost, were brought to this spot in the 4th century by a monk named St Rule. St Andrews is the ecclesiastical centre of Scotland and its ruined cathedral, begun in 1160, is THE LARGEST CATHEDRAL IN SCOTLAND. It was consecrated in 1318 by ROBERT THE BRUCE, who rode down the aisle on his horse.

In 1538 JAMES V of Scotland married MARY OF GUISE in the cathedral.

St Andrews is also known as the headquarters of golf, and is home to the ROYAL AND ANCIENT GOLF CLUB, the governing body of golf who write the rules of the game. Before 1764 the golf course at St Andrews had 22 holes, four of which were then merged with others to make 18 holes. Since most golf clubs took their lead from St Andrews, 18 became the accepted number of holes for a round of golf. THE OLD COURSE at St Andrews is THE OLDEST 18-HOLE GOLF COURSE IN THE WORLD.

The earliest known royal reference to golf dates from 1457, when James II of Scotland banned golf because it was distracting his men from their archery practice.

Well, I never knew this
about
ROYAL SCOTLAND – PRESENT

BRAEMAR, in Aberdeenshire, home of the famous Braemar Games, sits at a height of 1,100 ft (307 m) above sea level and is officially THE COLDEST PLACE IN BRITAIN, holder of the lowest recorded temperature in Britain on two occasions – minus 17°F (27.2°C) in 1895 and 1982.

BALLATER STATION, east of Balmoral, is perhaps the best-preserved Victorian railway station in Britain. Once famous as the backdrop to every royal arrival

and departure, the station remains exactly as it was when Queen Victoria was a regular visitor – the Queen insisted that the new railway line should not be extended west of Ballater so that it did not impinge on the quiet and privacy of Balmoral.

MARY, QUEEN OF SCOTS, often stayed in St Andrews, usually in the home of a local merchant called HENRY SCRYMGEOUR. The house is now known as QUEEN MARY'S HOUSE.

While she was there Mary must have learned to play golf, because in 1567, just a few days after the murder of her husband Lord Darnley, she played a round of golf at SETON CASTLE near Prestonpans in East Lothian, becoming both THE FIRST MONARCH AND THE FIRST WOMAN EVER TO BE RECORDED PLAYING GOLF.

The present Royal Family's best golfer is, appropriately enough, PRINCE ANDREW, a former captain of the Royal and Ancient Golf Club, who plays off a handicap of 4.

Seton Castle today

CHAPTER ELEVEN

ROYAL SCOTLAND – PAST

EDINBURGH ✦ STIRLING ✦ SCONE ✦ LINLITHGOW
✦ FALKLAND ✦ QUEEN MARY'S HOUSE, JEDBURGH
✦ LOCHLEVEN CASTLE ✦ GLAMIS ✦ IONA ✦ ROTHESAY

Scotland has a long royal history that dates back to the 6th century and before. Many of Scotland's royal palaces and castles are no longer used for royal purposes, but have become tourist attractions or evocative ruins. They still comprise a magnificent royal heritage.

Edinburgh Castle

In the Middle Ages EDINBURGH CASTLE was Scotland's chief royal castle. It was begun in 1128 when KING DAVID I of Scotland decided to make Edinburgh his principal residence and began the building of a powerful royal castle on Castle Rock. The first thing he did was to build a small stone chapel to replace the simple wooden one where his mother, Margaret, had heard the news of her husband Malcolm Canmore's death.

Castle Rock

The summit of CASTLE ROCK is 430 ft (131 m) above sea level with cliffs on three sides rising 260 feet almost sheer up from the ground, and the obvious strategic importance of the site suggests that it must have been used as a refuge since early times.

The first recorded evidence comes from the 7th century, when a hill fort on the rock was occupied as the northern outpost of Northumbria, ruled at that time by the Saxon KING EDWIN, hence 'Edwin's burgh' or Edinburgh.

In 973 KING EDGAR of England gave Edinburgh to KENNETH II of Scotland in return for Kenneth recognising Edgar's overlordship, and it remained in Scottish hands for the next 300 years.

First Parliament

In 1215 ALEXANDER II held SCOTLAND'S FIRST PARLIAMENT in the castle, and it was later used by his son ALEXANDER III for judicial courts and as a home for his wife QUEEN MARGARET, daughter of Henry III of England – she found it 'a sad and solitary place'.

During the Wars of Scottish Independence the castle changed hands several times. In 1291 Edward I of England received submissions from a number of Scottish magnates in the castle, but in 1312 the Scots recaptured it by scaling the cliffs. Robert the Bruce ordered all but St Margaret's Chapel to be destroyed so that the castle couldn't be used any more by the English.

In the 1360s Robert the Bruce's son DAVID II began rebuilding the castle but died there before it was finished.

Jacobean Edinburgh

In 1430 JAMES I constructed a new Great Chamber next to David's Tower, which forms the nucleus of the present castle, most of which took shape under James's Stewart successors, JAMES II to James VI. The young James II was held captive at Edinburgh for two years by the castle governor Sir William Crichton until James's mother finally managed to smuggle the infant king out in a box.

JAMES III imprisoned his feuding brothers the Earl of Mar and the Duke of Albany in the castle in 1479, but Albany escaped by slipping something into his guards' drinks and then setting the guards on fire before escaping down the cliffs on knotted sheets.

JAMES IV constructed the Great Hall, with its vast hammer-beam roof, in 1511, and Parliament sat here until the time of Charles I.

In 1517 the five-year-old JAMES V was brought to the castle for safe keeping during his minority. His wife, MARY OF GUISE, died there in 1560.

Six years later their daughter Mary, Queen of Scots, gave birth to her son, JAMES VI, in a tiny bedroom in the castle. The rumour that the baby was stillborn and that Mary had the tiny corpse dropped down the palace well, and a surrogate substituted, was given credence in 1830 when a child's bones were discovered at the bottom of the well along with a piece of cloth bearing the letter 'J'.

In 1617, as James I of England, James VI returned to the castle where he was born to celebrate 50 years as King of Scots.

CHARLES I was THE LAST MONARCH TO SLEEP IN EDINBURGH CASTLE – in 1633 on the eve of his coronation as King of Scotland. CHARLES II paid a brief visit to the castle, but apart from that no other monarch dropped in until George IV in 1822.

Stirling Castle

STIRLING CASTLE played a major role in the lives of all the Stewart monarchs from Robert II to James VI. It was home to the royal court and, to all intents and purposes, the capital of Scotland. Standing high on a rock between the Highlands and the Lowlands, at Scotland's narrowest point, Stirling was always known as the gateway to Scotland, with Stirling Castle the key.

Three Battlefields

The commanding, panoramic views from the castle battlements take in Scotland's rich central plains, the industrial reaches of the Forth, the stark Highland line to the north, and three famous battlefields, Stirling Bridge, Bannockburn and Sauchieburn.

The first proper records of life on the Rock of Stirling come from 1110, when ALEXANDER I dedicated a chapel there. Alexander died at Stirling in 1124, as did WILLIAM THE LION, in 1214.

During the War of Independence STIRLING WAS THE LAST LOWLAND CASTLE TO SURRENDER TO EDWARD I, in 1304.

Ten years later Stirling Castle looked on as EDWARD II of England came to rescue the besieged English garrison there, and was vanquished at Bannockburn by ROBERT THE BRUCE, who then demolished the castle and went on his way.

James I

The first Stewart Kings, Robert II and Robert III, began to rebuild the castle, and in 1425 James I took up residence at Stirling after his exile in England. One of his first acts was to execute his cousin the DUKE OF ALBANY, whose father had usurped the throne of James's weak father Robert III and run Scotland while James was in captivity. Albany was beheaded, along with his two sons, at a spot just north of the castle where you can still see the gruesome BEHEADING STONE.

James II

In 1437 the six-year-old JAMES II was brought to Stirling for safety after his father James I was murdered by disgruntled nobles at Perth. Not long afterwards, one of his murderers, Sir Robert Graham, was tortured and put to death himself, at Stirling. It was here, in 1452, that the 21-year-old James ran through the disagreeable Earl of Douglas with his dagger and tossed the body out of the window.

James III

JAMES III was born at Stirling in 1451 and grew to love the place so much he neglected all his other royal palaces. He died in sight of the castle, after the Battle of Sauchieburn in 1488, at the hands of an unknown assassin sent by supporters of his son James IV, who wore an iron belt in penance ever afterwards.

James IV

JAMES IV then started on a major building programme which included the original Chapel Royal and the Great Hall, where Parliament would sit. The Great Hall at Stirling is SCOTLAND'S GRANDEST MEDIEVAL HALL, and was described by Daniel Defoe as 'the noblest I ever saw in Europe'.

James V

JAMES V spent much of his childhood at Stirling and later built the fine Renaissance palace within the ramparts to impress his French wife Mary of Guise.

Mary and James

Their daughter MARY, QUEEN OF SCOTS, was crowned in the Chapel Royal at just nine months old, and in 1566 her son James was christened in the chapel. He returned in 1594 as JAMES VI OF SCOTLAND to have his own son PRINCE HENRY baptised in the new Chapel Royal, which was refurbished especially for the occasion.

After this, James's attention switched to London and the Union of Crowns, and Stirling's royal days were over. The castle went through a number of uses and rebuilding programmes before coming into the care of Historic Scotland.

Church of the Holy Rood

Just down the hill from the castle is the 16th-century CHURCH OF THE HOLY ROOD, THE ONLY CHURCH WHERE A SCOTTISH MONARCH WAS CROWNED STILL IN USE TODAY. The monarch was James VI, who was crowned King of Scotland in the church in 1567, to the accompaniment of a sermon from JOHN KNOX. The oak roof of the church is original and the best in Scotland.

Scone

KENNETH MACALPIN, THE FIRST KING OF THE SCOTS, made the Pictish capital of Scone THE FIRST CAPITAL OF SCOTLAND when he merged the Scots with the Picts in 843. He set up the Stone of Destiny there and for the next 450 years all the Kings of Scotland were enthroned on the Moot Hill at Scone.

In 1114 ALEXANDER I of Scotland founded an abbey on the site, which grew to be one of the largest and wealthiest in Scotland and was also home to many Scottish Parliaments in the Middle Ages.

In the early 17th century, after the Reformation, Scone Abbey came to the EARL OF GOWRIE, who rebuilt the Abbot's palace into a sumptuous residence. This house passed to SIR DAVID MURRAY, a friend of James VI (James I of England). His most celebrated descendant was WILLIAM MURRAY, 1ST EARL OF MANSFIELD, THE FIRST SCOT TO BECOME LORD CHANCELLOR.

JAMES STUART, THE OLD PRETENDER, son of James VII of Scotland and James II of England, held court here in 1715. The present Scone Palace, completed in 1802, is largely a Georgian Gothick refurbishment of the 17th-century house. Scone remains the home of the Earls of Mansfield.

A little to the north of the palace is the Moot Hill, where the enthronements took place, marked by a small chapel and a replica of the Stone of Destiny.

Linlithgow Palace

Even in ruin, LINLITHGOW PALACE, glowing golden on its promontory above Linlithgow Loch, is bewitching. There was a royal manor here from the time of David I in the 12th century but, like Stirling, Linlithgow was really a Stewart creation. JAMES I began what was to become the loveliest of all Scotland's royal palaces in 1425 on his return from 18 years of captivity in England, and his descendants carried on adding of their plenty for the next 100 years.

The centrepiece of James I's work was the Great Hall, still impressive today even though windowless and gaunt. JAMES III completed the south range and allowed Henry VI of England and his wife Margaret of Anjou to hide out there for over a year after they had fled from the Battle of Towton in 1461.

James and Margaret

JAMES IV built the west range in 1500 and strengthened the defences with a huge barbican, then gave the palace to his new young wife MARGARET TUDOR, who spent most of her time at Linlithgow and gave birth to James V there in 1512.

Legend has it that before James IV rode away to his needless death at the Battle of Flodden, Margaret arranged for him to see a vision of St John in the palace chapel, who warned him not to go. James didn't listen, and a few weeks later Margaret stood on the roof of the QUEEN'S BOWER, a small octagonal turret in the south-west corner of the palace, waiting in vain for news of her husband's return.

Birth of a Tragic Queen

Margaret's son JAMES V brought his wife MARY OF GUISE to Linlithgow and in 1542, in the same Queen's Bower where her husband had been born almost 30 years before, Mary gave birth to a daughter, MARY, soon to be Queen of Scots. James V died alone at Falkland Palace six days later.

The infant Mary was whisked away to Stirling Castle for safety and the Stewarts' love affair with Linlithgow was over. Mary rarely returned and her son James VI was indifferent. The last King to sleep in the crumbling palace was CHARLES I in 1633.

Fiery End

The final end came in 1746 when the Duke of Cumberland's troops camped in Linlithgow on their way home from Culloden. The Hanoverians' final insult was to burn down the once resplendent palace by omitting to smother the ashes of their camp fires as they left. The straw bedding they left behind caught fire and so did Linlithgow Palace.

Fortunately, the elaborate KING'S FOUNTAIN in the palace courtyard survived the fire. Built in 1538 for James V, it is THE OLDEST FOUNTAIN IN BRITAIN. It is said that on grand occasions the fountain flowed with wine – the last occasion was when BONNIE PRINCE CHARLIE stopped at Linlithgow on his way to Edinburgh in 1745.

Falkland Palace

FALKLAND PALACE in Fife, where JAMES V died, was largely his own creation. It began life as a hunting lodge and grew into a massive, turreted edifice that towers over the picturesque little town of FALKLAND, SCOTLAND'S FIRST CONSERVATION AREA. Still to be seen inside is the great black oak four-poster bed where James breathed his last.

Fifty years previously, the DUKE OF ALBANY had brought his nephew DAVID, DUKE OF ROTHESAY, heir to Robert III, to what was then Falkland Castle as a captive and starved him to death. In 1425 Albany's sons and grandsons were all executed by David's brother James I and Falkland became a royal property. JAMES IV transformed it into a palace and JAMES V frenchified it for his French bride PRINCESS MADELAINE.

Falkland Palace still belongs to the monarch but is home to the Crichton Stuart family, who are Hereditary Keepers. The chapel, built for James V, is THE ONLY ROMAN CATHOLIC CHURCH ON ROYAL PROPERTY IN BRITAIN.

In the grounds, and still used, is the

'Real' or 'Royal' Tennis Court, built in 1539. It is THE OLDEST TENNIS COURT IN SCOTLAND and THE SECOND OLDEST TENNIS COURT IN BRITAIN, after the one at Hampton Court.

Mary, Queen of Scots' House, Jedburgh

Mary stayed in this sturdy, 16th-century fortified tower house for five weeks in 1566 while she presided over the local assizes. While she was here she learned that her lover, the Earl of Bothwell, had been injured in a skirmish and rode over to Hermitage Castle to see him, a journey of some 20 miles (32 km) across wild and dangerous country. She insisted on returning the same day and grew so weary she fell off her horse and was thrown into a bog. From this she caught a bad fever, which almost killed her, and she had to spend many days convalescing in the house. In later life, when a prisoner in England, she reflected ruefully, 'Would that I had died in Jedburgh . . .'

The house belonged to the KERR family (later the Dukes of Roxburgh),

who lived in nearby Ferniehurst Castle, and has a left-handed staircase that spirals anti-clockwise so as to allow the left-handed Kerrs to freely wield their sword arms.

Lochleven Castle

MARY, QUEEN OF SCOTS, was brought as a prisoner to LOCHLEVEN CASTLE, a small 15th-century keep on an island in the middle of Loch Leven, in June 1567 after her defeat at Carberry Hill. Here she was pressured both to abdicate the throne and divorce the Earl of Bothwell, by whom she was pregnant. She refused to do either, until her will was finally broken when she gave birth to stillborn twins.

Amongst Mary's jailers at Lochleven were two young men who fell in love with their captive, GEORGE DOUGLAS and 16-year-old WILLIE DOUGLAS, sons of SIR WILLIAM DOUGLAS who owned the castle, and they both devised plans to help Mary to escape.

First Attempt

George had Mary swap clothes with the laundress who came to the island every morning. Thus disguised, she was being rowed across to the mainland when the boatman made a play for the 'laundress' and tried to strip the muffler from her face. Mary raised her arms defensively and revealed the fair white hands of someone who had never scrubbed laundry in her life. Her cover was blown and Mary was rowed back to the island, while George was sent away in disgrace.

Second Attempt

Next, Willie Douglas, an illegitimate son of Sir William who was employed at the castle as a page boy, devised his own plan. On the evening of 25 March 1568, while serving at dinner, he managed to pocket the keys to the castle's main door, which had been left on the dining table. He then led Mary down from her room above the dining hall, out through the castle gates and into a waiting boat, locking the castle door behind him and tossing the keys into the loch. Once ashore they were met by George Douglas and a troop of loyal soldiers and taken to hide at Lord Seton's seat, Niddrie Castle in West Lothian.

Early in the 19th century the loch was partially drained and a rusty set of door keys was retrieved from the muddy bottom – the very keys dropped into the water by young Willie Douglas during that dramatic escape. They are now kept in the Armoury at Abbotsford, Sir Walter Scott's home in Roxburghshire.

Glamis Castle

That first view of GLAMIS CASTLE, massive, pink-turreted and pinnacled,

sitting at the end of a long, sweeping, tree-lined driveway and framed by the blue Angus hills behind, is unforgettable. It is everything a Scottish castle should be. And some say it is THE MOST HAUNTED CASTLE IN THE WORLD.

The first building at Glamis was a royal hunting lodge, and it was there that KING MALCOLM II was murdered. His blood is said to seep through the floor of the castle's King Malcolm's Room.

The oldest part of the castle, DUNCAN'S HALL, dates from about 1400, and was built on the site of the hall where MACBETH, who according to Shakespeare was Thane of Glamis, is said to have murdered his cousin KING DUNCAN (although several other castles also claim that accolade, notably Cawdor and Inverness).

KING ROBERT II of Scotland, the first Stewart king, granted Glamis to his son-in-law SIR JOHN LYON OF FORTEVIOT in 1372, and it was his son who began to turn the old royal hunting lodge into the castle we see today. He constructed the east wing, while his son PATRICK, 1ST LORD GLAMIS, built the great tower, with its turrets and conical corner towers and great central stairway, which was completed in 1484.

Haunted

Many people have tried to count the windows at Glamis but no one seems to be able to make the number of windows tally with the number of rooms, indicating that there must be a secret room somewhere. In this secret room sits a guest earl who refused to stop playing cards on the Sabbath when asked to by his hosts. The earl declared that he would play until doomsday or with the Devil if he wanted to, at which point a stranger appeared and joined the earl at cards, and now the earl must play until doomsday. Legend has it that the secret has been passed down through the generations from the 15th century, and that only the current laird is ever allowed to know the true story.

In 1540 JANET DOUGLAS, widow of the 6th Lord Glamis, was burned as a witch on charges trumped up by James V, who was seeking revenge for past wrongs by the Douglas family. She was later pardoned, but her soul is said to haunt the chapel at Glamis, where one seat is reserved for her and has never been sat in to this day, even if the chapel is full.

Queen Mother's Home

The 9th Lord Glamis was created EARL OF KINGHORNE by James VI; and his grandson, who became EARL OF STRATHMORE AND KINGHORNE, added the west wing to balance the appearance of the castle at the end of the 17th century.

In 1767 the 9th Earl married MARY BOWES, heiress to rich coal-mines in Durham, and the family name became BOWES LYON. The 14th Earl had ten children, the ninth named Elizabeth, and she would eventually become affectionately known as the 'Queen Mum'.

She spent much of her childhood at Glamis and in 1930 gave birth to her younger daughter PRINCESS MARGARET in the royal apartments in the east wing at Glamis. This was the LAST TIME THAT A GOVERNMENT MINISTER WAS REQUIRED TO BE PRESENT AT A ROYAL BIRTH, to rule out any chance of the baby being substituted.

Iona

The tiny island of IONA, which lies close to the southwestern tip of Mull, off the west coast of Argyllshire, is Scotland's most sacred place, the birthplace of Christianity in Scotland and the burial place of her ancient kings. The first King of the Scots, Kenneth MacAlpin, was buried on the island in 858.

In 563 ST COLUMBA, exiled from Ireland, landed on Iona, which was then part of the Irish kingdom of Dalriada, and founded a monastery. St Columba chose Iona because it was the first island he had reached from where he could not see Ireland. From here St Columba went out to convert the heathen Picts.

Iona Abbey, which sits on the site of St Columba's wooden church, was built in 1203, and rebuilt in the 16th century. The nave of the church slopes downwards toward the wonderful altar of Iona marble, which lies below the level of the west door, a rare configuration found only in one other church in Scotland, St Mungo's Cathedral in Glasgow.

Forty-eight Scottish kings lie buried in the abbey's graveyard, along with eight Norwegian kings and four Irish kings. The last Scottish king to be buried on Iona was DUNCAN I in 1040.

Rothesay

ROTHESAY CASTLE, in the middle of Rothesay on the Isle of Bute, is one of the oldest and most remarkable royal castles in Scotland. Built around 1230 by Walter, 2nd High Steward of Scotland, it is notable for its round keep, consisting of a very high curtain wall protected by four drum towers enclosing a circular courtyard, all surrounded by a deep moat. The design is unique in Scotland.

Twice captured by King Haakon IV of Norway before his defeat at the Battle of Largs in 1263, Rothesay was eventually taken by Robert the Bruce. It became a favourite royal residence of the early Stewart kings, and a particular refuge for Robert III, who died there in 1406.

Scotland's Oldest Dukedom

Robert created his eldest son, David, DUKE OF ROTHESAY in 1398, making him SCOTLAND'S FIRST DUKE. When David was murdered the title passed to his brother James, later James I, and has been held ever since by the eldest son of the Kings of Scotland. The Prince of Wales is known as the Duke of Rothesay when in Scotland.

Well, I never knew this about
ROYAL SCOTLAND – PAST

Edinburgh Castle's most quirky attraction is MONS MEG, a huge bombard's gun given to James II in 1457 by his uncle-by-marriage the Duke of Burgundy. James only used the gun once, against Norham Castle on the River Tweed, and it was eventually retired to Edinburgh Castle and placed on guard outside St Margaret's Chapel. Since the gun was made in Mons in Belgium and Meg is short for Margaret it became known as Mons Meg.

In 1558 Mons Meg was fired to celebrate the marriage of Mary, Queen of Scots to the French Dauphin. The stone cannonball used was found almost 2 miles (3 km) away, in what is now the Royal Botanic Gardens.

JAMES IV had a 'laird's lug' built above the fireplace in the Great Hall at Edinburgh Castle, a small barred opening through which he could eavesdrop on his guests. When MIKHAIL GORBACHEV was coming to visit in

1984, the KGB asked that the laird's lug be blocked up for security reasons, but Gorbachev never got there – that morning he was told of the imminent demise of the Soviet leader Chernenko and he had to hurry back to Moscow.

JAMES VI's christening in the Chapel Royal at Stirling was celebrated with THE FIRST RECORDED PUBLIC FIREWORKS DISPLAY IN BRITAIN.

A highlight of the palace at SCONE, retained from the previous manor house, is the ROYAL LONG GALLERY, built in 1618, which is THE LONGEST ROOM IN SCOTLAND, 142 ft (43 m) in length. CHARLES II walked along the Long Gallery to his coronation in 1651.

In the billiard room at GLAMIS CASTLE is a full-length portrait of FRANCES

Dora Smith, wife of the 13th Earl of Strathmore, and great-grandmother of Elizabeth II. By a direct, if complicated, line through Frances Smith, the present Queen of England is one of the closest living relatives of the first President of the United States of America, George Washington.

Glamis Castle was the last household in Scotland to employ a jester.

During his progress through the Scottish borders during the second Jacobite Rebellion in 1745, Bonnie Prince Charlie paid a visit to his kinsman the Stuart Earl of Traquair at

Scotland's oldest inhabited house, Traquair House in Peeblesshire. When he departed, the Bear Gates at the end of the long drive to the house were closed and locked behind him, and the Earl declared that they would not be opened again until a Stuart sat upon the British throne once more. They have remained closed ever since.

After the Battle of Culloden in 1746, Bonnie Prince Charlie spent some time hiding on the island of Skye. As a thank you for helping him while he was there, the Prince gave his loyal supporter John MacKinnon the secret recipe to Drambuie, or 'an Dram Buidheach' – meaning 'the drink that satisfies'. The MacKinnon family still guard the secret and run the Drambuie company to this day – they brewed the first Drambuie for public consumption at the Broadford Inn on the Isle of Skye in 1893.

CHAPTER TWELVE

ROYAL WALES

PENMYNYDD ✦ PEMBROKE CASTLE ✦ OFFA'S DYKE
✦ FLINT CASTLE ✦ RHUDDLAN CASTLE ✦ CONWY CASTLE
✦ HARLECH CASTLE ✦ BEAUMARIS CASTLE
✦ CAERNARFON CASTLE ✦ LLWYNYWERMOD

When the DUKE AND DUCHESS OF CAMBRIDGE, Prince William and his new bride Kate, settled into their cottage on the island of ANGLESEY after their wedding in 2011, they were coming home. The corner of Wales is where his ancestors came from 700 years ago, for Anglesey is the birthplace of the royal Tudors.

Penmynydd

Anglesey

In the 13th century EDNYFED FYCHAN, Lord Steward to Llywelyn the Great,

was granted the lands around PENMYNYDD as a reward for his services and he built himself a small manor house there, Plas Penmynydd. Ednyfed's descendants pledged loyalty to Edward I when he conquered Wales and so retained their lands and influence.

In 1385 Ednyfed's great-great-great-grandson OWAIN AP MAREDUDD AP TUDUR was born at at Plas Penmynydd. Owain, known as the 'Rose of Mona', fought alongside HENRY V at the Battle of Agincourt in 1415 and later entered the service of Henry's queen, CATHERINE DE VALOIS.

After Henry's death in 1422,

Catherine and Owen Tudor, as he was now known, fell in love and secretly married. They had three sons, EDMUND, JASPER and OWEN. Edmund, created Earl of Richmond by Henry VI, married MARGARET BEAUFORT, great-granddaughter of John of Gaunt, fourth son of Edward III and founder of the House of Lancaster. In January 1457 Margaret Beaufort gave birth to a son, HENRY TUDOR, at Pembroke Castle in South Wales.

The current Plas Penmynydd was rebuilt in 1576 around the original home of the Tudors. Etched on to the stone wall inside the enormous inglenook, which survives from the older house, is the fleur-de-lys of Catherine de Valois, Owen Tudor's wife.

The house has been refurbished several times since and is now a private dwelling, but the windswept landscape and the spectacular views of Snowdonia across the Menai Strait that the early Tudors knew can have changed very little.

St Gredifael

In a side chapel of Penmynydd's little 14th-century village church of ST GREDIFAEL are the grand alabaster

tombs of Owen Tudor's brother, Henry VII's great-great-uncle, GRONW FYCHAN AP TUDOR, and his wife. Gronw, who was Forrester of Snowdonia, drowned in 1382. Over the years pilgrims have removed bits of the tombs in the belief that they are bestowed with healing powers.

There is also a colourful stained-glass window illustrating the Regalia of the English crown along with a Tudor rose and the portcullis badge of the Beaufort family. Welsh lettering round the window translates as 'Unity is like a rose on a river bank, and like a house of steel on a mountain top'. TY DUR, or Tudor, is Welsh for House of Steel.

First Tudor King

The first Tudor King, HENRY VII, was born at PEMBROKE CASTLE in 1457. The Wars of the Roses were going badly for the House of Lancaster, to which Henry's mother Margaret Beaufort belonged, and so Margaret, 13 years old and heavily pregnant, had been brought to Pembroke by her brother-in-law Jasper Tudor, Earl of Pembroke, for safe keeping. Her husband, Henry's father Edmund Tudor, was a prisoner of the Yorkists and was languishing in Carmarthen Castle, where he died shortly before his son was born.

As the war raged on, Henry grew up safe inside the castle walls, until the death of Henry VI and his heir Prince Edward elevated Henry to Head of the House of Lancaster. Because there was now a Yorkist King on the throne, Edward IV, Henry had to flee to France.

After 14 years he returned, landing in Wales at Mill Bay, on the tip of the Dale peninsula west of Pembroke, and marched through Wales under the banner of the Red Dragon, picking up Welsh support as he went. In 1485 he defeated Richard III at Bosworth Field and became THE FIRST TUDOR KING.

Pembroke Castle

PEMBROKE CASTLE dates mainly from the late 12th century and was built by RICHARD DE CLARE, 2ND EARL OF PEMBROKE, known as Strongbow and the man who led the Norman invasion of Ireland. The castle occupies an almost impregnable site on a rocky promontory, surrounded on three sides by water and defended against the land approach from the east by a huge gate with three portcullises.

Pembroke Castle is astonishingly intact, with miles of dark passageways to explore and an outstanding cylindrical keep, 60 ft (18 m) high with walls 18 ft (5.5 m) thick, topped by an unusual stone dome from which the views over Milford Haven are amazing. Pembroke

Castle is THE ONLY CASTLE IN BRITAIN CONSTRUCTED OVER A NATURAL CAVERN, a huge cave known as THE WOGAN, which used to allow access to the castle from the water.

Offa's Dyke

The earliest evidence we have of royal activity in Wales was built 700 years before Henry Tudor was born in Pembroke Castle. OFFA'S DYKE, THE LONGEST ARCHAEOLOGICAL MONUMENT IN BRITAIN, was the greatest achievement of Mercia's Saxon KING OFFA and is perhaps the most lasting and celebrated memorial of any Anglo-Saxon King.

The huge earth rampart stretched, as Offa had ordained, 'from sea to sea', from Sedbury Cliffs on the Severn estuary near Chepstow to the Irish Sea at Prestatyn. At some 150 miles (240 km) long it was almost twice the length of Hadrian's Wall, although the purpose of the dyke was not so much defensive as to clearly mark the agreed border between Mercia and the kingdoms of the Welsh.

According to the 19th-century writer George Borrow, 'It was customary for the English to cut off the ears of every Welshman who was found to the east of the dyke, and for the Welsh to hang every Englishman found to the west of it.'

There were some gaps, but for most of its length the dyke consisted of a ditch on the Welsh side and a rampart on the English side, and was about 89 ft (27 m) wide and 26 ft (8 m) high. Roughly 80 miles (130 km) of the dyke, from the Wye valley to Wrexham, are still traceable, with the best-preserved sections being found at LLANFAIR HILL above Clun in Shropshire, and at DISCOED near Presteigne, old county town of Radnorshire.

Offa's Dyke was THE FIRST OFFICIAL BORDER EVER DRAWN BETWEEN ENGLAND AND WALES, and the line of the border has remained substantially the same to this day.

The only town located actually on Offa's Dyke is KNIGHTON, home of the OFFA'S DYKE CENTRE, which provides information on the 177-mile (285-km) long OFFA'S DYKE PATH, THE ONLY NATIONAL TRAIL TO FOLLOW A MAN-MADE FEATURE.

Among the highlights to be seen along the path are BRITAIN'S FIRST STONE CASTLE AT CHEPSTOW, TINTERN ABBEY

in the Wye Valley, the county town of MONMOUTH, with BRITAIN'S LAST REMAINING FORTIFIED BRIDGE, Clive of India's POWIS CASTLE, CHIRK CASTLE and Thomas Telford's PONTCYSYLLTE AQUEDUCT, THE LONGEST AQUEDUCT IN BRITAIN.

The Conquest of Wales

EDWARD I's great ambition was to unite all of Britain under his rule, and to achieve this he first concentrated on conquering Wales, as Kings of England had been trying to do with not much success since William the Conqueror. Edward's particular bugbear was the Welsh prince LLYWELYN AP GRUFYDD, who had taken advantage of Henry III's weak rule to assume the title Prince of Wales, and had refused to attend Edward's coronation or pay homage to him in any way.

In 1277 Edward marched north to Chester, entered Wales along the Dee estuary, and began to build a castle on a rocky platform above the marshes at Flint.

Flint

FLINT CASTLE was the first in a remarkable series of castles Edward would build in Wales during what was to be the most prolific and ambitious programme of castle building in British or European history. It is THE ONLY CASTLE IN BRITAIN TO HAVE A SEPARATE

DONJON, or fortified keep, detached from the rest of the castle and surrounded by its own moat, filled from the Dee. The walls of the donjon, which was built in 1277–80, are 23 ft (7 m) thick, THE THICKEST CASTLE WALLS IN THE WORLD. The internal plan of the donjon at Flint is unique in Britain, with rooms arranged around a central shaft, designed to admit air and light to the interior.

The word 'donjon' became dungeon in English, but originally donjon meant the lord's residence within the castle, rather than a place of imprisonment.

In the shadow of the castle Edward constructed a bastide, or planned town, which became the town of Flint. Edward had learned about bastides while fighting in Gascony in south-west France. Protected by the castle and encircling town wall, they were designed as fortified centres of administration and as a safe place for people to settle and establish a market – in the case of Edward's Welsh bastides, they were to be occupied by English administrators and English merchants.

Rhuddlan

Edward then advanced along the Dee to RHUDDLAN. Sitting at the mouth of the River Clwyd, Rhuddlan had long been recognised for its strategically important position as a gateway to North Wales, and had changed hands between Saxon kings and Welsh princes many times. In 1076 William the Conqueror built a castle on top of a mound 60 ft (18 m) high beside the river known as TWTHILL, on the site of the palace of GRUFFYDD AP LLYWELYN (1007–64), THE ONLY WELSH PRINCE WHO COULD EVER CLAIM SOVEREIGNTY OVER ALL OF WALES.

Edward built his castle a little to the north of Twthill and also created a new bastide on the other side of the castle from the existing Norman town, which had been based around a Dominican friary.

The castle at Rhuddlan was the first of the concentric castles in Wales designed by Edward's military architect JAMES OF ST GEORGE, a master mason from Savoy, the home of Edward's maternal grandmother. Unlike James's later castles it had a UNIQUE DIAMOND LAYOUT with the gatehouses positioned at the corners rather than the sides of the bailey.

Because the mountainous territory of North Wales rendered overland travel hazardous, the castle was made accessible from the sea by canalising the final 3 miles (4.8 km) of the River Clwyd.

Powerless in the face of such military might, Llywelyn ap Grufydd backed down and signed the TREATY OF ABERCONWY, whereby he conceded all his lands to Edward save for the kingdom of Gwynedd. He was allowed to retain the title of Prince of Wales, and to marry Eleanor, the daughter of Simon de Montfort.

Statute of Rhuddlan

In 1282 Llywelyn's younger brother DAFYDD began his own rebellion, provoking Edward to launch a full-scale invasion. Dafydd was captured and hung, drawn and quartered at Shrewsbury Castle, while Llywelyn was killed in a skirmish (*see* Princes of Wales). His head was taken to Edward at Rhuddlan.

In 1284 Edward issued the STATUTE OF RHUDDLAN, the first step toward uniting England and the Principality of Wales, and effectively ending Welsh independence. It introduced a version of English Common Law into Wales, divided Llwyelyn's kingdom of Gwynedd into the new counties of Anglesey, Merioneth and Caernarfonshire, and created a number of further new Welsh counties, including Cardiganshire and Flintshire.

There is a plaque commemorating the event on the wall of Parliament House in Rhuddlan, which stands where Edward proclaimed the statute, at the same time promising to make his son 'Prince of Wales'.

Ring of Iron

Next, in order to intimidate the principality and subdue the Welsh once and for all, much as William the Conqueror had subdued the English, Edward embarked upon the construction of an iron ring of fortresses to encircle the heartlands of the Welsh princes, stretching from his existing castle at Flint in the east to Conwy and Harlech in the west. These lonely, isolated English outposts, standing alone against the wild might of North Wales, are the most supreme examples of the medieval castle to be found anywhere in the

world. They dominated their surroundings, were able to withstand any weapon of the age save treachery, and they achieved their purpose – never again would Wales be independent.

Conwy

Completed in less than six years between 1283 and 1289, CONWY's castle and town walls were designed and built as a single unit, and the result is THE MOST COMPLETE MEDIEVAL WALLED TOWN IN BRITAIN. You can walk virtually all the way around the town on the walls, which are three-quarters of a mile (1.2 km) long and incorporate three gates and 21 towers. They enclose a virtually unchanged medieval townscape with cobbled streets and narrow alleyways. Although the town was built by the English, who called it Conway, Conwy was soon occupied by the Welsh and is as close as you can get to a real medieval Welsh town.

The castle stands on a high rock promontory and guards the entrance to the River Conwy. With its eight massive towers it intimidates through its sheer size, and seen from the river, with the mountains as a backdrop, it looms over the town like a crouching bear guarding its cubs.

Although the Conwy we see today is the work of Edward I, the original settlement of Conwy grew up around a Cistercian abbey founded in 1199 by the Welsh prince LLWYELYN THE GREAT, who is buried there with his two sons.

Harlech Castle

HARLECH CASTLE was begun in 1283 and completed in 1290 at a cost of £8,000 – about £5 million in today's money. Its position is unsurpassed. Even in a country of such superlative panoramas as Wales, the view from the ramparts of Harlech Castle is special. The awestruck visitor stands teetering on a high wall, itself perched on a tall rocky crag – Harlech means 'bold rock' – and gazes across the shimmering sea to the gnarled receding coastline of the Lleyn Peninsula.

Laid out below, like a green and gold tapestry, the flat, sun-dappled marshes and sands of Morfa Harlech lead the

eye across Tremadog Bay to the brooding, thunderous mass of Snowdon, one moment standing stark, proud and clear, the next veiled in dark and swirling clouds. Professor Tolkien must have been standing right here when he thought of Mordor.

Harlech is the best of castles to explore, with dungeons and hidden passageways as well as spectacular walks around the square battlements. A challenging way to approach the castle is to climb the 'Way from the Sea', the old fortified stairway clinging to the western rock face that leads up from the harbour. Before the land was reclaimed for a golf course, waves used to lap against the foot of the cliff on which Harlech stands, and during sieges the castle could be supplied from the sea.

Although seemingly impregnable, Harlech was captured in 1404 by OWAIN GLYNDWR, during his conflict against Henry IV, when he was able to block off the sea route with help from the French navy. Glyndwr made Harlech his base and proclaimed himself Prince of Wales at the castle, in front of envoys from France and Scotland. When the castle was retaken in 1408, Glyndwr's rebellion collapsed.

During the Wars of the Roses, Harlech was a Lancastrian stronghold and held out under siege for seven years before finally falling to the Yorkists in 1468, a feat remembered in the song 'MEN OF HARLECH'.

During the Civil War, Harlech Castle was THE LAST CASTLE IN WALES TO FALL TO OLIVER CROMWELL.

Beaumaris

The Last Great Castle

BEAUMARIS, 'beautiful marsh', on Anglesey was chosen by Edward as the location for the last of his great castles in Wales. Built to guard the northern approach to the Menai Strait, it was begun in 1295 but never fully completed owing to lack of funds. Because of its low-lying position, Beaumaris Castle is less spectacular than Edward's other castles and, seen from the south against the backdrop of Snowdonia across the blue, dazzling waters of the Strait, it is quite beautiful rather than intimidating.

Further examination, however, reveals the remarkable strength and ingenuity of its design. An octagon, enclosing a rectangle, Beaumaris is considered THE MOST PERFECT EXAMPLE OF A CONCENTRIC CASTLE IN EUROPE, both technically and architecturally.

For anyone attempting to capture the castle there are some 14 obstacles to overcome. The first line of defence is a deep moat, connected to the sea by a canal – at high tide boats could sail right up to the castle walls, protected by guns sited on a raised platform on the 'Gunner's Walk'. The next defence is an octagonal curtain wall, punctuated with 16 drum towers and two gates. The main gate in the south wall is set slightly off centre, so that anyone who succeeded in getting through the gateway would have to execute a sharp right and left before setting about the barbican, all the while being subjected to boiling oil being poured on their heads through 'murder holes' in the walls.

The walls of the huge inner ward, 16 ft (5 m) thick and over 40 ft (12 m) high, are riddled with narrow passageways that cry out to be explored, and hidden away in one of the massive inner towers is the jewel of the castle, an exquisite vaulted chapel.

The town that grew up around Beaumaris Castle has an undeniably genteel, 'English' feel to it, which is hardly surprising since King Edward insisted that the Welsh inhabitants of the original village, called Llanfaes, were forcibly moved across Anglesey to start again at Newborough, since they were taking up space he wanted for his new fortress.

Caernarfon Castle

CAERNARFON CASTLE is the most imposing as well as THE LARGEST OF EDWARD'S CASTLES IN WALES. It was designed not just as a mighty fortress but as a palace and as the seat of English royal government in Wales. Begun in 1283, it took 50 years to build and, even then, was never finished. When it was built it was surrounded on three sides by water and owes its unusual elongated oval configuration to the shape of the rock on which it is built.

The first impression of Caernarfon Castle is the sheer size of it. The entrance arches soar higher than a cathedral, and the tall, grim walls darken the narrow streets below. Voices and footsteps echo in the hollow shadows. If the castle has that effect now, then it must have inspired considerable awe and fear 700 years ago.

But there is more to Caernarfon than simple brute power: there is subtle imagery at work here too. Edward built his castle near the site of the Roman fort of SEGONTIUM, guarding the northwest frontier of the Roman Empire. The remains can still be seen outside the town walls to the south. In AD 383 the commander of the Roman legions in Britain, MAGNUS MAXIMUS, declared himself 'Caesar' and went out from Segontium, accompanied by many Welsh warriors, to set himself up as Emperor of the West.

Although Maximus was eventually defeated and the Romans never returned to Wales, the symbolism of Welsh princes fighting alongside Roman legionaries was not lost on Edward, and Caernarfon was a powerful expression of Edward's desire to be seen as imperial Rome's natural successor in Wales.

The imperial imagery goes deeper still. The banded walls of the castle, lined with strips of dark sandstone and layers of decorative tiles, are reminiscent of the mighty Theodosian Wall at Constantinople, capital of the Eastern

Roman Empire, which Edward and his architect James of St George had admired while on crusade. Caernarfon would be the Constantinople of the West.

Further to emulate the walls of Constantinople, Caernarfon has polygonal towers rather than circular ones. The distinctive EAGLE TOWER, one of THE TALLEST MEDIEVAL TOWERS EVER BUILT, once had imperial eagles on each of its three turrets. Tradition has it that it was in the Eagle Tower that Edward's Queen Eleanor gave birth to their son, the future Edward II, in 1284.

The young Prince Edward was created THE FIRST ENGLISH PRINCE OF WALES in 1301, and ever since then the eldest son of the reigning monarch has been invested with the title Prince of Wales.

Llwynywermod

In 2007 the current Prince of Wales, who is the 21st English Prince of Wales, purchased LLWYNYWERMOD, a

small three-bedroomed farmhouse in Carmarthenshire to use as a base for visits and his annual summer tour of Wales. The house was once the coach house of a nearby manor and sits at the heart of a 200-acre (80 ha) estate of parkland and woods, which Prince Charles is managing organically, with the meadows set aside for wild flowers.

Local Welsh craftsmen were employed to renovate the house, and the furniture includes a Welsh dresser given to the Queen as a wedding present by the people of Meirionnydd.

Llwynywermod is THE FIRST HOME IN WALES EVER PRIVATELY OWNED BY AN ENGLISH PRINCE OF WALES.

Princes of Wales

LLYWELYN AP GRUFYDD (Llywelyn the Last) was THE ONLY CONSTITUTIONALLY RECOGNISED NATIVE-BORN PRINCE OF WALES. Before that Wales had been divided into a number of smaller territories, each with its own overlord, the most mighty of which was acknowledged as 'Prince of Wales'. Llywelyn the

Last was slain in a skirmish in the woods at CILMERY near Brecon in 1282. A monument of Caernarfonshire granite, 15 ft (4.6 m) high, was erected near the spot in 1956, encircled by 13 oak trees representing the 13 traditional Welsh counties.

Llywelyn ap Grufydd's father LLYWELYN AP IORWERTH (Llywelyn the Great), ruler of the most powerful of the Welsh kingdoms, Gwynedd, was recognised as the 'Prince of North Wales'. He was buried in 1240 in the abbey he founded at Conwy.

In 1401 OWAIN GLYNDWR, the son of a prosperous Welsh landowner, mustered an uprising against Henry IV and declared himself Prince of Wales at Harlech Castle, in front of delegates from both France and Scotland. In 1404 he held the last native Welsh parliament at MACHYNLLETH in Montgomeryshire, before his rebellion petered out.

The FIRST ENGLISH PRINCE OF WALES was EDWARD II, who was created Prince of Wales at Lincoln on 1 February 1301.

The second Prince of Wales was the BLACK PRINCE, eldest son of Edward III. He was the first of six Princes of Wales to die before becoming king. The other five were:

EDWARD OF WESTMINSTER (1453–71), only son of Henry VI. He was killed at the Battle of Tewkesbury during the Wars of the Roses and was buried in Tewkesbury Abbey. He is THE ONLY HEIR APPARENT TO THE ENGLISH THRONE EVER TO DIE IN BATTLE.

EDWARD OF MIDDLEHAM (1473–84), only legitimate son of Richard III. He died of ill health aged 11 and was buried in Sheriff Hutton church in Yorkshire, where there is an alabaster monument in his memory, THE ONLY PRINCE OF WALES BURIED IN A SIMPLE PARISH CHURCH.

PRINCE ARTHUR (1486–1502), eldest son of Henry VII. He was married to Catherine of Aragon, who would later become the first wife of Henry VIII, but died of ill health at Ludlow Castle, aged just 15. He is buried in Worcester Cathedral.

PRINCE HENRY STUART (1594–1612), eldest son of James I. He died of typhoid fever after swimming in the River Thames, at the age of 18. He was buried in Westminster Abbey.

PRINCE FREDERICK (1707–51), eldest son of George II. While playing a game of cricket in the garden at Cliveden in Buckinghamshire he was struck on the chest by a cricket ball, causing an abscess, which became fatally infected. The FIRST PERSON EVER KNOWN TO HAVE DIED FROM BEING HIT BY A CRICKET BALL, Prince Frederick succumbed to the infection in 1751 and was buried in Westminster Abbey.

JAMES STUART (1688–1766), eldest son of James II, forfeited the title Prince of Wales after his father was deemed to have abdicated in 1688.

Born in Wales

Only two English Princes of Wales were actually born in Wales, EDWARD II (*see* Caernarfon) and HENRY V, who was born in the Queen's Chamber of the Great Tower above the gate house of MONMOUTH CASTLE in 1387, the son of Henry Bolingbroke (later Henry IV) and his first wife Mary de Bohun. Mary died before her husband became King and hence was never a Queen. She was, however, descended from the last recognised Welsh-born Prince of Wales, Llywelyn the Great, and this, allied to the fact that Henry was born in Wales, made Henry, in the eyes of the Welsh people themselves, a very acceptable Prince of Wales, a title he received when his father won the throne from Richard II in 1399.

A Sign of the Times

Before the Battle of Agincourt in 1415, Henry V told his men
that the French intended to cut off two fingers from the right
hand of every Welsh and English archer they caught, so that he
would never be able to fire a longbow again. During the battle,
the archers raised two fingers to the French to show that they
were still in fighting form – the origin of the English 'V' sign.

A Couple of Edwards and a Charles

PRINCE EDWARD, later Edward VII, was
born at Buckingham Palace in 1841 and
created Prince of Wales at the age of
four weeks. He did not succeed to the
throne until nearly 60 years later and
is still THE LONGEST-SERVING PRINCE
OF WALES AND HEIR APPARENT IN
BRITISH HISTORY.

PRINCE EDWARD, later Edward VIII,
was THE FIRST PRINCE OF WALES EVER
TO BE INVESTED ACTUALLY AT
CAERNARFON CASTLE, in 1911.

The current Prince of Wales, PRINCE
CHARLES, was created Prince of Wales
in 1958 at the age of ten and was
invested as Prince of Wales at Caernarfon
Castle in 1969. In 2008 at the age of
60 he became THE OLDEST EVER PRINCE
OF WALES.

Well, I never knew this
about
ROYAL WALES

The hidden harbour village of NANT
GWRTHEYRN on the Lleyn peninsula
in Caernarfonshire is the burial place
of the Celtic KING VORTIGERN, who
was responsible for inviting the Saxons
into Britain in the 5th century. Not
far away, near Beddgelert, is the hill
fort of DINAS EMRYS where the Druid

Merlin revealed to Vortigern two
fighting dragons, one red representing
the British, one white representing the
treacherous Saxons. The red dragon
triumphed and the Saxons never did
conquer the British stronghold of
Wales, hence the red dragon on the
national flag of Wales.

EDWARD I gave a charter to FLINT in 1284, making it THE OLDEST CHARTERED TOWN IN WALES.

Richard II's reign came to an end when he was captured at FLINT CASTLE in 1399 and forced to surrender to his cousin Henry Bolingbroke, later Henry IV. The scene was re-enacted in Act III, Scene iii of Shakespeare's *Richard II*.

Down on the quayside at CONWY, beneath the castle walls, is THE SMALLEST HOUSE IN BRITAIN, just 10 ft 2 inches (3.1 m) high and 6 ft (1.8 m) wide. It has only two rooms, and the last tenant was a fisherman who was 6 ft 3 inches (1.9 m) tall.

Aberconwy House

Conwy also possesses THE OLDEST TOWN HOUSE IN WALES, ABERCONWY HOUSE. It dates from the 14th century and is now run by the National Trust.

In the porch of Beaumaris's 14th-century church of St Mary sits the stone coffin of 'SIWAN', OR JOAN (1195–1237),

illegitimate daughter of Edward's grandfather King John, and wife of Llywelyn the Great. Used for a long time as a drinking trough for horses, her coffin was moved to Beaumaris from Llanfaes Priory at the Dissolution of the Monasteries.

The Prince of Wales's badge of three ostrich feathers was said to have been adopted by the Black Prince, son of Edward III, and the second non-Welsh Prince of Wales, after the Battle of Crecy in 1346. The Prince removed a helmet lined with ostrich feathers from the body of the blind King of Bohemia, who had fought bravely, and used the feathers for his own badge as a tribute. He also took the King's motto 'Ich Dien', meaning 'I serve'.

In February 1896 the Prince of Wales, later Edward VII, became THE FIRST MEMBER OF THE BRITISH ROYAL FAMILY TO RIDE IN A MOTOR CAR, when he was a passenger in the FIRST CAR SEEN IN BRITAIN, a Panhard Levassor belonging to the Hon. Evelyn Ellis of Datchet, near Windsor.

Owing to his large 48-inch (120 cm) waist, EDWARD, PRINCE OF WALES, later Edward VII, began the tradition of men leaving undone the bottom button of a suit coat. He also first introduced the traditional English Sunday lunch of roast beef and horseradish sauce.

CHAPTER THIRTEEN

ROYAL VILLAINS

Ethelred the Unready ✦ Henry II ✦ John
✦ Richard III ✦ Henry VIII ✦ Mary I

Richard III

Modern monarchs don't have quite the same opportunities to become villains as their predecessors, who could slaughter entire communities, chop people's heads off or burn people at the stake with impunity. Health and Safety frown on that sort of behaviour today. There are, however, a few notable villains amongst the Queen's ancestors.

Ethelred the Unready

r. 978–1016

ETHELRED acquired the throne through treachery, and this overshadowed his entire reign, which would last for nearly 40 years, THE LONGEST REIGN OF ANY ANGLO-SAXON KING. Ethelred's mother

Elfrida, the original 'wicked step-mother', had her stepson King Edward, Ethelred's half-brother, brutally murdered at her home, Corfe Castle in Dorset, so that her own son Ethelred could become king.

Ethelred was only ten years old when he succeeded and it was for his weakness in the face of Danish aggression that he is condemned as a villain. During the peaceful years of his father Edgar's reign England had become rich and made a tempting target for the Danes. In 991 a Danish army landed on a muddy island in the Blackwater estuary near Maldon in Essex, marched across the causeway at low tide, and over-whelmed what was one of THE FIRST TRUE ENGLISH ARMIES, led by a heroic local earl called Brihtnoth, and made up of warriors from all across England.

The Battle of Maldon became the subject of an Anglo-Saxon poem, and Brihtnoth became THE FIRST ENGLISH HERO TO BE IMMORTALISED IN VERSE.

Danegeld

However, instead of resisting the Danes like his ancestors, Ethelred opted to pay them off, using the vast reserves of money built up during the previous years of peace. This Danegeld, as it became known, only encouraged the Vikings to come back for more, and soon England was bankrupt and desolate, easy prey for the Viking hordes.

Emma of Normandy

In 1002, in a desperate effort to dissuade the Norsemen of Normandy from helping their Danish cousins ransack England, Ethelred married Emma, the daughter of the Duke of Normandy, as his second wife. Although he didn't know it at the time, this would lead directly to another disaster for England, the Norman invasion of 1066, led by Emma's great-nephew, William.

Bring on the Danes

Ethelred then ordered the slaughter of all the Danes in England, which only enraged them further, and by 1013 the Danes had occupied London and taken control of the kingdom. Ethelred fled to join his wife Emma and their two sons in exile in Normandy, leaving England in the hands of the Danish King Sweyn.

Sweyn, however, died in the spring of 1014. The occupying Danes chose Sweyn's son Canute as king, but the English decided to invite Ethelred to return under certain conditions. Ethelred met with the English nobles in the Guildhall in London and was forced to promise not to reimpose high taxes or curtail the rights of free men. The text of the agreement, THE FIRST CONSTITUTIONAL SETTLEMENT IN ENGLISH HISTORY, and a precursor of Magna Carta, was written down in the Anglo-Saxon Chronicle.

Guildhall today

Ethelred died in London in 1016 after two years of constant fighting against Canute and was buried in Old St Paul's Cathedral. His nickname 'the Unready' means 'poorly counselled', and is a pun on the name Ethelred, which means 'noble counsel'.

Henry II

r. 1154–1189

HENRY II was one of our great monarchs, who ruled an empire stretching from Scotland to the Pyrenees, curbed the power of the barons, strengthened the law and established trial by jury as a right. However, although he did have a famous mistress and instigated the Norman invasion of Ireland, Henry will always be remembered as a villain for just one reason – the murder of Archbishop THOMAS BECKET.

It all began in 1164 when Henry issued what some regard as ENGLAND'S FIRST CONSTITUTION, the CONSTITUTION OF CLARENDON, which brought the Church back under the authority of the Crown and English law. This led to a dispute with his friend Thomas Becket, the Archbishop of Canterbury, who was eventually exiled for his dissent.

Unintentionally, this led to Henry II being responsible for the founding of ENGLAND'S FIRST UNIVERSITY at Oxford. On being exiled Thomas Becket took refuge in Paris, and in a fury Henry ordered all English students who were studying in Paris to return to England. They made their way to Oxford, already renowned as a place of learning since King Alfred had debated with the monks there in 872 while travelling up the Thames. In 1249 the first of Oxford's 38 colleges was founded by William of Durham and Oxford University was established as THE OLDEST UNIVERSITY IN THE ENGLISH-SPEAKING WORLD.

Murder in the Cathedral

Once he had calmed down, Henry invited Thomas Becket back to England. The archbishop still refused to back down and berated Henry from the pulpit until finally, in exasperation,

Henry cried out, 'Will no one rid me of this turbulent priest?'

Four knights took him at his word and gathered at SALTWOOD CASTLE, a few miles from Canterbury, to plot Becket's demise. The following afternoon the knights entered the archbishop's palace and demanded to be taken to Becket, who had been hurried out through the cloisters by his monks and taken into the cathedral. Becket, however, refused to bar the door of the cathedral to the knights, who burst in and hacked him to death with their swords.

The awful spot in the north transept of Canterbury Cathedral where Thomas Becket was murdered is today marked with a plaque and a sculpture.

In 1174 Henry II did penance for Becket's murder by travelling to Canterbury and entering the cathedral barefoot before being whipped by the clergy as he knelt at his friend's tomb.

Canterbury Tales

The deed shocked Christendom and within two years Becket had been made into a saint by the Pope and given a sumptuous, bejewelled tomb next to the high altar. His shrine became the focus of one of the great medieval pilgrimages, with pilgrims coming to Canterbury from all over Europe. At the end of the 14th century, in one of the first great works of English literature, GEOFFREY CHAUCER immortalised the Canterbury pilgrimage in his *Canterbury Tales*, in which members of a group of pilgrims recount stories while journeying to Canterbury from Southwark in London.

Becket's tomb was destroyed by Henry VIII, and the site in the cathedral where it stood is now marked with a candle.

King John

r. 1199–1216

JOHN, born at Beaumont Palace in Oxford in 1166, was the youngest of Henry II's five sons by Eleanor of Aquitaine. He was scheming, deceitful, cruel, and embittered by the fact that since he was the youngest, there was no kingdom left for him to inherit. Henry jokingly named John 'Sans Terre'

or 'Lackland'. In fact, because all of his older brothers died young, John came to inherit his father's whole empire – and managed to lose most of it.

When John's brothers began to rebel against their father in 1173, John became Henry's favourite, and in 1185 he was made LORD OF IRELAND, with a view to being crowned King of Ireland. However, John made himself so unpopular that within six months he was recalled and his coronation was cancelled.

While his brother Richard I was on crusade, John manoeuvred to put himself on the throne of England, and when Richard died in France in 1199 John finally got his chance. He was crowned in Westminster Abbey on 27 May.

Losing France

While there was not much opposition in England, there was open rebellion in John's French territories, where the barons supported the claims of John's nephew PRINCE ARTHUR, the son of John's deceased elder brother Geoffrey, Duke of Brittany, who had been designated Richard's heir in France. Then John succeeded in uniting pretty much all of France against him by stealing the 12-year-old fiancée of a French count,

the heiress ISABELLA OF ANGOULEME, and marrying her.

When John was suspected of having Prince Arthur murdered, that was the final straw and the French barons rose up against him, forcing him to flee to safety in England. By 1206 John had lost almost all his French territory, including Normandy, and the rest of his reign was spent trying to find ways of raising the money to win them back again – usually by fleecing the English barons.

Losing England

Not content with just upsetting the English barons, John then upset all his English subjects, getting himself and the whole of England excommunicated by refusing to accept the Pope's nomination for Archbishop of Canterbury, STEPHEN LANGTON.

John eventually repented and recognised Langton, but he continued to levy huge taxes on the barons for his wars in France, which might just have been accepted had he been successful, but in 1214 John was comprehensively defeated by the King of France at the Battle of Bouvines and the English barons could take no more. They occupied London and then summoned John to come to Runnymede and sign Magna Carta.

Magna Carta

'No freeman shall be seized, or imprisoned or diseased or outlawed, or any way destroyed, nor will we go upon him, except by the lawful judgement of his peers, or by the law of the land. To none will we sell, to none will we deny, to none will we delay right of justice.'

from Magna Carta

In June 1215, John reluctantly travelled to Windsor to meet with the rebel barons, mustered on the lush green meadows of Runnymede, beside the River Thames in Surrey. It took several days for the King, representatives of the nobility and the Church, led by Archbishop Stephen Langton, merchants from London and even some ordinary English yeomen to thrash out an agreement that would answer 49 grievances drawn up by the barons. Finally, on 15 June John angrily stamped his royal seal on the preliminary draft of the Great Charter that forms the foundation stone of English liberty.

Although Magna Carta is rough and clumsy, and by no means the most effective or far-reaching declaration of basic freedoms and rights ever written, it is nonetheless amongst the most revered by virtue of its being the first.

It was heavily influenced by Henry I's Charter of Liberties of 1100, but Henry's charter had been voluntarily issued by the King, while John had to be coerced into agreeing Magna Carta – THE FIRST DOCUMENT EVER FORCED ON AN ENGLISH KING BY HIS SUBJECTS. Most of the clauses didn't last for very long but Magna Carta did re-establish one very important principle that survives to this day – that THE MONARCH IS SUBJECT TO THE LAW OF THE LAND.

Runnymede

Magna Carta underlies constitutions and statutes all over the world from the European Convention on Human Rights to the American Constitution and Bill of Rights. The simple but classical MAGNA CARTA MEMORIAL, which sits on the lower slopes of Cooper's Hill above Runnymede, was presented by the American Bar Association in 1957 as a tribute to 'freedom under the law'.

John, needless to say, had no intention of abiding by the agreement to which he had given his seal, and civil war broke out again. The barons reneged on their promise to give up London, and invited the French Dauphin, Prince Louis, to come to England to lead them.

Losing the Crown

In the autumn of 1216 John found himself in King's Lynn in Norfolk after having successfully lifted the rebel siege of Lincoln. Here he contracted dysentery, but instead of recuperating he hurriedly set out again, heading north at the head of a train containing the Crown Jewels, other household valuables and the booty he had looted from the wealthy farmers of East Anglia.

Ever impatient, John attempted to cross the wide, treacherous estuary known as the Wellstream, without waiting for a guide. In the days before the Fens were drained, this stretch of water and mudflats, where the rivers meet the sea, was a maelstrom of whirlpools and shifting currents. The horse-carts, heavy with plunder, sank into the mud and stuck fast, leaving them at the mercy of the incoming tide, which swept in and overwhelmed everything. The king himself had to swim, barely escaping with his life, and leaving behind all his worldly treasures, including his magnificent jewel-encrusted crown. It lies there to this day, sunk beneath the mud at Foul Anchor, along with the rest of King John's goods.

The area still attracts bounty hunters and is a melancholy place. Just occasionally, above the howling of the chill sea winds and the cries of the scavenging gulls, the choked sobs of drowning men and the pitiful whinnies of frightened horses can be heard echoing across the empty marshes.

Bedraggled, ill and in despair, King John dragged himself into the abbey at SWINESHEAD, on the other side of Boston, and feasted, it was said, on a 'surfeit of peaches'. Two days later he was carried beneath the yawning arch of the main gateway at NEWARK CASTLE and into the south-west tower where he died on the night of 18 October 1216.

John was buried, at his own request, in WORCESTER CATHEDRAL, near the shrines of his two favourite Anglo-Saxon saints, St Wulfstan and St Oswald. His tomb rests in the chancel and is crowned with THE OLDEST ROYAL EFFIGY IN BRITAIN, created in 1232.

Richard III

r. 1483–1485

RICHARD III ranks alongside King John as one of Royal Britain's greatest villains.

His notoriously bad press as the murdering 'wicked uncle' might just be Tudor propaganda, for it suited Henry Tudor to blacken the name of the King whom he had deposed in battle. However, even the saintly Sir Thomas More described Richard as 'ill featured' and 'crookbacked', while Shakespeare paints him as a monstrous deformed hunchback. Whatever the truth, Richard certainly had the motive to murder the Princes in the Tower and, rightly or wrongly, will always be history's prime suspect, particularly as he had form – Richard was also suspected of the murder in the Tower of the last Lancastrian King, HENRY VI, on the orders of his brother the Yorkist Edward IV.

In April 1483 EDWARD IV died suddenly in the Palace of Westminster and his son and heir EDWARD V set out from his home at Ludlow Castle accompanied by his younger brother RICHARD, DUKE OF YORK, and their uncle ANTHONY WOODVILLE, and headed for London to be proclaimed King. They never made it. Their party was ambushed at Stony Stratford by their other uncle, Edward IV's brother Richard of Gloucester. Woodville was escorted away, to be beheaded later, and the princes were eventually put in the Tower of London 'for their own safety'.

Princes in the Tower

At first, the two princes were often seen playing in the Tower gardens. Then Richard of Gloucester set about discrediting the princes' mother Elizabeth Woodville, declaring that Edward IV had already been engaged to another, Lady Eleanor Butler, and therefore his marriage to Elizabeth was null and void and their children illegitimate.

After this the princes were confined to an inner room and seen less and less frequently. The occasional appearance of a white, boyish face at a window confirmed the boys were still alive, and their doctor reported that he had seen them but that they seemed to be living in constant fear. Then their uncle Richard became King Richard III and the princes were never seen again.

In 1674 workmen restoring a staircase to the chapel in the White Tower discovered the skeletons of two children buried in an elm chest, about 10 ft (3 m) below the floor. The bones were examined and declared to be the remains of Edward V and his brother. The king at the time, Charles II, had Sir Christopher Wren design a marble casket and the children were reburied in Innocents' Corner in Westminster Abbey.

It is thought that the princes were smothered with a pillow while sleeping, probably in the tower set in the curtain wall behind Traitors' Gate, later known as the Bloody Tower.

Henry VIII

r. 1509–1547

HENRY VIII is arguably England's most famous king and the most colourful royal villain. He was born in Greenwich Palace in 1491, the second son of Henry VII and Elizabeth of York, and became Prince of Wales at the age of ten, when his older brother Prince Arthur died at Ludlow.

Henry was crowned at Westminster Abbey in 1509 and within two months, in accordance with his father's dying wishes, married his brother's widow, CATHERINE OF ARAGON, the daughter of the Spanish king. They would be married for 24 years.

From then on, most of Henry's reign was devoted to the pursuit of a son and heir, for which he married six times, unleashed the Reformation, split England from the Church of Rome and the authority of the Pope for the first time since the Synod of Whitby in 664, established the Church of England, and initiated the Dissolution of the Monasteries.

Act of Supremacy

Catherine of Aragon failed to provide Henry with a son. Although she bore six children, only one survived, her daughter MARY. Henry began to believe the marriage was cursed because Catherine was his brother's widow, and in 1527 he sought an annulment from the Pope. The Pope refused, so Henry dismissed the chancellor who had failed him, Cardinal Wolsey, and in 1533 appointed a smart-thinking Cambridge lecturer called THOMAS CRANMER as Archbishop of Canterbury.

Later that year, at Dunstable Priory, Cranmer found a way to have Henry's marriage to Catherine annulled and Henry married ANNE BOLEYN, who gave birth to another daughter, ELIZABETH. The Pope then excommunicated Henry, and so in 1534 Henry passed the ACT OF SUPREMACY, which made him Supreme Head of the Church in England and gave him authority to begin the Dissolution of the Monasteries.

In 1536 Anne Boleyn was beheaded – ostensibly for adultery but in all likelihood for failing to have a son. The very next day Henry proposed to JANE

Dissolution of the Monasteries was THE BIGGEST LEGALISED TRANSFER OF PROPERTY IN ENGLAND SINCE THE NORMAN CONQUEST.

SEYMOUR, and a mere ten days after Anne's execution they were married. In 1537 Jane gave Henry the son he craved, but she herself died of post-natal fever a fortnight later.

Next Henry tried an arranged marriage with ANNE OF CLEVES, known as the 'Mare of Flanders', but she was too ugly for him, and so after three months he divorced Anne and married her maid of honour, the buxom CATHERINE HOWARD. When Henry learned that Catherine was far from chaste he sent her to the Tower, where she was beheaded. Henry's sixth wife was CATHERINE PARR, who nursed him through his final years.

When Henry died, his body was laid to rest at one of the abbeys he had destroyed, Syon Abbey by the River Thames at Brentford, before being taken for burial at Windsor. The abbot of Syon had cursed Henry, foretelling that dogs would one day lick at his blood, and indeed that night his corpse, bloated and pustulous from his final years of dissolute living, burst open, spilling blood and guts on to the ground, which were gleefully lapped up by the household hounds.

Dissolution of the Monasteries

Between 1536 and 1540 over 800 monasteries were effectively nationalised, their income acquired by the King, their buildings and estates either demolished, abandoned or given to the King's supporters, and the monks pensioned off or retained to serve in the new cathedrals and parish churches. The

Mary I

r. 1553–1558

MARY, the daughter of Henry VIII and his first wife Catherine of Aragon, was born at Greenwich in 1516. Humiliated and declared illegitimate by her father when he divorced Catherine, Mary grew up defiantly Catholic and resisted all attempts to convert her. In Henry's last years he relented and made Mary

WALTHAM ABBEY in Essex was the unlikely cradle of the English Reformation. In the summer of 1529 THOMAS CRANMER, a lecturer at Cambridge University, was staying in Waltham Abbey with his relatives the Cressys when two of Henry VIII's counsellors, EDWARD FOXE and DR GARDINER, the King's secretary, paid a visit. They were trying to find a way of legitimising Henry's divorce from Catherine of Aragon and fell into conversation with Cranmer, who suggested that the matter should be decided by 'the Word of God, which is above the Church and above the Pope'. King Henry was delighted with this idea and three years later he appointed Cranmer Archbishop of Canterbury, with a mandate to make sure the Word of God came up with the right answer. One unfortunate consequence of this meeting in Waltham Abbey was the Dissolution of the Monasteries, which would result in the destruction of most of Waltham Abbey itself – but Henry VIII was so grateful to Waltham that he made it THE LAST MONASTERY IN ENGLAND TO BE DISSOLVED.

QUEEN OF ENGLAND TO BE CROWNED IN HER OWN RIGHT.

Joy turned to anger, however, when Mary declared her intention to marry the Catholic PRINCE PHILIP OF SPAIN, son of the holy Roman Emperor Charles V. Thomas Wyatt, a minor nobleman, raised a Protestant rebellion against the marriage, and although Mary's sister Elizabeth had nothing to do with it, Mary imprisoned her in the Tower of London, lest she become a focus of Protestant unrest.

the rightful heir if her brother Edward VI should die childless. Edward's attempt to disinherit Mary and install LADY JANE GREY on the throne was thwarted and Mary was proclaimed as the rightful Queen. She was crowned in Westminster Abbey on 1 October 1553, amidst much rejoicing, THE FIRST

Bloody Mary

On 25 July 1554, Mary married Philip of Spain in Winchester Cathedral, making Philip THE ONLY SPANISH KING OF ENGLAND. Mary immediately set about returning England to Roman Catholicism. In the next three years she had 287 leading Protestants and architects of the Reformation, including Archbishop Cranmer, burnt at the stake for heresy, most of them at Smithfield in London and often with Mary looking on. These persecutions earned her the name BLOODY MARY.

Immediately after Cranmer's death Mary appointed REGINALD POLE, a grand-nephew of Edward IV, as Archbishop of Canterbury.

In the meantime Philip's father abdicated and Philip went back to Spain to be crowned King of Spain. He never returned to England. He did, however, drag England into war with France, which resulted in the loss of Calais, England's last possession in France. This did not endear him to his English subjects, or to Mary, who declared that when she was dead they would find the word 'Calais' engraved on her heart.

Saddened by her husband's lack of interest and her own inability to produce a Catholic heir, Mary died at St James's Palace on 17 November 1558. Cardinal Pole died on the same day – THE LAST ROMAN CATHOLIC ARCHBISHOP OF CANTERBURY.

Well, I never knew this about
ROYAL VILLAINS

When ETHELRED THE UNREADY returned to England in 1014, his progress into London was blocked by Danish forces who occupied London Bridge. So Ethelred, aided by King Olaf of Norway, sailed up the Thames, tied his fleet to the wooden supports of the bridge and rowed away, pulling the bridge down behind him, thus prompting the nursery rhyme 'London Bridge is falling down . . .'

In 1170 HENRY II had his eldest surviving son, Henry, crowned, THE ONLY HEIR TO THE ENGLISH THRONE TO BE CROWNED IN HIS FATHER'S LIFETIME. This

was common practice amongst French kings as a way of ensuring the succession. Young Henry became known as HENRY THE YOUNG KING, to distinguish him from his father, but he died in 1183 at the age of 28, predeceasing his father and leaving his brother Richard (Lionheart) as heir to the throne.

KING JOHN demonstrated his boorishness by reportedly giggling throughout his coronation service at Westminster Abbey, which he left before receiving the Sacrament.

KING JOHN only ever built three castles, and of those his favourite was ODIHAM, in Hampshire, halfway between Winchester and Windsor. It was completed in 1214, and it was from here the following year that John rode out to seal Magna Carta at Runnymede. KING DAVID II of Scotland was imprisoned here by Edward III for much of his 11 years in captivity after being defeated at the Battle of Neville's Cross in 1346. Odiham Castle has THE ONLY OCTAGONAL KEEP IN ENGLAND, the shell of which survives and can be visited.

King John is condemned to be remembered only for his negative qualities, and most notably as the villain of the Robin Hood tales. In these he is perhaps most associated with NOTTINGHAM CASTLE, the base of his evil henchman the Sheriff of Nottingham, and indeed, in 1212, while he was in conflict with the Welsh prince Llywelyn the Great, and in perfect keeping with his cruel reputation, John had 12 young Welsh hostages hanged from the ramparts of Nottingham Castle.

SWINESHEAD, where King John indulged in a surfeit of peaches after losing his Crown Jewels in the Wash, was the birthplace of HERBERT INGRAM (1811–60), founder of the *Illustrated London News*.

In 1535, as part of his plan to anglicise the Church, Henry VIII authorised the GREAT BIBLE, which was prepared by MILES COVERDALE and was THE FIRST AUTHORISED EDITION OF THE BIBLE IN ENGLISH – although it included the work of WILLIAM TYNDALE who had completed the translation into English of the New Testament in 1524. Henry ordered that the Great Bible be read aloud in Church of England services.

ST BENET'S ABBEY in Norfolk was THE ONLY MONASTERY IN BRITAIN NOT TO BE DISSOLVED DURING THE DISSOLUTION OF THE MONASTERIES. Instead, Henry VIII exchanged it for lands owned by the diocese of Norwich.

There is only one statue of Henry VIII in London. It stands above the gateway of St Bartholomew's Hospital in London – Henry refounded the hospital after the dissolution of St Bartholomew's Priory.

Henry VIII was THE FIRST MONARCH TO BE ADDRESSED AS 'YOUR MAJESTY' rather than 'Your Highness'.

Henry VIII made himself THE FIRST ENGLISH KING OF IRELAND – formerly English Kings were known as Lord of Ireland.

Henry VIII was THE LAST MONARCH TO FOUND A CAMBRIDGE COLLEGE. In 1546 he endowed what is now the UNIVERSITY'S LARGEST COLLEGE, TRINITY COLLEGE, and his statue still gazes benevolently down from the college gatehouse.

Henry VIII was responsible for more executions at the Tower of London than any other monarch.

CHAPTER FOURTEEN

ROYAL ROGUES

EADWIG ✦ HENRY II ✦ CHARLES II ✦ GEORGE I
✦ GEORGE IV ✦ WILLIAM IV ✦ EDWARD VII
✦ EDWARD VIII

Charles II

Since royal history began, mistresses have been an occupational hazard for kings, despite the fact that illegitimate children can play havoc with an orderly succession. HENRY I, for instance, fathered 29 ILLEGITIMATE CHILDREN, MORE THAN ANY OTHER ENGLISH KING, and yet lost his only legitimate son and heir Prince William in the wreck of the *White Ship* off Barfleur, leading to years of anarchy while his daughter Matilda and nephew Stephen battled it out for the throne.

There are perhaps four kings known

not to have had at least one mistress: Charles I, George III, George V and George VI. Henry VIII got round the problem by having six wives. Some royals, however, have been less restrained.

Eadwig

r. 955–959

The Saxon KING EADWIG of Wessex, a great-grandson of Alfred the Great, was only 15 when he became King. At his coronation dinner at Kingston, Eadwig was caught by Dunstan, the pious Archbishop of Canterbury, indulging in a threesome with his future wife and mother-in-law, and was dragged ignominiously back to the celebrations by his ear. In a fury, Eadwig had Dunstan exiled, and would probably have done much more damage if he had lived long enough. However, he died suddenly in October 959 and was succeeded by his popular younger brother EDGAR, who would go on to be crowned the first King of England.

Henry II

r. 1154–1189

Where HENRY II found the courage to defy his redoubtable wife Eleanor of Aquitaine and embark upon an affair with ROSAMUND CLIFFORD, whose father owned Clifford Castle near Hay-on-Wye on the Welsh border, is unclear. However, it would lead to his downfall, for Eleanor turned all their sons against him, and their plotting eventually lost the family their empire, which stretched from Scotland to the Pyrenees.

Fair Rosamund, as she became known, was born in the beautiful black-and-white timbered Manor Farm in Frampton-on-Severn in Gloucestershire, where the village green, covering 22 acres (9 ha) and THE LONGEST VILLAGE GREEN IN ENGLAND, is called ROSAMUND'S GREEN. She may have been baptised at the rare Norman lead font in St Mary's Church, one of only 38 left in England.

Henry met Rosamund while walking along the banks of the Thames at GODSTOW, near Oxford, where she was studying at the nunnery. He instantly fell in love with her and carried her off to his palace at Woodstock where, according to legend, he built a bower for her, hidden in an impenetrable maze. His jealous Queen Eleanor found her way through the maze by following a loose silken thread from Rosamund's dress that had been caught in one of Henry's spurs, and furiously challenged her rival to either drink poison or 'get thee to a nunnery!'

Godstow

Rosamund chose the nunnery, and returned to Godstow where she had been educated. She died not long afterwards in 1176 and was buried there in a magnificent tomb before the high altar, which every day was strewn with flowers sent by Henry. In 1191 the high-minded Bishop Hugh of Lincoln visited Godstow and ordered 'that Harlot's body' to be removed to a smaller chapel so that 'other women, warned by her example, may refrain from unlawful love'.

The small chapel where she ended up is roofless now, and is all that remains of the nunnery. 'Fair Rosamund' is said to haunt the famous Trout hostelry just across the River Thames, appearing as a White Lady and smelling of the heather which lined her tomb.

Although there is nothing left of

Rosamund's bower at Woodstock, the site of it, in the park across the lake from Blenheim Palace, is marked by a stone pillar. Not far from the bridge over the lake is ROSAMUND'S WELL, fed by a spring that has never been known to dry up since the time when Rosamund lived there in her bower.

Charles II

r. 1660–1685

CHARLES II was the doyen of royal womanisers, known to have had at least 14 MISTRESSES, MORE THAN ANY OTHER BRITISH KING. His activities actually produced a number of the members of the present Royal Family.

Charles got to work early. In 1640, while staying with his sister Mary and her husband William of Orange at The Hague, he began an affair with a Welsh girl called LUCY WALTER, by whom he had a son, who would grow up to be the DUKE OF MONMOUTH. Lucy Walter claimed that Monmouth was legitimate because she and Charles had secretly married, and Monmouth later made a bid to take the throne from his uncle James II, but was defeated at the Battle of Sedgemoor in 1685.

Charles's reign as king was the polar opposite of the dour and joyless Commonwealth of Oliver Cromwell that had preceded it. The fun-loving Charles had a string of mistresses by whom he had numerous children to whom he gave dukedoms.

By BARBARA VILLIERS he had Charles Fitzroy, 2ND DUKE OF CLEVELAND, Henry Fitzroy, 1ST DUKE OF GRAFTON, and George Fitzroy, 1ST DUKE OF NORTHUMBERLAND. Diana, Princess of Wales was a descendant of Barbara Villiers, through Henry Fitzroy.

By his French mistress LOUISE DE KEROUAILLE he had Charles Lennox, 1ST DUKE OF RICHMOND. Sarah, Duchess of York, Camilla, Duchess of Cornwall, and Princess Diana are all descendants of Charles and Louise.

By his favourite mistress of all, NELL

GWYN, he had Charles Beauclerk, 1ST DUKE OF ST ALBANS.

Prince William, grandson of Elizabeth II, is likely to be the first monarch descended directly from Charles II, through his mother Diana, Princess of Wales, who was descended from two of Charles II's illegitimate children, the Duke of Grafton and the Duke of Richmond.

George I

r. 1714–1727

GEORGE I brought his mistresses with him when he arrived from Hanover to take over the British throne. Twenty years earlier he had divorced his wife SOPHIA and locked her up for the rest of her life in Ahlden Castle, after she had admitted to a scandalous affair. George forbade his children ever to see her, which turned his son, the future George II, against his father for ever. George also secretly arranged to have Sophia's lover done away with.

To compensate for the loss of his wife, George took up with two completely mismatched mistresses. One, EHRENGARD MELUSINE VON DER SCHULENBURG, was so tall and thin she was named 'The Maypole'. The other, George's illegitimate half-sister SOPHIA VON KIELMANSEGG, was short and dumpy and known as 'The Elephant'. Both mistresses stayed with George for life, and after his death in 1727 The Maypole carried around with her a pet raven, which she believed to be George's reincarnation.

George IV

r. 1821–1830

GEORGE IV got things a little muddled and in 1785, while still Prince of Wales, he actually married his mistress, the twice-widowed MARIA FITZHERBERT, at her house in Mayfair's Park Street. Their marriage was doubly illegal, because firstly, Maria was a Roman Catholic and hence barred from succeeding to the throne, and secondly, George failed to get the King's permission for the marriage, as required by the Royal Marriages Act of 1772.

Caroline of Brunswick

In 1795, in order to pay off his debts, Prince George was forced into an arranged marriage with his unattractive and unhygienic cousin CAROLINE OF BRUNSWICK – on their first meeting George was so shaken he turned to Lord Malmesbury and whispered audibly, 'I am not well, pray get me a glass of brandy.'

Marble Hill House

After Prince George reluctantly married Caroline of Brunswick, Mrs Fitzherbert retired to live in MARBLE HILL HOUSE, a simple Palladian villa set back from the River Thames in 66 acres (27 ha) of beautiful parkland near Richmond. It was a rather appropriate place for her to go, having been built in the 1720s as a royal pay-off to Henrietta Howard, Countess of Suffolk, a former mistress of George II.

Mrs Fitzherbert's exile was only temporary, as Prince George soon dismissed Caroline and spent as much time as he could enjoying the delights of Marble Hill, before they both eventually moved down to Brighton, where George built her a house on the sea front near his exotic Pavilion.

William IV

r. 1830–1837

WILLIAM IV would have liked to marry his mistress, the Irish actress DOROTHY JORDAN, but he knew he would never get permission from his strait-laced father George III to marry an actress. So they just lived together and had ten children, who were all given the surname FITZCLARENCE. Prime Minister David Cameron is a descendant of William IV and Dorothy Jordan through their 3rd daughter Elizabeth Hay, Countess of Errol.

Edward VII

r. 1901–1910

EDWARD, or 'Bertie' as he was known, from his first name Albert, was a disappointment to his strict parents, lacking in a sense of duty, and was kept away from any role in government throughout his mother's reign. Being sociable and well liked, he threw himself into a life of gambling, horse-racing and the theatre and had a string of affairs with actresses, the first being NELLIE CLIFDEN, who was smuggled into Edward's tent while he was on manoeuvres with the Grenadier Guards in Ireland. Prince Albert was very distressed when he heard of the affair. He hurried off to Cambridge, where Edward was studying, and they had a long talk while walking in the rain. Soon afterwards Prince Albert died of typhoid, and Queen Victoria subsequently blamed her husband's death on Bertie.

Marriage

Edward married Princess Alexandra of Denmark in 1863, and it proved a happy marriage despite Bertie's continued affairs, notably with the actresses LILLIE LANGTRY and SARAH BERNHARDT, and with ALICE KEPPEL, the great-grandmother of Camilla, Duchess of Cornwall, whom he used to visit regularly at her home, Pleasure House in East Sutton, near Maidstone in Kent.

Alice Keppel

Scandal

Edward was also involved in two embarrassing scandals, which led to him being THE FIRST MEMBER OF THE BRITISH ROYAL FAMILY TO BE CALLED AS A WITNESS IN COURT. In 1869 Lady Harriet Mordaunt named Edward as one of her lovers, and her husband Sir Charles Mordaunt, MP, threatened to

name Edward in his divorce suit. In 1891 Edward was embroiled in the Royal Baccarat Scandal during which the Prince of Wales was found to have been involved in an illegal card game at Tranby Croft in Hull, the home of Arthur Wilson of the Wilson shipping line.

Edward VIII

r. 1936

EDWARD VIII was the only British monarch who gave up his throne for his mistress. She was WALLIS SIMPSON and was on her second marriage when she met the then Prince of Wales. Edward seemed to favour married women. His most prominent mistress before Wallis Simpson was FREDA DUDLEY WARD, wife of the Liberal MP William Dudley Ward. The Dudley Wards lived in a lovely house called Monksbridge by the River Thames at Sunbury, and Edward used to rent a cottage nearby as a cover for their dalliances. The couple were often seen taking a dip in the river together, and in the garden of Monksbridge there is still a topiary bear created by Edward as a love token for Freda.

*Well, I never knew this
about*
ROYAL ROGUES

HENRY II had two acknowledged illegitimate children, GEOFFREY PLANTAGENET, who became Archbishop of York, and WILLIAM LONGSPEE, who became Earl of Salisbury. Neither of them was by his principal mistress Rosamund.

While on the run after the Battle of Worcester in 1651, CHARLES II spent a lot of time in hostelries. One of them was WHITTINGTON MANOR, north of Kidderminster, once the home of London mayor Dick Whittington's grandfather and now the Whittington Inn. Queen Anne later spent a night there in 1711, and her seal can be seen on the oak front door of the house, ONE OF ONLY TWO OF QUEEN ANNE'S ROYAL SEALS IN BRITAIN.

While he was in exile during the Commonwealth, Charles II spent some time in the Channel Islands. In 1649 the staunchly Royalist Governor of Jersey, Sir George Carteret, had Charles proclaimed King in St Helier's Royal Square, making Jersey THE FIRST PLACE IN BRITAIN TO RECOGNISE CHARLES II AS KING. Later, in return, Charles gave Carteret a land grant in the New World, where he founded what became the state of NEW JERSEY.

One lady who refused to become a mistress of Charles II was FRANCES STUART, DUCHESS OF RICHMOND AND LENNOX. Known as La Belle Stuart, she was the model for the portrait of Britannia as she appears on British coins, currently to be seen on the reverse of the 50 pence coin.

The only partner by whom Charles II had no children was his wife, the Portuguese princess CATHERINE OF BRAGANZA. However, she did help to bring something just as important into Charles's kingdom – tea. Portugal was the first European country to import tea, from China, and Catherine did much to make it fashionable.

The first person to be knighted by a Hanoverian monarch was the architect and playwright SIR JOHN VANBRUGH, who was knighted by George I in 1714.

Such was GEORGE IV's reputation with the women, even when he was old and immensely fat, that he became the butt of much ribaldry, including the famous rhyme: 'Georgie Porgie, pudding and pie, kissed the girls and made them cry. When the boys came out to play, Georgie Porgie ran away.'

In his declining years and after a glass or two of brandy, George IV, who likened himself to Napoleon, would often regale his dinner guests with the story of how he had single-handedly won the Battle of Waterloo – among the guests on one famous occasion was the man who actually had won the Battle of Waterloo, the DUKE OF WELLINGTON.

WILLIAM IV was 64 when he became King, THE OLDEST PERSON EVER TO ACCEDE TO THE BRITISH THRONE, and he relished every moment of it – when he was woken up to be told that his brother had died, he rushed back to bed declaring that he had been longing to sleep with a Queen.

GEORGE V, despairing of his dissolute son the future Edward VIII, claimed, 'After I am dead, the boy will ruin himself in 12 months.' And so Edward did, abdicating the throne less than 11 months after his father's death.

In 1936 Edward VIII became THE FIRST BRITISH MONARCH TO FLY IN AN AEROPLANE when he flew from Sandringham to London to be proclaimed King in St James's Palace.

CHAPTER FIFTEEN

ROYAL STICKY ENDS

ENGLISH ✦ SCOTTISH ✦ BRITISH

Perhaps one of the reasons that Elizabeth II has managed to become the longest living British monarch of all time is that she doesn't have to lead her troops into battle, as most of her predecessors did – GEORGE II WAS THE LAST BRITISH MONARCH TO LEAD HIS MEN INTO BATTLE, at the BATTLE OF DETTINGEN in 1743, during the War of Austrian Succession, when he was aged 60.

JAMES IV OF SCOTLAND WAS THE LAST BRITISH MONARCH TO DIE IN BATTLE

when he was killed at the BATTLE OF FLODDEN FIELD in 1513.

RICHARD III WAS THE LAST ENGLISH MONARCH TO DIE IN BATTLE, at the BATTLE OF BOSWORTH FIELD in 1485, the action that ended the Wars of the Roses.

Nor does Queen Elizabeth face the prospect of being murdered by a rival claimant to the throne, like Richard II or Henry VI, or a family member, like Edward the Martyr or Edward V – although in 1981 she did survive an assassination attempt in the Mall when Marcus Sarjeant fired six blanks at her as she was riding to the Trooping the Colour ceremony.

And taking into account the fact that the Queen is reputed to survive on a diet of Malvern Water and organic Duchy Original produce from Prince Charles's farm at Highgrove, she is unlikely to die of strong drink like Harthacanute and George IV, or from a surfeit of lampreys like Henry I, or a surfeit of peaches like King John or, indeed, a surfeit of fruit like poor George I.

However, as a keen rider, Queen Elizabeth *is* at risk of falling off her horse, which is what did for three of her predecessors, Alexander III of Scotland, William the Conqueror and William III.

However, many of her ancestors have not been so fortunate and have come to a very sticky end.

English Sticky Ends

King Edwin of Northumbria (r. 616–633) – died in battle

EDWIN gave his name to Edinburgh (Edwin's Burgh), which lay at the northernmost border of his kingdom. He was THE FIRST CHRISTIAN KING OF NORTHUMBRIA and was baptised in a little wooden church where York Minster, THE LARGEST MEDIEVAL CATH-EDRAL IN NORTHERN EUROPE, now stands. The well from which the water came for Edwin's baptism can still be seen in the crypt of York Minster.

Edwin was killed at the BATTLE OF HATFIELD CHASE, fought against the heathen King Penda of Mercia somewhere in the forests on the Northumbrian border, near Cuckney, in what is now Nottinghamshire. His body was carried away from the scene by his supporters and buried in a clearing to conceal it from Penda. When they returned to carry Edwin off to his final resting place in Whitby Abbey, his followers raised a wooden chapel over the place, which became 'Edwin's Holy Place', or EDWINSTOWE.

In 1175 the wooden chapel was replaced by a stone church and it was in this 'church in the forest', St Mary's at Edwinstowe, that ROBIN HOOD AND MAID MARIAN WERE SAID TO HAVE BEEN MARRIED.

King Oswald of Northumbria (r. 634–642) – died in battle

OSWALD was responsible for converting to Christianity, at Dorchester-on-Thames, KING CYNEGILS OF WESSEX,

THE FIRST CHRISTIAN KING OF THE LINE FROM WHICH OUR PRESENT ROYAL FAMILY DESCEND, hence QUEEN ELIZABETH'S FIRST CHRISTIAN ANCESTOR. In 642 Oswald was killed fighting the heathen King Penda of Mercia (him again) at the Battle of Maserfield on the Welsh border. The place where he fell became known as Oswald's Tree, now OSWESTRY. Oswald soon came to be regarded as a saint and miracles occurred around the tree. His relics were taken to BARDNEY ABBEY in Lincolnshire and, in 909, were removed from the threat of Viking raids to a new church in Gloucester, renamed ST OSWALD'S PRIORY in his honour.

Aethelbald of Mercia (r. 716–757) – murdered

AETHELBALD, self-styled Rex Britanniae, or King of the Britons, ruled for an incredible 41 years before he was

murdered by his own men at SECKINGTON, near his seat of power at Tamworth. The murder was probably orchestrated by his eventual successor Offa who, perhaps to allay suspicion, organised a lavish funeral for Aethelbald at Repton.

The superb Saxon crypt at REPTON, with its swirling pillars and dusty arches, that served as the mausoleum of the Mercian kings, survives remarkably intact beneath St Wystan's Church. Built on Aethelbald's orders around 750, it has, alas, been stripped of the jewels and treasures that would have lined the alcoves and shelves, but nonetheless remains one of the most thrilling and atmospheric ancient places in England.

In 850 WYSTAN, to whom the church is dedicated, was murdered by his own bodyguard before he could inherit the crown of Mercia, and was buried in the crypt. Miracles were ascribed to his remains, and the crypt became a place of pilgrimage. Wystan was later made a saint and his relics were moved to the abbey at Evesham by King Canute in the 11th century.

Repton's market cross, heavily restored, is said to mark the spot where King Peada, son of the powerful pagan King Penda, was converted to Christianity in 653, thus bringing Christianity to Mercia.

St Edmund the Martyr, King of East Anglia (r. 855–870) – died in battle

EDMUND gave himself up to the Danish Great Heathen Army to save his kingdom from further slaughter.

Refusing to denounce his Christian faith, he was tied to a tree and shot through with arrows. His grave at Bury St Edmunds became a shrine, and many historians regard St Edmund as the true Patron Saint of England.

His body was later found by Elfrida's servants, following the bloody trail, and the wicked Queen had Edward buried without ceremony in WAREHAM.

Soon, miracles were being attributed to Edward by visitors to his simple grave in Wareham, and in 980 Dunstan had Edward's remains transferred to SHAFTESBURY ABBEY. In 1008 Edward was made a saint.

When Shaftesbury Abbey was dissolved by Henry VIII in 1539, Edward's casket was hidden out of harm's way, and lay undiscovered for nearly 400 years, until an archaeological investigation of the site in 1931 uncovered the crude casket containing his bones.

In 1984 adherents to the Christian Orthodox faith in England, attached to the Russian Orthodox Church in Exile, took possession of Edward's bones and had them enshrined in a chapel of the St Edward Brotherhood in BRITAIN'S LARGEST CEMETERY, the BROOKWOOD CEMETERY in Woking, Surrey.

Edward the Martyr (r. 975–978) – murdered

While hunting in Purbeck Forest, the 16-year-old EDWARD stopped off for refreshment at CORFE CASTLE in Dorset, the home of his stepmother Elfrida and her son, his half-brother Ethelred. While downing the proffered cup of wine, Edward was brutally stabbed, probably by someone in the pay of his wicked stepmother, and his horse bolted, with Edward still on its back.

Badly wounded, Edward eventually fell from the saddle and was dragged along the ground for miles to a spot on the road to Wareham marked today by a little house called St Edward's Cottage.

Harthacanute (r. 1040–1042) – surfeit of drink

HARTHACANUTE, son of Canute, was responsible for the heavy taxes that prompted Lady Godiva to ride naked through the streets of Coventry in protest. He died of a seizure after a drinking bout.

Harold II (r. 1066) – died in battle

HAROLD, the last Saxon King of England, was killed while fighting the forces of William the Conqueror at the Battle of Hastings. After the battle Harold's body was claimed by both his mother and his wife Edith Swan Neck, but no one knows for sure where he was taken. There is a tradition that he is buried at WALTHAM ABBEY in Essex.

Waltham Abbey was originally founded in 1030 to house a piece of the Holy Cross found at Montacute in Somerset by Tovi, standard bearer to Canute. Harold, it was said, had been cured of a crippling illness by praying before this cross, and so he had richly endowed and extended the abbey and stopped to pray there on his way to meet William at Hastings. After Hastings some say his corpse was carried back to Waltham and secretly buried beneath the high altar.

In 1120 Harold's abbey was demolished and replaced by a huge Norman building that was at one time as long as Norwich Cathedral. What remains is considered to possess THE FINEST NORMAN NAVE IN THE SOUTH OF ENGLAND. Harold's gravestone can now be found outside the east wall where the high altar of his church once stood.

William I (the Conqueror, r. 1066–1087) – fell off his horse

WILLIAM I died in France, after falling from his horse during an attack on Nantes. He was buried in St Stephen's Abbey in Caen, THE FIRST KING OF ENGLAND TO BE BURIED ABROAD. During his funeral his bloated body burst open the sarcophagus, emitting a foul stench.

William II (r. 1087–1100) – hunting accident

On 2 August 1100, WILLIAM RUFUS was hunting in the forest with friends when a deer broke cover and startled them. A knight called WALTER TIREL loosed off an arrow, which missed the deer and glanced off an oak tree, hitting William in the chest and wounding him fatally. Tirel rode off, crossing the River Avon at a spot now called Tyrell's Ford, and escaped to safety in France, while the rest of William's party went to find the King's brother Henry who, fortuitously, was hunting elsewhere in the forest.

Henry, instead of pursuing Tirel, went swiftly to Winchester to secure the royal treasury and then rode on to London, where he was crowned Henry I, just three days after his brother's death.

William's body was left where it had fallen until found some time later, apparently by a local charcoal burner called Purkis, who hoisted it on to the back of his cart and trundled it into Winchester. William II, the second Norman king, was buried beneath the central tower of Winchester Cathedral without a single mourner present, a testimony to his unpopularity. The following year the tower fell down.

The story of William's death is inscribed on a stone memorial erected by Earl de la Warr in 1745 near where the incident occurred. Known as the RUFUS STONE, it stands in a clearing about 1 mile (1.6 km) north of the village of MINSTEAD – where SIR ARTHUR CONAN DOYLE, creator of Sherlock Holmes, the one man who might have been able to solve this royal mystery, lies buried beneath an oak tree in the churchyard.

Henry I (r. 1100–1135) – surfeit of lampreys

HENRY I died in 1135 in Normandy, apparently from food poisoning caused by a 'surfeit of lampreys' (a small eel-like fish). He was taken back to England and

buried in a silver coffin before the high altar of the great abbey he had founded at Reading as a royal mausoleum.

Henry had founded READING ABBEY in 1121 on high ground between the River Kennet and the Thames. He presented it with a valuable relic, the 'Hand of St James', which had been given to him by his daughter Matilda, who was married to the Holy Roman Emperor, and this ensured that the abbey became rich as a place of pilgrimage, with an abbey church almost the size of Durham Cathedral.

In 1359, at Reading Abbey, Edward III's son JOHN OF GAUNT married Blanche, daughter of the Duke of Lancaster, thus founding the LANCASTRIAN ROYAL DYNASTY. Their son became Henry IV.

In 1453 the abbey hosted a meeting of Parliament, and in 1464 EDWARD IV brought his secret new bride ELIZABETH WOODVILLE to the abbey for a thanksgiving service.

Reading Abbey was almost totally destroyed at the Dissolution of the Monasteries, but Henry I's burial place is marked among the ruins by a plaque.

Somewhere nearby lies his daughter the Empress Matilda, and at his feet lies his great-grandson William of Poitiers, first son of Henry II.

Berkshire's county town is not famous for its antiquities, and the ruins of the great abbey, which can be explored, come as something of a surprise, hidden away behind the town's bustling commercial centre. Only the inner gateway, home of the Abbey School, attended by Jane Austen, remains intact.

church, is the lion heart of England's warrior king Richard Coeur de Lion.

Edward I (r. 1272–1307) – died of dysentery

It was while travelling north to Scotland to confront the rebellious Scottish king Robert the Bruce that EDWARD I met his end. In 1307 he held a parliament in Carlisle Cathedral before riding away on his white horse to punish Robert the Bruce for his insolence.

Richard I (r. 1189–1199) – died in battle

RICHARD I died while fighting at Chalus in France, when he was struck by an infected arrow. Historians will tell you that Richard I's lion heart is buried in Rouen Cathedral. Some believe, however, that his heart was smuggled out of France and buried beneath the lady chapel that Richard had built at All Hallows by the Tower in London. The lady chapel has gone, but it could be that, buried under the flagstones of the tiny garden beneath the east window of London's oldest

He made it as far as the windswept marshes of Burgh-by-Sands, on the Solway Firth, just south of the border by Hadrian's Wall, before succumbing to dysentery and dying in the arms of his faithful earls. Today, a lonely monument stands tall in the empty fields, far from the road, on the bleak spot where Edward, Hammer of the Scots, breathed his last. A plaque at its base reads:

> Edward I fought a long bitter
> campaign to conquer Scotland
> Old and sick he made camp
> on these marshes whilst
> Preparing to subdue his
> enemy Robert the Bruce
> Edward died here on July 7 1307

It is a melancholy, yet strangely moving place, imbued with the defiant spirit of England's most formidable and unquenchable medieval king. Despite requesting that his son, Edward II, carry his bones with the army until the Scots had been subdued, Edward I was buried in Westminster Abbey.

Eleanor of Castile – died of fever

When Edward I's beloved wife ELEANOR OF CASTILE succumbed to a fever at Harby in Nottinghamshire in 1290, Edward was inconsolable, declaring, 'I loved her dearly during her lifetime and I shall not cease to love her now she is dead.' Eleanor was taken to Lincoln to be embalmed and then by a slow procession to Westminster Abbey, where she lies near the Coronation Chair. At each place where the Queen's coffin rested overnight Edward had memorial crosses set up, the last of which gave its name to Charing Cross, in London. Only three of the original 12 crosses survive, at Geddington, Northampton and Waltham.

Edward II (r. 1307–1327) – murdered

On 21 January 1327, in the Great Hall at Kenilworth Castle, EDWARD II was forced

to renounce the throne in favour of his son Edward – THE FIRST TIME A KING OF ENGLAND HAD BEEN DETHRONED SINCE ETHELRED THE UNREADY in 1013. The deposed Edward was then removed to Berkeley Castle in Gloucestershire.

Berkeley Castle

BERKELEY CASTLE was built in the early 12th century, on the site of a Saxon fortification and Norman motte and bailey, by the de Berkeleys, ONE OF ONLY THREE FAMILIES IN ENGLAND WHO CAN TRACE THEIR ROOTS DIRECTLY BACK TO THEIR SAXON ANCESTORS. It is THE OLDEST HOUSE IN ENGLAND STILL INHABITED BY THE FAMILY THAT BUILT IT.

Unlike most British castles, Berkeley survived the Civil War intact and it is still possible to stand in the room where one of the most foul murders in royal history was perpetrated.

On a dark September night in 1327, as the mist rolled in off the River Severn, shrouding the grey walls of the castle in a ghostly hue, two men crept into the cell where the toppled King Edward II was sleeping fitfully and hauled him from his bed. They taunted the King for his homosexuality, put flowers in his hair, and finally inserted a red-hot poker deep into his bowels, laughing as the King died in agony.

The murderers, Sir Thomas de Gurney and Sir John Maltravers, were sent by Edward's estranged queen Isabella and her lover Roger Mortimer to dispose of the King without leaving a mark. Since they had deposed Edward in favour of his son Edward III, Isabella and Mortimer had been hoping Edward would starve to death, but he had refused to co-operate and stronger measures were called for.

The following morning Edward's corpse was displayed for all to see and England was convulsed with horror. The Abbot of Gloucester came in reverence to claim the body and Edward III, shocked by the cruelty of his father's murder, built a grand tomb for him in the Abbey of St Peter in Gloucester, now Gloucester Cathedral.

Richard II (r. 1377–1399) – murdered

Deposed by his cousin Henry of Lancaster (Henry IV), whose lands he had seized, RICHARD II was imprisoned in Pontefract Castle in Yorkshire. Rather as his great-grandfather Edward II had been, Richard, while still alive, was an embarrassment to his successor, and in 1400 he was found in his cell dead from starvation. There are still a few traces to be seen of the Gascoigne Tower at Pontefract in which he languished.

After his body had lain in state in Old St Paul's Cathedral, to prove that he was dead, Richard II was buried in the friary beside the royal palace at KING'S LANGLEY in Hertfordshire, the home of his uncle, Edmund of Langley, but was later moved to Westminster Abbey.

Henry VI (r. 1422–1461 and 1470–1471) – murdered

After being defeated at the Battle of Tewkesbury by the Yorkist King Edward IV, the last Lancastrian King HENRY VI was thrown into the Tower of London. On 21 May 1471 he was found dead behind a painted timber screen in an oratory on the upper floor of the WAKEFIELD TOWER, on the inner curtain wall just behind Traitors' Gate. Yorkist history states that Henry died of melancholy after hearing of the death of his son Edward at Tewkesbury. It was widely believed, though, even at the time, that Henry was murdered by Richard, Duke of Gloucester (later Richard III) on the orders of Richard's brother Edward IV.

Henry was buried inside the Lady Chapel at Chertsey Abbey beside the River Thames in Surrey, but his tomb rapidly became a place of pilgrimage, and in 1484 Richard III decided it would be wise to move the body to St George's Chapel at Windsor Castle, where it would be out of the public gaze.

Edward V (r. 1483) – murdered

EDWARD V and his brother Richard, Duke of York, were sent to the Tower of London and never seen again, presumed murdered by their uncle, Richard of Gloucester, who ascended Edward's throne as Richard III.

Richard III (r. 1483–1485) – died in battle

RICHARD III died at the Battle of Bosworth Field in 1485. He was THE LAST PLANTAGENET KING and THE LAST ENGLISH KING TO DIE IN BATTLE. Richard spent the night before the battle in the Blue Boar Inn in Leicester, the site of which is now marked with a plaque. As he rode out to Bosworth over the River Soar, his spur caught a stone on the parapet of Bow Bridge and an old woman who was watching predicted that soon his lifeless head would be dashed against the same stone. She was right. At the end of the battle Richard's body was stripped naked, tied to the back of a horse and dragged back into Leicester, where it hung on the parapet of Bow Bridge for two days before being buried in Greyfriars Church.

At the Dissolution of the Monasteries Richard's body was dug up and flung into the River Soar, but his bones were later recovered and buried somewhere near Bow Bridge, not far from the burial place of Leicester's mythical founder King Leir.

There is a memorial to Richard III in Leicester Cathedral.

Lady Jane Grey (r. 1554) – beheaded

LADY JANE GREY, placed on the throne against her will by her father-in-law the Duke of Northumberland, reigned for only nine days before she was deposed by Henry VIII's rightful heir Mary I. On 12 February 1554, Jane was beheaded in her private apartments in the Tower of London. An observer at the scene wrote of the pathetic moment when Jane, a handkerchief tied across her eyes, had to grope to find the block on which to rest her head.

Scottish Sticky Ends

Scottish kings didn't have it any easier than their English counterparts. Indeed, THE VERY FIRST RECOGNISED KING OF THE SCOTS, KENNETH MACALPIN (r. 834–858) set the tone, securing his throne by inviting all his Pictish rivals to a banquet at their own Pictish capital of Scone. There he sat them on specially prepared benches that on his signal collapsed and sent his unfortunate opponents plunging into a pit full of sharpened stakes.

Tanistry

The early Scottish kings also had to contend with the LAW OF TANISTRY, introduced by Kenneth MacAlpin's son DONALD I (r. 858–863). Under tanistry a King's heir was elected during the King's lifetime from members of his family, usually a brother. As most kings didn't live for very long in those days, this prevented the succession going to a child, but it did also have the unfortunate drawback of encouraging the different branches of the family to kill off possible successors from the other branches.

Kenneth II (r. 971–995) – murdered by an Infernal Machine

A great-great-grandson of Kenneth MacAlpin, KENNETH II died in a most unusual way. In 995 he went to stay with Finella, the daughter of the Earl of Angus, at her castle near Fettercairn in Kincardineshire. Kenneth had earlier condemned Finella's son to death, and she was thirsting for revenge, but instead of allowing her anger to show she pretended to be reconciled with the King and threw a lavish banquet for him. In honour of the occasion she even had a statue of Kenneth made, representing him as a Greek god bearing a golden apple in his hand.

Kenneth was naturally flattered, and when Finella invited him to take the apple as a gift, he willingly plucked it from the statue's hand. It was the last thing he ever did. Finella had concocted a booby trap, designed so that when the apple was removed a golden arrow would shoot out and pierce the heart of whomsoever had taken it. Her 'infernal machine' worked to perfection, and so died King Kenneth II.

Duncan I (r. 1034–1040) – died in battle

DUNCAN I was killed by his cousin Macbeth at the Battle of Elgin in 1040. Duncan was not, in fact, murdered in his bed by Macbeth, as Shakespeare would have us believe, although the Bard's portrayal of the scheming Lady Macbeth is possibly quite accurate. Lady Macbeth's brother, a claimant to the throne, had been murdered by Malcolm II so that his own grandson Duncan could succeed, and this was Lady Macbeth's motive for encouraging Macbeth to topple Duncan.

Macbeth (r. 1040–1057) – died in battle

MACBETH was himself killed, by Earl Macduff, on behalf of Duncan's son Malcolm Canmore (Big Head or Chief). After being defeated by Malcolm at Dunsinane, near Dunkeld in Perthshire, Macbeth went on the run, but he was eventually caught at LUMPHANAN on Deeside in Aberdeenshire. There he was slain by Earl Macduff, who presented Malcolm with Macbeth's head on a stake in nearby Kincardine O'Neil, the oldest village on Deeside.

A cairn ringed with trees on a farmland slope just to the north of Lumphanan is said to mark the spot where Macbeth was buried. Not far away is the stone where he fell, and the well at which he took his last drink. It is a cold and sorrowful spot, hard to reach and steeped in melancholy.

Malcolm III Canmore (r. 1058–1093) – died in battle

MALCOLM III also died a violent death. It was his own fault really. Despite signing the Treaty of Abernethy with William the Conqueror in 1072, in which Malcolm and the English King agreed a truce, secured by William keeping Malcolm's son Duncan as a hostage, Malcolm kept making incursions into English territory. While returning from a harrying of Northumbria, Malcolm was ambushed near Alnwick Castle and killed, along with another son Edward. A cross, just to the north of Alnwick, marks where they fell.

Alexander III (r. 1249–1286) – fell off his horse

ALEXANDER III died while galloping along the cliff tops in a storm to see his new wife Yolande at Kinghorn in Fife. He was thrown from his horse and fell to his death on the beach below.

Alexander had been married to Margaret, sister of Edward I of England, and had established good relations with his brother-in-law, even attending Edward's coronation in Westminster Abbey in 1274, along with Margaret. Six months later Margaret died, leaving Alexander with three children.

Tragically for Scotland, in the early 1280s all three children died within a short time of each other, so Alexander married again in 1285, but fell off his horse before he could father another heir.

A Celtic cross, set up beside the road at Pettycur, near Kinghorn, by the Jacobite Earl of Mar, marks exactly the spot from where Alexander III fell to his death.

Maid of Norway – died young, from sea-sickness

And so it happened that Alexander's heir was his granddaughter MARGARET, the daughter of King Eric of Norway. Known as the MAID OF NORWAY, she was only three years old at the time of Alexander's death and living in Norway, so various other claimants to the Scottish throne began to come forward, including ROBERT BRUCE, grandfather of the future Robert I (the Bruce) and JOHN BALLIOL. Six guardians were appointed by the Scottish Parliament to look after Margaret's interests, and Edward I of England agreed to have his own son Edward (later Edward II) betrothed to Margaret and to act as her ward, while respecting Scottish independence.

In 1290, four years after Alexander's death, King Eric sent Margaret to Scotland to claim her throne but she died from the effects of sea-sickness after storms had driven her ship to seek shelter on Orkney. And with her ended the Royal Scottish House of Dunkeld.

Had Margaret lived, the thrones of England and Scotland would have been united 300 years earlier than they were. As it was, England and Scotland were plunged into war.

James Stewart

All the Scottish kings called James came to a sticky end, except for James VI who would go on to become Scotland's longest reigning monarch – and King of England to boot.

James I of Scotland (r. 1406–1437) – murdered

In February 1437 JAMES I and Queen Joan went to stay in the Black Friar's monastery in Perth. James had made Perth the centre of his royal court, and the effective capital of Scotland, holding several parliaments and councils there in Parliament Close, off the high street, in a building demolished in 1818.

Supporters of the Earl of Atholl, a legitimate son of King Robert II and a claimant for James's throne, broke into the monastery and began battering at the door to get at James and the Queen. James tried to escape by climbing down into a sewer beneath the tennis courts, while one of the Queen's ladies-in-waiting barred the door with her arm, in place of the bar, which had been secretly removed the night before by one of the plotters. Unfortunately, that very day James had ordered the sewer tunnel to be sealed off with a grill, to prevent tennis balls getting lost down there, and he was thus trapped – and hacked to death most foully.

Queen Joan, niece of Henry IV of England, fled to Stirling with their son, now James II. James I was buried in his beloved Perth.

James II of Scotland (r. 1437–1460) – blown up

In 1460 JAMES II decided to try and win back the border castle at Roxburgh, near Kelso, which had been in English hands for quite some years. The English garrison proved stubborn, so James called for his secret weapon, a great cannon called THE LION, with which he intended to reduce the stronghold to rubble. He bent down to train the gun and then fired it himself, but the weapon exploded and blew his leg off, causing the King to bleed to death on the spot – marked today by a holly tree in the grounds of FLOORS CASTLE, the present-day home of the Dukes of Roxburghe. Floors, a 17th-century tower house enlarged in 1721 by William Adam and then added to in 1840 by William Playfair, is THE LARGEST INHABITED CASTLE IN SCOTLAND.

James III of Scotland
(r. 1460–1488) – murdered

In 1488 JAMES III rode forth from Stirling Castle, brandishing the sword of Robert the Bruce, to confront his nobles, who had come to do battle in the name of James's heir the Duke of Rothesay (future James IV). With both sides flying the Royal Standard, they met at Sauchieburn, close to the site of the Battle of Bannockburn, and the King's men were routed.

James was forced to flee, but fell off his horse near Beaton's Mill and was carried into a hut, where he called for a priest. A man dressed as a priest

arrived, but instead of tending to the King's soul he drew a dagger and plunged it into James's heart. The King was succeeded by his son, who became James IV but was plagued by guilt for the rest of his days for having helped cause his father's death.

James III, and his queen, Margaret, were secretly buried in Cambuskenneth Abbey and forgotten about, until their tomb was rediscovered in 1865 under a blue marble slab in front of the high altar. They were reburied under a fine monument on the orders of Queen Victoria.

Cambuskenneth
Abbey

CAMBUSKENNETH ABBEY, located by the Forth below Abbey Craig, was named after Kenneth MacAlpin. It was founded by David I in 1147 and grew wealthy from its proximity to the royal court at Stirling. Robert the Bruce stored his reserves of arms in the abbey during Bannockburn, and then called

a parliament there in 1326 to acknowledge David II as his heir – THE FIRST SCOTTISH PARLIAMENT WHERE REPRESENTATIVES FROM THE BURGHS WERE RECORDED AS PRESENT.

The great campanile at Cambuskenneth, which is almost all that survives of the abbey, dates from the 14th century and is THE ONLY FREE-STANDING MEDIEVAL BELFRY LEFT IN SCOTLAND.

James IV of Scotland (r. 1488–1513) – died in Battle

JAMES IV became THE LAST BRITISH MONARCH TO DIE IN BATTLE when he was killed in 1513, along with 10,000 other Scots, including three bishops, 13 earls and the flower of the Scottish nobility, fighting against Henry VIII's men at the Battle of Flodden Field in Northumberland.

James V of Scotland (r. 1513–1542) – died of despair

When Henry VIII of England suggested to JAMES V OF SCOTLAND that he should follow Henry's example and break with the Church of Rome, James refused, declining to meet Henry in York to discuss the matter – and instead had a number of leading Scottish Protestants executed. The most high profile of these was PATRICK HAMILTON, nephew of the 2nd Lord Hamilton and SCOTLAND'S FIRST PROTESTANT MARTYR, who was burned at the stake in St Andrews in 1528. Hamilton took six hours to die because the fire burned out too quickly and he was left badly scorched, but alive. His agonising martyrdom ignited the first flames of the Scottish Reformation.

King Henry, who was not a forgiving man, responded by invading Scotland. James sent his army south to head him off and the Scots suffered a heavy defeat at the BATTLE OF SOLWAY MOSS in November 1542.

James, although not present at the battle, took the setback badly and retired to Falkland Palace with a high fever. As he lay on his deathbed he was told the awful news that his wife, Mary of Guise, had given birth to a daughter at Linlithgow. At that he turned his face to the wall and died.

Mary, Queen of Scots (r. 1542–1567) – beheaded

After being defeated at the Battle of Langside in 1568, MARY, QUEEN OF SCOTS fled to Dundrennan Abbey, where she was received by one of her few remaining supporters, Edward Maxwell, the Abbot of Dundrennan. Next morning she made her way down the burn to a creek on the Solway Firth, where she boarded a small fishing boat and sailed away to England, never to return.

As she stepped on to a rock to climb into the boat, Mary left her last footprint on Scottish soil and it is said that this footprint can still be seen when the rock is exposed at low tide. The lonely, desolate place is now called PORT MARY.

In England, however, Mary became the focus of numerous Catholic plots to unseat her cousin Elizabeth I, and after nearly 20 years of being held under house arrest in various castles and stately homes around the country,

Mary, who never actually met Elizabeth, was executed in the banqueting hall at Fotheringhay Castle in Northamptonshire in February 1587.

It took three strokes of the axe to remove Mary's head – after which came the pathetic discovery of the Queen's little terrier Geddon, covered in blood, hidden under her gown.

Mary's body lay at Fotheringhay for six months before it was taken by night to Peterborough Cathedral for burial.

British Sticky Ends

Charles I (r. 1625–1649) – beheaded

On the morning of 30 January 1649, after taking Communion in the Chapel Royal in St James's Palace, KING CHARLES I was escorted across St James's Park to the Banqueting House of Whitehall Palace, where a special scaffolding had been erected in preparation for the first and only official execution of a British monarch.

It was a bitterly cold morning and Charles had donned two shirts so that he wouldn't shiver from the cold and give the impression that he was shivering with fear.

At 2 p.m. Charles stepped out of the first floor of the Banqueting House on to the scaffolding, handed his gloves to Bishop Juxon (they can be seen in the library at Lambeth Palace), lay down, positioned himself and gave a pre-arranged signal for the axe to fall. His head was cut off with a single blow. The executioner held up the King's head and cried 'Behold the head of a traitor' – at which point a great groan went up from the crowd as they realised the enormity of what they had just witnessed.

Charles I was THE ONLY BRITISH MONARCH TO BE TRIED AND EXECUTED BY HIS OWN SUBJECTS.

William III (r. 1689–1702) – fell off his horse

In 1702 WILLIAM III broke his collarbone when his horse stumbled on a molehill while he was out riding at Hampton Court. He was taken back to Kensington Palace, but caught a chill while resting beside an open window, and died.

George I (r. 1714–1727) – surfeit of fruit

GEORGE I died in his beloved Hanover, in 1727, the immediate cause being a 'surfeit of fruit', which caused agonising diarrhoea. He was buried in Leinesschloss Church in Hanover.

George II (r. 1727–1760) – aneurysm

GEORGE II died of an aneurysm at Kensington Palace in October 1760 while sitting on the lavatory or, as Elizabeth I would have called it, his 'throne'.

George IV (r. 1821–1830) – died of drink

After a triumphant visit to Edinburgh, GEORGE IV, who was getting more rheumaticky and bloated with every passing day, virtually retired from public life and spent most his time at Windsor, where he died in June 1830 from what his doctor described as 'strong liquors taken too frequently and in too large quantities'.

Well, I never knew this about
ROYAL STICKY ENDS

William Rufus was not the only one of William the Conqueror's four sons to die in the New Forest. In 1081 the Conqueror's second son PRINCE RICHARD was killed in a hunting accident in the forest and then buried in Winchester Cathedral.

In 1240, JOHN OF FORNSETE, a monk at Reading Abbey where Henry I is buried, wrote down the music for a song called 'Sumer is icumen in' – THE FIRST EVER RECORDED ENGLISH SONG. A memorial plaque on the wall of the ruined chapter house displays a copy of the music, while the original manuscript, which was found amongst the leaves of an abbey journal, is now in the British Museum.

It was on a visit to PONTEFRACT CASTLE, where Richard II was starved to death,

that CATHERINE HOWARD, the fifth wife of Henry VIII, first committed adultery with THOMAS CULPEPER, an act that led her to the Tower of London and execution.

Pontefract Castle is now known across the world, for its image appears on the product for which the town of Pontefract is world famous – liquorice, which was once grown amongst the castle ruins.

The old Pictish capital of ABERNETHY, where Malcolm III signed a treaty with William the Conqueror in 1072, possesses ONE OF ONLY TWO IRISH-STYLE ROUND TOWERS IN SCOTLAND, the other being at Brechin. The quite beautiful, pencil slim tower at Abernethy is 75 ft (23 m) tall with Romanesque windows in the belfry which suggests that it was built, or at least remodelled, around the same time that the Treaty was being signed. A Pictish stone at the foot of the tower reflects Abernethy's importance as a Pictish stronghold.

Malcolm III's wife Margaret, who would later be canonised as Scotland's only royal saint, heard the news of the deaths of her husband and son while she was praying in her little wooden chapel on top of the rock at Edinburgh. She died soon afterwards, it is said of a broken heart. The little chapel was rebuilt by her son David I and ST MARGARET'S CHAPEL is now SCOTLAND'S SMALLEST ROYAL CHURCH, THE OLDEST BUILDING IN EDINBURGH and THE OLDEST ECCLESIASTICAL BUILDING STILL STANDING INTACT IN ALL SCOTLAND. Although restored, the chapel is virtually unchanged, the interior perfection, with a small nave, Romanesque chancel arch with chevron mouldings and a tiny sanctuary with apse.

Alexander III's death was foretold by a famous Scottish seer THOMAS THE RHYMER, the day before it occurred. 'On the morrow, afore noon, shall blow the greatest wind that ever was heard before in Scotland' – and indeed, not only did Alexander die in a storm, but his death precipitated Scotland into a crisis of hurricane proportions.

Famous Last Words

'It cam wi' a lass and it will gang wi' a lass' – 'it started with a girl and it will end with a girl' – JAMES V OF SCOTLAND, AT FALKLAND PALACE in 1542. As he lay on his deathbed James was told the news that his wife, Mary of Guise, had given birth to a daughter at Linlithgow. His last words were a mournful prophecy on the fate of the Stewart royal dynasty. He was right: the Stewarts had come in with the daughter of Robert the Bruce, Princess Marjorie, but ended, not with his daughter Mary, Queen of Scots, as James feared, but over 170 years later with Queen Anne, in 1714.

'All my possessions for a moment of time' – ELIZABETH I

'I shall go from a corruptible to an incorruptible Crown, where no disturbance can be' – CHARLES I, on the scaffold at Banqueting House in 1649.

'Let not poor Nellie starve' – CHARLES II, at Whitehall Palace in 1685.

'No, I shall not give in. I shall go on. I shall work to the end' – EDWARD VII

'My dear boy! This is death!' – GEORGE IV, at Windsor Castle in 1830.

'Bugger Bognor' – GEORGE V, at Sandringham in 1936. Purported response to his doctor's suggestion that he might feel better in the sea air at Bognor Regis.

Gazetteer

Interesting locations and places open to the public.
Please telephone or check websites for opening times
and admission costs which are subject to change.

CHAPTER ONE: QUEEN ELIZABETH II

BROADLANDS

Romsey, Hampshire SO51 9ZD
Currently undergoing
refurbishment
Tel: 01794 529750
www.broadlandsestates.co.uk

WHITE LODGE, RICHMOND

Richmond Park, Richmond,
Surrey TW10 5HR
Occupied by the Royal Ballet
School
Tel: 020 8392 8440
*www.royal-ballet-school.org.uk/
wl_museum*

ROYAL LODGE, WINDSOR

Windsor Great Park, Windsor,
Berkshire SL4 2HW
Not open to the public

CHAPTER TWO: ROYAL CELEBRATIONS & PAGEANTRY

DUNADD HILL FORT

4 miles north of Lochgilphead,
Argyllshire
Ancient Monument in the care of
Historic Scotland

CHAPTER THREE: ROYAL WESTMINSTER

WESTMINSTER ABBEY

20 Dean's Yard, London SW1P 3PA
Nearest underground: St James's
Park or Westminster
Tel: 020 7222 5152
www.westminster-abbey.org

PALACE OF WESTMINSTER

London SW1A 0AA
Nearest underground: Westminster
UK residents can visit Parliament
for free, including taking a tour of

the Chambers and Westminster Hall by contacting their MP. Paid tours are available for any visitors
www.parliament.uk

JEWEL TOWER (ENGLISH HERITAGE)

Abingdon Street, Westminster, London SW1P 3JX
Nearest underground: Westminster
Tel: 020 7222 2219
www.english-heritage.org.uk

ST JOHN'S SMITH SQUARE

London SW1P 3HA
Nearest underground: Westminster
Used as a concert venue. Contact box office for events
Box office tel: 020 7222 1061
www.sjss.org.uk

CHAPTER FOUR: ROYAL ST JAMES'S & WHITEHALL

BUCKINGHAM PALACE

London SW1A 1AA
Nearest underground: Green Park, Hyde Park Corner or Victoria
Tel: 020 7766 7300
www.royalcollection.org.uk

Royal Mews, Buckingham Palace
Tel: 020 7766 7302
www.royalcollection.org.uk

Queen's Gallery, Buckingham Palace
Tel: 020 7766 7301
www.royalcollection.org.uk

ST JAMES'S PALACE

Not open to the public except for services

CLARENCE HOUSE

Nearest underground: Green Park or St James's Park
Tel: 020 7766 7303
www.royalcollection.org.uk

MARLBOROUGH HOUSE

Pall Mall, London SW1Y 5HX
Nearest underground: Green Park
Tel: 020 7747 6491
www.thecommonwealth.org

BANQUETING HOUSE

Whitehall, London SW1A 2ER
Nearest underground: Westminster or Charing Cross
Tel: 0844 482 7777
www.hrp.org.uk/BanquetingHouse

ST MARTIN-IN-THE-FIELDS

Trafalgar Square, London WC2N 4JJ
Nearest underground: Embankment or Leicester Square
Tel: 020 7766 1100
www.smitf.org

CHAPTER FIVE: ROYAL LONDON

ST PAUL'S CATHEDRAL

St Paul's Churchyard, London EC4M 8AD
Nearest underground: St Paul's
Tel: 020 7246 8357
www.stpauls.co.uk

TOWER OF LONDON

London EC3N 4AB
Nearest underground: Tower Hill
Tel: 0844 482 7777
www.hrp.org.uk/TowerOfLondon

KENSINGTON PALACE

Kensington Gardens, London W8 4PX
Nearest underground: High Street
Kensington or Queensway
Tel: 0844 482 7777
www.hrp.org.uk/KensingtonPalace

ROYAL ALBERT HALL

Kensington Gore, London SW7 2AP
Nearest underground: South
Kensington or High Street
Kensington
Contact box office for events
Box office tel: 0845 401 5045
www.royalalberthall.com

ROYAL HOSPITAL, CHELSEA

Royal Hospital Road, London SW3 4SR
Nearest underground: Sloane
Square
Tel: 020 7881 5298
www.chelsea-pensioners.co.uk

CHAPTER SIX: ROYAL THAMES

HAMPTON COURT PALACE

Surrey KT8 9AU
Tel: 0844 482 7777
www.hrp.org.uk/
HamptonCourtPalace

KEW PALACE

Royal Botanic Gardens, Kew,
Richmond, Surrey TW9 3AB
Tel: 0844 482 7777
www.hrp.org.uk/KewPalace

GREENWICH PALACE

Greenwich, London SE10 9LW
Nearest station (DLR): Cutty Sark
Tel: 020 8269 4747
www.oldroyalnavalcollege.org

QUEEN'S HOUSE AND NATIONAL MARITIME MUSEUM, GREENWICH

Greenwich, London SE10 9NF
Nearest station (DLR): Cutty Sark
Tel: 020 8858 4422
www.nmm.ac.uk

CHAPTER SEVEN: ROYAL WINDSOR

WINDSOR CASTLE

Windsor SL4 1NJ
Tel: 020 7766 7304
www.royalcollection.org.uk

FROGMORE HOUSE

Windsor Home Park, Windsor
SL4 1NJ
Tel: 020 7766 7302
www.royalcollection.org.uk

CHAPTER EIGHT: ROYAL ENGLAND HOMES & PALACES

SANDRINGHAM HOUSE

Sandringham, Norfolk PE35 6EN
  Tel: 01485 545408
  www.sandringhamestate.co.uk

HIGHGROVE

Nr Doughton, Tetbury,
  Gloucestershire GL8 8PH
  Tel: 020 7766 7310
  www.highgrovegardens.com

OSBORNE HOUSE
(ENGLISH HERITAGE)

The Avenue, East Cowes, Isle of
  Wight PO32 6JX
  Tel: 01983 200022
  www.english-heritage.org.uk

ROYAL PAVILION

Brighton BN1 1EE
  Tel: 03000 290900
  *www.brighton-hove-rpml.org.uk/
  RoyalPavilion*

HATFIELD PALACE

Hatfield, Hertfordshire AL9 5NQ
  Tel: 01707 287010
  www.hatfield-house.co.uk

CLARENDON PALACE

2 miles east of Salisbury, Wiltshire

CLAREMONT LANDSCAPE GARDEN
(NATIONAL TRUST)

Portsmouth Road, Esher, Surrey
  KT10 9JG
  Tel: 01372 467806
  www.nationaltrust.org.uk

ELTHAM PALACE
(ENGLISH HERITAGE)

Court Yard, Eltham, Greenwich,
  London SE9 5QE
  Tel: 020 8294 2548
  www.english-heritage.org.uk

CLIVEDEN
(NATIONAL TRUST)

Taplow, Maidenhead,
  Buckinghamshire SL6 0JA
  Tel: 01494 755562
  www.nationaltrust.org.uk

FISHBOURNE ROMAN PALACE

Roman Way Road, Fishbourne,
  Chichester, West Sussex PO19 3QR
  Tel: 01243 789829
  www.sussexpast.co.uk

PEVENSEY CASTLE

Castle Road, Pevensey, East Sussex
  BN24 5LE
  Tel: 01323 762604
  www.english-heritage.org.uk

CHAPTER NINE: ROYAL ENGLAND, BIRTHS, BURIALS & BETWEEN

ST AUGUSTINE'S ABBEY, CANTERBURY (ENGLISH HERITAGE)

Monastery Street, Canterbury, Kent
CT1 1PF
Tel: 01227 767 345
www.english-heritage.org.uk

CANTERBURY CATHEDRAL

Canterbury, Kent CT1 2EH
Tel: 01227 762862
www.canterbury-cathedral.org

WINCHESTER CATHEDRAL

9 The Close, Winchester, Hampshire
SO23 9LS
Tel: 01962 857200
www.winchester-cathedral.org.uk

GREAT HALL, WINCHESTER

Castle Avenue, Winchester,
Hampshire SO23 8PJ
Tel: 01962 846476
www.hants.gov.uk/greathall

WORCESTER CATHEDRAL

College Yard, Worcester WR1 2LA
Tel: 01905 732900
www.worcestercathedral.co.uk

GLOUCESTER CATHEDRAL

College Green, Gloucester GL1 2LX
Tel: 01452 528095
www.gloucestercathedral.org.uk

TEWKESBURY ABBEY

Tewkesbury, Gloucestershire GL20 5RZ
Tel: 01684 850959
www.tewkesburyabbey.org.uk

HEVER CASTLE

Hever, Nr Edenbridge, Kent TN8 7NG
Tel: 01732 865224
www.hevercastle.co.uk

LEEDS CASTLE

Maidstone, Kent ME17 1PL
Tel: 01622 765400
www.leeds-castle.com

QUEEN ELIZABETH'S HUNTING LODGE

Rangers Road, Chingford,
Essex E4 7QH
Tel: 020 8529 6681
www.cityoflondon.gov.uk

KING'S COLLEGE CHAPEL

Cambridge CB2 1ST
Tel: 01223 331212
www.kings.cam.ac.uk

WIMBORNE MINSTER

Wimborne, Dorset BH21 1HT
Tel: 01202 884753
www.wimborneminster.org.uk

ALLERTON CASTLE

Allerton Park, Knaresborough, North
Yorkshire HG5 0SE
Tel: 01423 331123
www.allertoncastle.co.uk

CHAPTER TEN: ROYAL SCOTLAND – PRESENT

PALACE OF HOLYROODHOUSE

Canongate, The Royal Mile,
Edinburgh EH8 8DX
Tel: 0131 556 5100
www.royalcollection.org.uk

BALMORAL CASTLE

Ballater, Aberdeenshire AB35 5TB
Tel: 013397 42534
www.balmoralcastle.com

BIRKHALL

Not open to the public

CASTLE OF MEY

Thurso, Caithness KW14 8XH
Tel: 01847 851473
www.castleofmey.org.uk

CHAPTER ELEVEN: ROYAL SCOTLAND – PAST

EDINBURGH CASTLE

Castlehill, Edinburgh EH1 2NG
Tel: 0131 225 9846
www.edinburghcastle.gov.uk

STIRLING CASTLE

Castle Esplanade, Stirling, FK8 1EJ
Tel: 01786 450 000
www.stirlingcastle.gov.uk

SCONE PALACE

Perth PH2 6BD
Tel: 01738 552300
www.scone-palace.co.uk

LINLITHGOW PALACE
(HISTORIC SCOTLAND)

Linlithgow, West Lothian EH49 7AL
Tel: 01506 842896
www.historic-scotland.gov.uk

FALKLAND PALACE
(NATIONAL TRUST FOR SCOTLAND)

Falkland, Cupar, Fife KY15 7BU
Tel: 0844 493 2186
www.nts.org.uk

QUEEN MARY'S HOUSE, JEDBURGH

Queen Street, Jedburgh TD8 6EN
Tel: 01835 863331
www.scotborders.gov.uk

LOCHLEVEN CASTLE
(HISTORIC SCOTLAND)

Kinross KY13 8UF
Tel: 01577 862670
www.historic-scotland.gov.uk

GLAMIS CASTLE

Angus DD8 1RJ
Tel: 01307 840393
www.glamis-castle.co.uk

IONA
(HISTORIC SCOTLAND)

Argyllshire PA76 6SQ
Tel: 01681 700512
www.isle-of-iona.com

ROTHESAY CASTLE
(HISTORIC SCOTLAND)

Isle of Bute PA20 0DA
Tel: 0131 668 8600
www.historic-scotland.gov.uk

TRAQUAIR HOUSE

Innerleithen, Peeblesshire, EH44 6PW
Tel: 01896 830323
www.traquair.co.uk

CHAPTER TWELVE:
ROYAL WALES

PENMYNYDD

Anglesey, North Wales LL61
Plas Penmynydd is not open to
the public. To visit church contact
Friends of St Gredifael
Tel: 01248 712988

PEMBROKE CASTLE

Pembroke, Pembrokeshire SA71 4LA
Tel: 01646 684585
www.pembroke-castle.co.uk

OFFA'S DYKE

Offa's Dyke Centre, Knighton, Powys
LD7 IEN
Tel: 01547 528753
www.offasdyke.demon.co.uk

CADW
(WELSH HISTORIC MONUMENTS)

Tel: 01443 33 6000

FLINT CASTLE
(CADW)

Flint, Flintshire, North Wales
www.cadw.wales.gov.uk

RHUDDLAN CASTLE
(CADW)

Hylas Lane, Rhuddlan,
Denbighshire LL18 5
Tel: 01745 590777
www.rhyl.com/rhuddlan

CONWY CASTLE
(CADW)

Conwy, Caernarfonshire, North Wales
Tel: 01492 592358
www.conwy.com

HARLECH CASTLE
(CADW)

Harlech, Merioneth
Tel: 01766 780552
www.harlech.com

BEAUMARIS CASTLE
(CADW)

Beaumaris, Anglesey, North Wales
Tel: 01248 810361
www.beaumaris.com

CAERNARFON CASTLE
(CADW)

Caernarfon, Caenarfonshire,
North Wales
Tel: 01286 677617
www.caernarfon.com

LLWYNYWERMOD

Llandovery, Carmarthenshire
www.princeofwales.gov.uk

ABERCONWY HOUSE
(NATIONAL TRUST)

Castle Street, Conwy, Caenarfonshire,
   North Wales LL32 8AY
   Tel: 01492 592246
   www.nationaltrust.org.uk

CHAPTER THIRTEEN: ROYAL VILLAINS

RUNNYMEDE
(NATIONAL TRUST)

Old Windsor, Surrey
   Tel: 01784 432891
   www.nationaltrust.org.uk

ODIHAM CASTLE (HAMPSHIRE
COUNTY COUNCIL)

Off Tunnel lane, North
   Warnborough, Odiham,
   Hampshire
   Tel: 0845 603 5636
   www.hants.gov.uk

NOTTINGHAM CASTLE

Nottingham NG2 3NG
   Tel: 0115 915 3700
   www.mynottingham.gov.uk

CHAPTER FOURTEEN: ROYAL ROGUES

GODSTOW ABBEY

Wolvercote, near Oxford, Oxfordshire

BLENHEIM PALACE

Woodstock, Oxfordshire OX20 1PP
   Tel: 01993 810 500
   www.blenheimpalace.com

MARBLE HILL HOUSE
(ENGLISH HERITAGE)

Richmond Road, Twickenham,
   London TW1 2NL
   Tel: 020 8892 5115
   www.english-heritage.org.uk

CHAPTER FIFTEEN: ROYAL STICKY ENDS

ST WYSTAN

Repton, Derbyshire
   Tel: 01283 702159
   www.reptonchurch.org.uk

CORFE CASTLE
(NATIONAL TRUST)

Corfe Castle, Wareham,
   Dorset BH20 5EZ
   Tel: 01929 481 294
   www.nationaltrust.org.uk

WALTHAM ABBEY

www.walthamabbeychurch.co.uk

READING ABBEY

36 Kings Road, Reading,
   Berkshire RG1 4AE
   Tel: 0845 765 4321
   www.readingmuseum.org.uk

BERKELEY CASTLE

Berkeley, Gloucestershire GL13 9PJ
   Tel: 01453 810332
   www.berkeley-castle.com

PONTEFRACT CASTLE

Castle Chain, Pontefract WF8 1QH
   Tel: 01977 723440
   www.wakefield.gov.uk

FLOORS CASTLE

Kelso, Roxburghshire TD5 7SF
   Tel: 01573 223 333
   www.roxburghe.net

CAMBUSKENNETH ABBEY
(HISTORIC SCOTLAND)

Cambuskenneth, Stirling, Stirlingshire
   Tel: 0131 668 8600
   www.historic-scotland.gov.uk

Index of People

Aberdeen, Lord 113
Adam, Robert 54
Adam, William 180
Addington, Henry 7
Adelaide, Princess 39, 41, 66
Adelaide, Princess Mary 7
Adelaide, Queen 60, 83
Aethelbald of Mercia, King 169
Aidan, King 14
Aiton, William 37
Albany, Duke of 120, 122, 124
Albert Victor, Prince 74, 85
Albert, Duke of York 7, 78
Albert, Prince 7, 36, 39, 41, 54, 76, 77, 83, 84, 87, 107, 111, 112, 113, 114, 115, 163
Alexander I 14, 122, 123
Alexander II 120
Alexander II, Tsar 40
Alexander III 168, 178, 179, 184
Alexandra, Princess 38, 163, 164
Alexandra, Queen 18, 41, 42, 85
Alfred the Great 17, 19, 61, 81, 82, 97, 147
Alice, Princess 8
Althorp, Viscount 94
Amelia, Princess 7, 66
Andrew, Prince 2, 8, 25, 118
Anne of Bohemia 27, 65, 102, 106
Anne of Cleves 31, 32, 63, 65, 68, 105, 154
Anne of Denmark 6, 69
Anne, Princess 2, 25, 38, 40, 66, 94, 95, 109

Anne, Queen 4, 26, 28, 33, 38, 39, 47, 52, 64, 70, 81, 109, 165, 184
Archer, Thomas 33
Arlington, Earl of 35
Armstrong-Jones, Anthony 25
Arne, Thomas 92
Arthur of Brittany, Prince 80, 149
Arthur, Duke of Connaught 40, 78, 94
Arthur, King 73, 80, 98
Arthur, Prince of Wales 47, 98, 99, 141, 153
Astor, William Waldorf 105
Astors 92
Athelstan 16, 83
Atholl, Earl of 179
Augusta, Princess 40, 66, 67, 93
Augustine, St 96
Austen, Jane 45, 173

Badlesmere, Bartholomew de 105
Baldwin, Stanley 78
Balliol, John 14, 79, 179
Banks, Joseph 67
Barrie, J. M. 83, 116
Barry, Sir Charles 92
Beatrice, Princess 38
Beauclerk, Charles, Duke of St Albans 162
Beaufort, John, Duke of Somerset 108
Beaufort, Margaret 132
Beck, Anthony 91
Becket, Thomas 147, 148

Black Prince 19, 97, 140, 143
Blair, Tony 9
Blake, William 51
Blore, Edward 36
Boleyn, Anne 32, 38, 43, 49, 50, 60, 68, 104, 105, 106, 153
Boleyn, Mary 104
Bolingbroke, Lord 109
Bonnie Prince Charlie 112, 124, 130
Borrow, George 133, 134
Bothwell, Earl of 111, 112, 125
Boudicca, Queen 80, 81
Bowes, Mary 127
Boyle, Henry, Baron Carleton 42
Bradford, John 57
Bramah, Joseph 95
Brewster, Sir David 116
Bridgeman, Charles 91
Brihtnoth 146
Brown, Capability 91
Brown, John 114
Brown, Sir Samuel 89
Bruce, Robert 179
Bruce, Sir William 112
Buckingham, Duke of 35, 92
Burgundy, Duke of 129
Bute, 3rd Earl of 7
Butler, Lady Eleanor 152
Butler, RAB 95
Byron, Lord 113

Caithness, Earl of 115
Cambridge, Duke of 53
Cameron, David 9, 163
Canute, King 98, 108, 146, 147, 169, 171
Capability Brown 67, 70
Caroline of Ansbach 28, 66
Caroline of Brunswick 22, 39, 42, 162, 163
Caroline, Princess 66
Caroline, Queen 7, 88
Carrick, John, Earl of 79
Carteret, Sir George 165
Catherine de Valois 27, 106, 131, 132
Catherine Howard 154
Catherine of Aragon 32, 47, 62, 68, 103, 105, 153, 154, 155
Catherine of Braganza 60, 64, 165
Cecil, Robert, Earl of Salisbury 90
Cenwahl 97

Cerdic 81
Charles I 5, 6, 9, 18, 21, 30, 31, 39, 44, 45, 62, 63, 64, 74, 81, 83, 93, 104, 111, 120, 122, 124, 159, 182, 185
Charles II 4, 6, 14, 19, 20, 37, 39, 45, 54, 55, 56, 60, 64, 69, 76, 77, 79, 104, 112, 122, 129, 152, 159, 161, 162, 165, 185
Charles, Prince of Wales 2, 13, 20, 47, 52, 66, 86, 94, 114, 115, 116, 139, 140, 142
Charlotte, Princess 41, 42, 77, 91
Charlotte, Queen 7, 35, 39, 66, 67, 77, 83
Chichester, Sir Francis 68
Chirac, Jacques 6
Churchill, Sir Winston 31
Clarence, George, Duke of 103
Clark, Sir James 115
Claudius 5
Clifden, Nellie 163
Clifford, (Fair) Rosamund 160, 161
Clive of India 91
Cobham, Sir John de 105
Coggan, Donald 105
Cogidubnus 94
Conan Doyle, Sir Arthur 83, 172
Cook, Captain James 67
Cornwall, Duchess of 93, 114, 115, 116, 161
Courtauld, Samuel 95
Courtaulds 92
Coverdale, Miles 157
Cowper, Charles Spencer 84
Cox, Judge 95
Cranmer, Archbishop Thomas 63, 153, 155, 156
Crevecoeur, Robert de 105
Crichton, Sir William 120
Croft, Sir Richard 91
Cromwell, Oliver 14, 17, 18, 19, 20, 31, 55, 65, 83, 108, 161
Cromwell, Thomas 49
Cubitt, Thomas 86
Culpeper, Thomas 183
Cumberland, Duke of 78, 87, 124
Cynegils of Wessex 168, 169

Dafydd, ap Llyewlyn 135, 136
Darnley, Lord 104, 111, 112, 118
David I 79, 91, 111, 119, 123, 180, 184
David II 112, 120, 157
David, King of Israel 17

De Montfort, Simon 30
Defoe, Daniel 122
Diana, Princess of Wales 24, 25, 39, 44, 47, 51, 86, 94, 161, 162
Douglas, Earl of 122
Douglas, George 125, 126
Douglas, Janet 127
Douglas, Sir William 125, 126
Douglas, William 125, 126
Downshire, Lady 88
Drake, Sir Francis 68
Drayson, Lord 95
Dudley Ward, Freda 164
Dudley Ward, William 164
Duncan I 128, 177
Duncan, King 126
Duncan, Prince 178
Dunstan, Archbishop 160, 170

Eadred 16
Eadred, Archbishop of York 21
Eadward the Martyr 16
Eadweard the Elder 16
Eadwig of Wessex 159, 160
Ecgfrith 21
Edgar 16, 17
Edgar, King 22, 120, 160
Edmund of Langley 101, 102, 103
Edmund the Magnificent 16
Edward I 14, 15, 27, 49, 56, 64, 79, 105, 107, 120, 134, 137, 138, 139, 142, 143, 173, 174, 178, 179
Edward II 30, 91, 99, 101, 102, 105, 122, 139, 140, 141, 179, 174, 175
Edward III 12, 30, 32, 56, 57, 65, 73, 91, 98, 102, 106, 157, 175
Edward IV 9, 10, 30, 57, 73, 74, 92, 102, 103, 152, 156, 172, 175
Edward of Middleham 141
Edward of Westminster 2, 102, 140, 141
Edward the Confessor 17, 19, 24, 25, 26, 27, 28, 30, 34, 100, 107
Edward the Martyr 146, 167
Edward V 10, 17, 28, 50, 63, 152, 167, 176
Edward VI 28, 68, 106, 155
Edward VII 18, 19, 22, 31, 36, 41, 42, 74, 76, 80, 84, 85, 86, 87, 108, 114, 115, 142, 144, 163

Edward VIII 1, 7, 17, 20, 77, 78, 85, 142, 164, 166
Edward, Prince of Wales 7, 54
Edwin, King of Northumbria 120
Egbert of Wessex, King 62
Egbert, King 97, 107
Eleanor of Aquitaine 148, 160
Eleanor of Castile 27, 102, 105, 139, 174
Eleanor of Provence, Queen 90
Elfrida 146
Elizabeth I 6, 9, 17, 18, 19, 28, 34, 39, 50, 65, 68, 71, 76, 79, 81, 90, 104, 106, 108, 109, 153, 181, 182
Elizabeth II 11, 13, 16, 17, 19, 25, 38, 40, 47, 61, 68, 71, 72, 76, 81, 83, 85, 86, 94, 95, 109, 110, 111, 114, 140, 167, 168
Elizabeth of York 10, 28, 59, 68, 153
Elizabeth Woodville 152, 172
Elizabeth, Queen Mother 8, 9, 31, 32, 40, 41, 44, 115, 116
Emma, Queen 146
Eric of Norway, King 179
Esledes 105
Essex, Richard Devereux, Earl of 50
Ethelbert, King of Kent 47, 96, 97
Ethelfleda, Princess 100
Ethelred I 107, 108
Ethelred the Unready 16, 145, 146, 147, 156
Ethlred, King of Mercia 99

Ferdinand of Portugal, Prince 87
Fergus I 112
Ferguson, Sarah 25
Finella of Angus 177
Fisher, Cardinal John 49
Fitzherbert, Maria 88, 162, 163
Fitzroy, Charles, Duke of Cleveland 161
Fitzroy, George, Duke of Northumberland 161
Fitzroy, Henry, Duke of Grafton 161, 162
Flambard, Ranulf 49, 50
Foley, J. H. 54
Fornsette, John of 183
Fortrey, Samuel 66
Foxe, Edward 155
Franklin, Benjamin 116
Frederick, Duke of York 108
Frederick, Prince of Wales 42, 66, 71, 92, 93, 107, 141

Frideswalde, Princess 61
Fychan, Ednyfed 131

Gainsborough, Thomas 42
Gardiner, Dr 155
Gaunt, John of 172
Gaveston, Piers 102
Geddon 5
Geoffrey, Count of Anjou 78
Geoffrey, Duke of Brittany 149
George I 53, 60, 64, 70, 110, 162, 166, 168, 182
George II 7, 22, 28, 53, 57, 58, 60, 64, 66, 81, 162, 167, 183
George III 3, 7, 12, 35, 39, 45, 48, 57, 64, 66, 67, 71, 74, 76, 77, 80, 93, 95, 159, 163
George IV 4, 8, 22, 29, 35, 36, 37, 39, 40, 41, 42, 45, 57, 74, 76, 78, 87, 110, 112, 122, 162, 163, 166, 168, 183, 185
George of Denmark 39, 52
George V 1, 3, 19, 20, 31, 36, 37, 39, 41, 42, 74, 76, 78, 79, 85, 107, 111, 114, 159, 166, 185
George VI 1, 4, 7, 8, 9, 19, 31, 40, 74, 76, 78, 85, 114, 115, 159
George, Duke of Kent 78
George, Duke of York 7
Gibbons, Grinling 64, 76
Gibbons, Grinling 76
Gibbs, James 45
Gilbert, Sir Alfred 42
Gladsone, William 31
Glamis, Lord 126, 127
Gloucester, Duke of 53
Gloucester, Humphrey, Duke of 67
Glyndwr, Owain 137, 140
Godiva, Lady 170, 171
Godwinson, Harold 26
Gorbachev, Mikhail 129
Gordon, Sir Robert 113
Goring, Lord 35
Goring. Otto 32
Gowrie, Earl of 123
Graham, Sir Robert 122
Graves, Robert 87
Grey, Lady Jane 50, 60, 155, 176
Grey, Walter de 43
Gruffydd ap Llywelyn 135

Gundulf, Bishop of Rochester 49
Gurney, Sir Thomas de 175
Gwyn, Nell 45, 54, 75, 161, 162

Haakon IV 5, 128
Hamilton, Duke of 93
Hamilton, Patrick 181
Handel, Frideric 22, 58, 60
Harcourt, Robert 108
Hardy, Thomas 83
Harefoot, King Harold 58
Harington, Sir John 65
Harold II 17, 108, 171
Harry, Prince 13, 52, 86
Harthacanute, King 170, 171
Hawksmoor, Nicholas 31, 69
Hay, Elizabeth Hay, Countess of 163
Henrietta Maria, Queen 18, 39, 62, 64, 69, 81, 107
Henry I 5, 19, 49, 61, 64, 79, 100, 101, 159, 168, 171, 172, 173
Henry II 23, 61, 73, 90, 147, 148, 156, 160, 161, 165, 173
Henry III 12, 21, 26, 27, 31, 49, 50, 51, 73, 74, 90, 97, 101, 102, 103, 120, 134
Henry IV 21, 27, 31, 47, 49, 50, 94, 95, 97, 106, 137, 143, 172, 175
Henry V 19, 27, 47, 102, 106, 131, 132, 141, 142
Henry VI 28, 47, 50, 67, 74, 91, 106, 123, 132, 133, 140, 152, 167, 175
Henry VII 10, 27, 28, 47, 65, 67, 71, 74, 108, 132, 133, 152, 153
Henry VIII 29, 35, 38, 43, 49, 51, 59, 62, 65, 68, 74, 76, 90, 98, 101, 103, 104, 106, 148, 153, 154, 155, 157, 158, 159, 170, 181
Henry, Duke of Gloucester 78
Henry, Prince of Wales 6, 60, 122, 141
Henry, the Young King 157
Herschel, William 80
Hess, Rudolph 50
Hillary, Sir Edmund 9
Hilliard, Nicholas 90
Holbein, Hans 38
Holland, Henry 42, 87, 88
Hood, Robin 168
Howard, Catherine 32, 49, 50, 63, 183
Howard, Henrietta 163

Hugh, Bishop of Lincoln 160
Humbert, A. J. 85

Ingram, Herbert 157
Irving, Washington 28
Isabella, Queen 105, 175

James I 3, 4, 6, 12, 18, 21, 28, 34, 35, 37,
    39, 43, 50, 60, 63, 65, 68, 81, 90
James I of Scotland 80, 120, 123, 124, 179
James II 3, 19, 22, 39, 50, 81, 161
James II of Scotland 80, 111, 117, 120, 122,
    123, 129, 179, 180
James III of Scotland 80, 111, 120, 122,
    123, 180
James IV of Scotland 20, 65, 80, 111, 120,
    122, 123, 124, 129, 167, 181
James Stuart, Old Pretender 123
James V of Scotland 20, 80, 112, 117, 120,
    122, 123, 124, 127, 181, 184
James VI of Scotland 110, 112, 120, 121,
    122, 123, 124, 127, 128, 129, 179
James VII of Scotland 80
Jenner, Edward 116
Joan of Navarre, Queen 97, 106
Joan, Princess 143
Joan, Queen 179
John of Gaunt 47
John, Augustus 41
John, King 19, 21, 61, 79, 80, 98, 143,
    148–151, 157, 168
John, King of France 91
John, Prince 79
Jones, Inigo 6, 44, 68, 93
Jonson, Ben 6
Jordan, Dorothy 163
Jorry, Ulrich 53
Joyson-Hicks, Sir William 1
Judith, Princess 103
Juxon, Bishop 182

Keeler, Christine 92
Kenneth II 120, 177
Kent, Duchess of 8, 40, 53, 53, 77
Kent, Edward, Duke of 66
Kent, William 38, 42, 53, 91
Keppel, Alice 93
Keppel, George 93
Kerouaille, Louise de 161

Kielmansegg, Sophia von 162
King of Prussia 42
Kipling, Lockwood 87, 94
Kipling, Rudyard 83, 87, 116
Knox, John 122
Kray Ronnie 50
Kray, Reggie, 50

Lamb, Lady Caroline 42
Langton, Stephen 149, 150
Lawrence, Sir Thomas 76
Leir, King 176
Lennox, Duke of Richmond 161,
    162
Leopold, Prince 41, 42, 74, 77, 91
Leopold, Prince, Duke of Albany 91
Llywelyn ap Gruffudd 20, 134, 135, 136,
    140
Llywelyn the Great 137, 140, 141, 143, 157
Longspee, William 165
Louis IX 5
Lovat, Lord 50
Lulach 14
Lutyens, Sir Edwin 36, 83
Lyon, Sir John of Forteviot 126

MacAlpin, Kenneth 14, 15, 122, 127, 176,
    177, 180
Macbeth 14, 114, 126, 177, 178
Macbeth, Lady 177
Macduff 178
MacKinnon, John 130
Macmillan, Harold 86, 92
Macmillan, Maurice 86
Madelaine, Princess 124
Magnus Maximus 139
Malcolm II 126, 177
Malcolm III 114, 119, 178, 184
Malmesbury, Lord 162
Maltravers, Sir John 175
Mar, 6th Earl of 114
Mar, Earl of 120
Marain, Maid 168
Maredudd, Owain ap 131
Margaret of Anjou, Queen 67, 123
Margaret, Maid of Norway 179
Margaret, Princess 3, 9, 25, 53, 127
Margaret, Queen 119, 120, 178, 180
Marie Alexandrova 40

Marina of Greece, Princess 2
Marjorie, Princess 184
Marlborough, Duke of 48
Mary I 9, 28, 39, 50, 57, 63, 65, 68, 79, 90, 98, 105, 153, 154, 155, 156
Mary of Guise 117, 120, 122, 124, 181, 184
Mary of Modena 3
Mary of Teck, Princess 7, 39
Mary, Princess 7, 28
Mary, Queen 9, 31, 42, 83, 111
Mary, Queen of Scots 3, 20, 28, 68, 79, 103, 104, 111, 112, 117, 120, 122, 124, 125, 129, 181, 182, 184
Matilda, Empress 107, 159, 173
Matilda, Queen 98
Maugham, Somerset 83
Maxwell, Edward 181
May, Brian 13
McCartney, Paul 13
Mehemet 53
Merlin 142
Merrick, Joseph 23
Michael of Kent, Prince 53, 94, 95
Middleton, Kate 24, 32, 109, 110, 116, 131
Middleton, Pippa 24
Milne, A. A. 87
Monmouth, Duke of 50
Monmouth, Duke of 161
Mordaunt, Lady Harriet 164
Mordaunt, Sir Charles 164
More, Sir Thomas 49, 152
Mortimer, Roger 57
Mortimer, Roger 175
Morton, Cardinal 90
Mountbatten, Earl 77
Murray, Sir David 123
Mustapha 53

Napier, John 116
Napoleon, Emperor 38
Nash, John 8, 35, 39, 42, 88
Navarre, Joan of 31
Nelson, Admiral Lord 7, 71, 74
Newbury, Jack Oí 109
Newcastle, Duke of 91
Nicolls, Richard 4
Nightingale, Florence 115
Northumberland, Duke of 77, 176
Nottingham, Earl of 52

Offa, King 21, 133, 134, 169
Oglethorpe, James 81
Oliver, Isaac 90
Orwell, George 107

Paine, James 93
Palladiom Andrea 69
Parr, Catherine 32, 63, 154
Peade, King 169
Peel, Sir Robert 43
Pelham-Holles, Thomas, Earl of Clare 91
Pelham, Lady Joan 95
Pembroke, Richard de Clare, Earl of 133
Penda of Mercia, King 168, 169
Pennethorne, Sir James 41
Pepys, Samuel 60
Perrers, Alice 56
Peter the Wild Boy 53
Philip of Spain, King 63, 65, 98, 155, 156
Philip, Duke of Edinburgh 2, 25, 37, 40, 72, 111
Philippa of Hainault 27
Phillips, Captain Mark 25, 95
Philpot, John 57
Piper, John 41
Plantagenet, Geoffrey 165
Plantagenet, Richard 108
Playfair, William 180
Pole, Archbishop Reginald 156
Porden, William 88
Profumo, John 92

Raedwald, King of East Anglia 107
Raleigh, Sir Walter 50, 68
Raphael 77
Regent, Prince 8
Reynolds, Sir Joshua 42, 58
Rhymer, Thomas the 184
Richard I 19, 23, 61, 79, 90, 149, 157, 173
Richard II 21, 27, 30, 32, 47, 50, 56, 65, 101, 106, 143, 167, 175, 183
Richard III 10, 50, 59, 74, 100, 103, 133, 141, 145, 151, 152, 153, 167, 176
Richard, Duke of Bernay 98, 183
Rizzio, David 112
Robert I (the Bruce) 14, 115, 117, 120, 128, 179, 180, 184
Robert II 14, 113, 122, 122, 126, 179
Robert III 122, 124, 128

Robert of Curthose 100, 101
Rogue 5
Rollie, Lord 22
Rothesay, Duke of 128
Rubens, Peter Paul 44

Salisbury, Marquess of 90
Sarah, Duchess of Marlborough 41
Sarjeant, Marcus 168
Schrijver, Herman 78
Schulenburg, Ehrengard Melusine von der 162
Scott, Sir George Gilbert 54
Scott, Sir Walter 81, 110, 112
Scrymgeour, Hnery 117
Sebbi, King of Essex 47
Sebert, King 25
Senlis, Simon de 103
Seymour Conway, General Henry 93
Seymour, Jane 32, 43, 63, 74, 154
Shah of Persia 36
Shakespeare, William 6, 63
Sickert, Walter 41
Simon of Sudbury 56
Simpson, Wallis 77, 78, 164
Smith, Frances Dora 129, 130
Soane, Sir John 93
Sophia Charlotte von Kielmansegg 60
Sophia, Princess 28
Sophia, Queen 162
St Columba 128
St Edmund the Martyr 169, 170
St George, James of 135, 139
St Margaret 184
St Oswald 98, 100, 151, 168, 169
St Peter 26
St Rule 117
St Wulfstan 151
St Wystan 169
Stephan, Henri 43
Stephen, King 19, 159
Strathmore and Kinghorne, Earl of 127
Strathmore, Earl and Countess 1
Straw, Jack 56
Stuart, Frances, Duchess of Richmond 165
Stuart, James 141
Stuart, James ëAtheniani 70
Stubbs, George 42

Sutherland, Duke of 92
Sutherland, Graham 41
Sweyn, King 146

Tallis, Thomas 71
Tensing, Sherpa 9
Thomas of Woodstock 100
Thomason, James 92
Thornhill, Sir James 70
Thornycroft, Hamo 97
Thornycroft, Thomas 81
Tijou, Jean 64
Tovi 171
Traquair, Earl of 130
Treves, Sir Frederick 23
Tsar of Russia 42
Tudor, Edmund 132, 133
Tudor, Gronw Fychan 132
Tudor, Jasper 132, 133
Tudor, Margaret 112, 123
Tudor, Owen 132
Tyler, Wat 56, 58
Tyndale, William 157

Vanbrugh, Sir John 52, 64, 91, 165, 166
Verrio, Antonio 64, 76
Victoria, Queen 1, 7, 8, 11, 13, 19, 22, 36, 37, 39, 40, 41, 48, 53, 54, 57, 64, 66, 74, 76, 77, 80, 81, 83, 85, 87, 89, 91, 93, 107, 112, 113, 114, 117, 163
Villiers, Barbara 77, 104, 161
Vortigern 142

Waldegrave, Sir Edward 105
Wallace, William 56, 65
Wallworth, William 56, 58
Walpole, Sir Robert 41
Walter, 2nd High Steward of Scotland 128
Walter, Lucy 161
Warr, Earl de la 172
Wastell, John 106
Weldon, Fay 116
Wellington, Duke of 54, 166
Wessex, Earl of 81, 93
Wilhelm, Kaiser 85
William and Mary 18, 22, 28, 38, 52, 64, 69, 70, 161
William I (the Conqueror) 9, 17, 19, 21, 26, 29, 48, 73, 78, 79, 98, 100, 135, 168,

171, 178, 184
William II 19, 30, 79, 98, 171, 172, 183
William III 19, 81, 111, 168, 182
William IV 8, 22, 29, 36, 38, 39, 40, 60,
    66, 74, 89, 93, 163, 166
William of Poitiers 173
William the Lion 23, 122
William, Prince 13, 24, 25, 52, 86, 110, 116,
    131, 162
William, Prince of Wales 159
Wilson, Arthur 164
Winchcombe, Frances 109
Winchcombe, John 109
Witt, Jacob de 112
Wolsey, Cardinal 43, 62, 65, 68, 74, 153
Woodville, Anthony 152

Woodville, Sir Richard 104
Wren, Sir Christopher 41, 47, 52, 54, 56,
    64, 69, 152
Wulfstan, St 98, 99
Wyatt, Benjamin 42
Wyatt, James 77
Wyatt, Thomas 155
Wyattville, Sir Jeffrey 8, 73, 75, 76,
    78

Yeoman Warders 51
York, Grand Old Duke of 42
York, Richard, 3rd Duke of 102, 103
York, Richard, Duke of 28, 50, 152, 176
York, Sarah, Duchess of 161
Yvele, Henry 106

Index of Places

Abbey Craig, Stirling 180
Abbotsford 126
Abernethy, Angus 184
Adelaide, South Australia 83
Agincourt, Battle of 142
Ahlden Castle, Hanover 162
Albemarle Street 57
All Hallows by the Tower, London 173
Allerton Castle, North Yorks 108
Alnwick Castle 178
Althorp, Northants 94
Anglesey 131, 132
Anglesey, Penmynydd 131, 132
Anglesey, Penmynydd, St Gredifael 132
Annapolis, Maryland 81
Arbroath Abbey 15
Ardverikie, Castle, Inverness-shire 113
Arlington House 35

Bagshot Park, Surrey 93, 94
Ballater 117
Balmoral 2, 36, 76, 111–114
Bannockburn, Battle of 180
Banqueting House, Whitehall 6, 43, 44, 182, 185
Bardney Abbey 169
Bath 14
Bath Abbey 16, 17, 22
Beaumaris Castle 138
Beaumaris, St Mary's Church 143
Berkeley Castle 174, 175

Berkeley Square House 9
Berkhamsted 102
Birkhall 2, 114, 115
Blenheim Palace 161
Bognor Regis, Sussex 107, 185
Bombay 64
Boscobel House 55
Bosham, Sussex 108
Bosworth Field, Battle of 108, 167, 176
Braemar, Aberdeenshire 114, 117
Brandenburgh House 22
Brechin, Angus 184
Brighton 163
Brighton, Chain Pier 89
British Museum 57, 58, 183
Broadlands, Hampshire 2
Brocket Hall 42
Brookwood Cemetery 170
Bruton Street, Mayfair 1, 9
Buckingham Palace 2, 11, 12, 13, 23, 25, 34–38, 44, 76, 87, 89, 142
Buckingham Palace, Queen's Gallery 37
Buckingham Palace, Royal Mews 37
Bucklebury, Berks 109
Burgh-by-Sands, Cumberland 173
Bury St Edmunds 170

Caernarfon Castle 138, 139, 142
Caernarfon Castle, Eagle Tower 139
Cambridge 163
Cambridge, King's College 74

Cambridge, Trinity College 158
Cambuskenneth Abbey, Stirling 180, 181
Canterbury 14, 96, 97
Canterbury Cathedral 97, 148
Canterbury, St Augustine's Abbey 96, 97
Canterbury, St Martin's Church 97
Cape Charles 81
Cape Henry 81
Cardiff Castle 100
Cardiff, National Museum of Wales 20
Carisbroke Castle, Isle of Wight 64
Carlisle Cathedral 173
Carlton House 35, 42, 43, 45
Carlton House Terrace 42
Castle of Mey 115, 116
Channel Islands 165
Charing Cross, London 174
Chelsea Physic Garden 67
Chepstow Castle 134
Chertsey Abbey 74, 176
Chester 134
Chirk Castle 134
Cilmery, Breconshire 140
Claremont 77, 91
Clarence House 2, 39, 40, 41
Clarendon Palace 90, 91
Clarendon Park 91
Clifford Castle 160
Cliveden House 92
Clwyd, River 135
Colchester Castle 49
Constantinople 139
Conwy 136, 137, 140, 143
Conwy Castle 136, 137
Conwy, Aberconwy House 136, 143
Conwy, River 136
Cooper's Hill, Runnymede 150
Corfe Castle 16, 146, 170
Covent Garden 58
Coventry 170, 171
Crinan Moss 13

Datchet, Berks 144
Deptford 68
Diana, Princess of Wales Fountain 57
Dorchester-on-Thames, Oxon 168
Dove, Pub, Hammersmith 92
Dunadd 13, 14
Dundrennan Abbey 181

Durham Cathedral 172
Dymock, Glos 29

East Cote 4
Eastwell, Kent 108
Edinburgh 184
Edinburgh Castle 15, 20, 110, 119, 120, 121, 129
Edinburgh Castle, St Margaret's Chapel 120, 129, 184
Edinburgh, Royal Botanic Gardens 129
Edwinstowe, Notts 168
Edwinstowe, St Mary's Church 168
Egypt 15
Elgin, Battle of 177
Eltham Palace 91, 92, 94
Evesham Abbey 169

Falkland Palace 124, 125, 181, 184
Fettercairn, Kincardineshire 177
Fishbourne Palace, Sussex 94
Flint 134, 135, 136
Flint 142, 143
Flint Castle 134, 135
Flint Castle 143
Flodden, Battle of 65, 123, 167, 181
Floors Castle 180
Fort Belvedere 77, 78
Fotheringhay 103
Fotheringhay Castle 5, 28, 103, 182
Frampton-on-Severn, Manor Farm 160
Frampton-on-Severn, Rosamund's Green 160
Frampton-on-Severn, St Mary's Church 160
Frogmore House 77
Frogmore, Royal Mausoleum 77

Gatcombe Park, Glos 94, 95
Geddington, Northants 174
Georgia 81
Ghana 2
Glamis Castle 3, 126, 127, 129, 130
Gloucester 14, 99, 100
Gloucester Cathedral 100, 101, 175
Gloucester, St Peter's Abbey 99
Gloucester, St Oswald's 100
Godstow 160
Goring Hotel, London 33

Grafton Regis, Northants 104
Greenwich 47, 59, 60
Greenwich Palace 6, 67–71, 153, 154
Greenwich, National Maritime Museum 70, 71
Greenwich, Painted Hall 70, 71
Greenwich, Queen's Chapel 70
Greenwich, Queen's House 44, 68–69
Greenwich, Royal Hospital 69–70
Greenwich, Royal Observatory 67
Greenwich, St Alfege Church 71
Griffin, Pub 4
Guildhall, London 146

Hammersmith 22
Harby, Notts 174
Hampton Court 6, 60, 62, 63, 64, 71, 182
Hanover 162
Harlech 136
Harlech Castle 137, 140
Hastings, Battle of 171
Hatfield Chase, Battle of 168
Hatfield Palace 9
Heathrow Airport 83
Hermitage, Grafton Regis 104
Hever Castle, Kent 104, 105
Highgrove 86, 94, 168
Hyde Park 52
Hyde Park Barracks 52

Iona 14
Iona 127, 128
Iona Abbey 128
Ireland 15

James, River 81
Jamestown, Virginia 81

Kenilworth Castle 174
Kennet, River 172
Kensington Palace 36, 40, 51, 52, 53, 64, 182, 183
Kenya 2
Kew Gardens 37, 66, 67
Kew Palace 66
Kew, White House 67
Kincardine O'Neill, Aberdeenshire 178
King's College Chapel, Cambridge 106
King's Langley, Herts 101, 102, 175

King's Lynn, Norfolk 151
Kinghorn, Fife 178
Kings Cross Station 81
Kingston-upon-Thames 14, 16, 62, 160
Kingston, All Saints 16
Kingston, St Mary's 16
Knighton, Radnorshire 134

Lake Victoria 82
Lambeth 60
Lambeth Palace 182
Langside, Battle of 181
Leamington Spa, Warks 107
Leeds Castle, Kent 105, 106
Leicester Cathedral 176
Leicester, Blue Boar Inn 176
Leicester, Bow Bridge 176
Leicester, Greyfriars Church 176
Leinesschloss Church, Hanover 182
Lichfield, Staffs 21
Lincoln Cathedral 47, 174
Linlithgow Palace 123, 124, 181, 184
Linlithgow Palace, King's Fountain 124
Llanfaes Priory 143
Llanfair Hill, Salop 134
Llwynywermod, Carmarthenshire 139, 140
Lochgilphead 13
Lochleven Castle 125, 126
London Bridge 20, 60, 156
Ludlow Castle 98, 141, 152, 153
Lumphanan, Aberdeenshire 114

Machynlleth, Montgomeryshire 140
Maldon, Battle of 146
Maldon, Essex 146
Marble Arch 36
Marble Hill House 163
Marlborough House 41, 42
Mary, Queen of Scots, House, Jedburgh 125
Maryland 81
Menai Strait 132
Monmouth 134
Monmouth Castle 141
Montacute, Somerset 171

Nant Gwrtheyrn, Caenarfonshire 142
National Portrait Gallery 10
Nene, River 104
Nether Lypiatt, Glos 94, 95

New Forest 183
New Jersey 165
New York 81
Newark Castle, Notts 151
Newburgh Priory, North Yorks 108
Newmarket 4
Niddrie Castle 126
North Carolina 81
Norwich Cathedral 171
Nottingham Castle 157

Oatlands Palace 63
Odiham Castle 157
Offa's Dyke 133, 134
Old Bond Street 57
Old Windsor 73
Orkney 179
Osborne House, Isle of Wight 12, 86, 87, 89, 95
Oxford 61–62
Oxford University 147
Oxford, Ashmolean Museum 61
Oxford, Beaumont Palace 61, 148
Oxford, Bodleian Library 67

Palace of Holyroodhouse 110, 111, 112
Pall Mall 41
Park Place, Berks 93
Park Street, Mayfair 162
Pembroke Castle 132, 133
Perth 179
Peterborough Cathedral 28, 32, 103, 182
Pettycur, Kinghorn, Fife 179
Pevensey, Sussex 95
Piccadilly Circus 74
Plantagenet Cottage, Eastwell, Kent 108
Pleasure House, East Sutton, Kent 164
Pontcysyllte Aqueduct 134
Pontefract Castle 175, 183
Port Victoria, Seychelles 82
Powis Castle 134
Prestatyn, N. Wales 133
Presteigne, Radnorshire 134
Prestonpans, Battle of 58

Queen Elizabeth's Hunting Lodge, Chingford 106
Queensland, Australia 82
Queenstown, South Africa 82

Reading Abbey 172, 183
Reading, Berks 82
Regent Street 45
Regent's Park 45, 51
Regina, Saskatchewan 82
Rhuddlan 135, 136
Rhuddlan Castle 135
Richmond Green 65
Richmond Lodge 66, 67
Richmond Palace 64, 65
Richmond Park 7, 65, 71
Richmond, Old Deer Park 65, 66
Rochester Cathedral 49
Rosamund's Well, Woodstock 161
Rothesay Castle 128
Rotten Row, Hyde Park 52
Rouen Cathedral 173
Round Pond, Hyde Park 53
Roxburgh 179, 180
Royal Academy of Arts 58
Royal Albert Hall 53, 54, 57
Royal Albert Memorial 54
Royal Arcade 57
Royal Crescent, Bath 107
Royal Hospital, Chelsea 54, 56, 60
Royal Lodge, Windsor 2, 7, 76
Royal Pavilion, Brighton 87–90
Runnymede, Surrey 149, 150, 157

Sandringham 79, 84, 85, 86, 166, 185
Sandringham, Park House 94
Sandringham, St Mary Magdalene 79
Sandringham, Wood Farm 79
Savoy Palace 56
Scone 14, 15, 122, 123
Scone Abbey 123
Scone, Moot Hill 14, 122
Scone, Royal Long Gallery 129
Scotland Yard 43
Sedbury Cliffs, Chepstow 133
Sedgemoor, Battle of 161
Segontium 139
Serpentine, Hyde Park 38, 53
Seton Castle 118
Severn, River 99, 174
Shaftesbury Abbey 170
Sheen 65
Sheriff Hutton, North Yorks 141
Shifford, Oxon 61

Shoreham, Sussex 55
Sicily 15
Sitirling, Church of the Holy Rood 122
Skye, Isle of 130
Smithfield 56, 57, 58, 156
Snowdonia 132
Soar, River 176
Solway Moss, Battle of 80, 181
Somerset House 60
South Carolina 81
Southwark 148
Spain 15
St Albans, Battle of 104
St Andrews University 110, 116
St Andrews, Fife 116, 117, 181
St Bartholomew's Hospital 158
St Bartholomew's House 57
St Benet's Abbey, Norfolk 157
St Bride's, Fleet Street 93
St Clement Danes 58
St Helier, Jersey 165
St James's 34–45
St James's Palace 3, 37, 38, 40, 43, 43, 52, 156, 166
St James's Palace, Chapel Royal 5, 25, 38, 39, 182
St James's Palace, Queen's Chapel 39
St James's Park 6, 35, 39
St John's Smith Square 33
St Martins-in-the-Field 44, 45
St Paul's Cathedral 11, 13, 46, 47, 71, 74, 91, 92, 101, 147, 175
St Stephen's Abbey, Caen 171
St Wystan's Church, Repton, Derbys 169
Stanton Harcourt, Oxon 108
Stirling Castle 20, 121, 122, 180
Stirling Castle, Chapel Royal 122, 129
Sudeley Castle, Glos 32
Sunbury 164
Sutton Courtenay 107
Sutton Hoo, Suffolk 107
Swan, The 4
Swineshead Abbey, Lincs 151
Syon Abbey 154
Syon House 60

Tetbury 86
Tewkesbury Abbey 102, 103, 175
Tewkesbury, Battle of 141

Thames, River 20, 22, 56, 59–71, 92, 141, 156, 160, 163, 164, 172, 176
Theatre Royal, Drury Lane 58
Theobalds 90
Thorney Island 25
Tintern Abbey, Monmouthshire 134
Tower Green 50, 68
Tower Hill 56
Tower of London 5, 17, 18, 21, 22, 48–51, 56, 59, 60, 152, 154, 155, 158, 175, 176, 183
Tower of London, Bloody Tower 50, 153
Tower of London, Chapel of St Peter ad Vincula 32, 50
Tower of London, St John's Chapel 49
Tower of London, Traitors' Gate 49, 50, 153, 175
Tower of London, Wakefield Tower 175
Tower of London, Waterloo Block 51
Tower of London, White Tower 152
Towton, Battle of 123
Trafalgar Square 43, 44, 45
Tranby Croft, Hull, East Yorks 164
Traquair House 130
Tremadog Bay 137
Tunbridge Wells 107
Tyrell's Ford 171

Versailles 64
Victoria Falls 82
Victoria Memorial 13, 37
Victoria, British Columbia 82
Victoria, Virginia, USA 82
Virginia, USA 81

Waltham Abbey 155, 171
Waltham Cross 174
Wareham, Dorset 170
Warwick 102
Wash, The 151
Waterloo, Battle of 109, 166
West Tilbury, Essex 108, 109
Westminster 24–33
Westminster Abbey 2, 12, 15, 17, 21, 22, 24, 25, 26, 27, 28, 29, 31, 32, 39, 47, 74, 101, 102, 141, 149, 153, 155, 157, 174, 175, 178
Westminster Abbey, Chapter House 25, 27
Westminster Abbey, Henry VII's Chapel 28

Westminster Abbey, Jerusalem Chamber 31
Westminster Bridge 20, 81
Westminster Hall 17, 22, 29, 30, 31, 32
Westminster, Palace of 28, 36, 43, 152
Westminster, Palace of, Jewel Tower 29, 31
Westminster, Palace of, St Stephen's Chapel 27
Weymouth, Dorset 95
Whitby Abbey 168
White City 83
White Lodge, Richmond Park 7
Whitehall 34–45, 52, 60
Whitehall Palace 6, 29, 38, 43, 52, 64, 68, 185
Whittington Manor, Kidderminster 165
Williamsburg, Virginia 81, 95
Wilton House 32
Wimborne Minster, Dorset 107, 108
Winchester 14, 97, 98, 171, 172
Winchester Castle 73, 89
Winchester Cathedral 63, 97, 98, 156, 172, 183
Winchester, Hyde Abbey 97

Winchester, Old Minster 107
Winchester, Wolvesey Palace 98
Windsor 59, 66, 72–83, 150, 154
Windsor Castle 4, 5, 8, 36, 72–76, 78, 82, 83, 91, 185
Windsor Castle, Albert Memorial Chapel 74, 75
Windsor Castle, Queen Mary's Dolls House 83
Windsor Castle, Waterloo Chamber 6, 38, 75, 76
Windsor Great Park 8, 72, 75
Windsor, Home Park 72, 75, 76, 77
Windsor, St George's Chapel 25, 32, 73, 74, 101, 176
Woodstock Palace 160, 161
Woodstock, Oxon 5
Woolwich 68
Worcester Cathedral 98, 99, 141, 151

Y Bwthyn Bach 8, 9
York 181
York Minster 168

Acknowledgements

My thanks go to all the amazing team at Ebury, Carey Smith and Roxanne Benson-Mackey in particular for their patience, wise advice and hard work.

Thanks also to Steve Dobell for his usual excellent editing and to my inspirational agent Kevin Conroy Scott.

And to Mai, my eternal love and thanks.